SOCIAL PROBLEMS
IN THE WORLD TODAY

Edited by
JOHN W. KINCH
California State University at San Francisco

ADDISON-WESLEY PUBLISHING COMPANY
Reading, Massachusetts • Menlo Park, California • London
Don Mills, Ontario

This book is in the
ADDISON-WESLEY SERIES IN SOCIOLOGY

ISBN 0-201-03706-8
ABCDEFGHIJ-DO-79876543

To Linda Kay,
Cathy,
Sally Jo,
and Carol Ann

PREFACE

Social Problems in the World Today is part of a series of readers in sociology which is being compiled with one central idea in mind —to bring the perspectives of sociology into the world of the student. More specifically, this book attempts to make the analysis of social problems relevant for the student by enabling him to relate those problems and perspectives to his own experience and to those social problems he will confront in his real-life experience. The book is designed for students who have little academic experience in sociology; it draws its material almost exclusively from nonprofessional popular sources. The criteria used for selection of these articles were as follows: (1) they must have appeared in a popular source with a wide distribution (usually a national magazine), (2) they should be of high literary quality and sociologically sound, and (3) they must be relevant and interesting to the students using the text and related to their understanding of social problems.

It might well be asked, "Why select articles of this type rather than the conventional articles from professional journals? Do journalists and others in fact have more to say on social problems than the sociologists who are scientifically investigating these problems?" Several considerations went into the decision to use nonprofessional sources in this book of readings. First of all, it should be recognized that professional journals provide articles which are written by sociologists for other sociologists, not for college freshmen. Therefore, they frequently turn out to be less than satisfactory for our purpose. It is no insult to the student to suggest that he would find their technical jargon and occasional low literary quality difficult and perhaps boring.

However, there are other considerations which are just as important and central to our concern. Most of the students who will be using this reader will never become professional sociologists, but will go on to various other fields of their choice. This means that their exposure to social problems throughout their lifetime will not come through the reading of professional journals or other academic sources, but rather through their exposure to popular magazines, newspaper articles, and the like—the types of material presented in this book. Therefore, it is our feeling that a course in social problems which enables the student to systematically analyze and understand material presented in this fashion will be far more beneficial than a course that exposes the student exclusively to professional material. It is our hope that these students will become skillful in their ability to interpret and garner the value of the material available from these types of sources, and as a consequence be able to use their sociological understanding and knowledge to help them cope with the world in their everyday life experiences.

A third factor that went into our selection of the articles was the consideration that sociological concepts and understandings could be best understood in the context of material that would be meaningful and relevant to the lives of the students taking the course. We were careful to select a large number of articles with which the student could identify, or at least feel are relevant to his own life experiences. It was felt that articles of this kind would enable him to better understand sociological concepts as they are presented in typical courses in social problems.

In this book the student will be confronted with contrasting ideologies, competing views, and opinionated materials. He will read articles written by psychiatrists, journalists, and politicians, as well as by sociologists and various practitioners who are working directly with social problems. It is expected that the student will read the articles carefully, looking for the biases of the authors, their motivation and aims. The authors, of course, are only human and are frequently trying to persuade the reader of their particular point of view. It must be up to the student to appraise the material critically, evaluate it, and determine its validity. We encourage the use of the articles for open discussion in classrooms as a valuable aid to developing the student's ability to make these critical judgements. It is our hope that this book will help the student to better understand himself, his society, and the problems that the individual and the society are confronted with in the world today. If it is used in one of his first courses in his college career, we hope that it will instill in him the idea that college can be an exciting adventure, but most important that education can and should be a stimulating lifetime experience which never ends.

San Francisco, California
May 1973   J.W.K.

CONTENTS

INTRODUCTION

INTRODUCTION

The study of social problems has always been a very central part of sociological analysis. Many of the pioneers of sociology were deeply influenced by the social problems of their day and were motivated to study sociology in hopes of finding means of relieving these problems. For them, the purpose of sociology was to resolve social problems.

As sociology became deeply concerned with its image as a science, there was a trend away from direct involvement in the solution of social problems towards a detached "scientific" interest in the subject. The investigator might still be interested in contributing to the solution to society's problems, or he might simply find social problems a convenient source of data for his sociological investigation. In either case he felt that detachment was a necessary consideration for objective study. In more recent years a more liberal trend within sociology has suggested that not only is it possible for a sociologist to involve himself in the social problems which he studies, but that this involvement can enhance his study. Even further, some have suggested that the investigator has a moral obligation to become involved. They feel that it is not proper for him to study his subject just because it is fascinating or to use subjects just because they provide valuable data for the test of his hypothesis. He should feel an obligation either to the individuals or the society he studies and use his expertise to help alleviate these problems.

Just as there are many motivations for the interest in and study of social problems, so there are many approaches to and perspectives for the analysis of social problems. Because of the lack of consistency among those studying social problems, placing labels on various approaches can prove very misleading. To avoid this problem we would caution the reader to become familiar with the basic premises of the approach and attach little significance to its name. The reader should be sensitive to the differences between the various approaches, for the approach one uses will affect the method of analysis, the data that are relevant for the investigation, and the implications for cures or remedies.

For example, let us first consider two directions from which we approach social problems—the personal disorganization approach and the social disorganization approach. These two approaches explain the existence of social problems from exactly opposite directions. The first suggests that individuals' problems cause social problems, and the second implies that society's problems cause individuals' problems.

The personal disorganization approach starts out with the assumption that the social order is basically sound. The goals and the means of arriving at those goals which have been laid down by the established social organization are adequate and need not be questioned. This approach then attempts to explain and analyze why individuals have problems in conforming to the demands of the social order. Problems are seen in terms of the individuals' failures, and cures are looked for in either greater social control or improvements in the socialization of the potential deviant, so that he will be more likely to follow the acceptable norms and values of the existing system.

Competing with this view is the approach that suggests that social problems exist because of the inability of the established society to fulfill the needs and demands of the individual and to adapt to the changes necessary in a fluid, ever-changing society. In this case social disorganization might be seen as a disjunction between institutions. For example, the innovations and improvements in the economic-political scheme of a society may outstrip the ability of the family and the religious institutions to adjust and thereby create a type of disorganization. You can see that this approach to studying the disorganization of society requires quite a different remedy. It suggests that the solution to social problems comes not in the changes imposed upon individuals who deviate from the values of society, but rather from basic institutional changes in established patterns. It suggests that there is something wrong with the society that leads to social problems rather than something wrong with individuals which causes disruption of the society.

As an example of the way in which these two approaches might deal with a social problem, consider the problems of drug use. The personal disorganization approach would consider addiction to dangerous drugs as indicative of defects in the personality of the addict. Perhaps he was not properly trained to understand the consequences of their use, or he may have a weak personality which allows him to easily give in to temptations. A cure that might be recommended by proponents of this view might be to increase the education of the effects of drugs or to make the punishment for the use of drugs more severe. Both attempts deal with the individual and heighten his awareness of the values that the established society places on the use of drugs.

The social disorganization approach would be more likely to see the problems of drugs in terms of questions like, "What is it about the demands and stress of modern society that lead large numbers of persons to look for life's satisfactions through the use of drugs?" They might also be concerned with the consequences of drug use on other dimensions of society. Does the abuse of drugs undermine the effectiveness of the family in fulfilling its function in society? Here the cure might be to change the social structure so that stress is reduced, or if that cannot be accomplished, a cure might be sought by introducing substitutes and less dangerous forms of satisfaction.

We have briefly described these contrasting approaches to the study of social problems because they exemplify the relationship between approach, investigation, analysis, and cure. Of course, these are not the only ways of approaching the study of social problems. One other approach, which is sometimes simply labeled the social-problems approach, suggests that a very important dimension in studying social problems is the perception which society, or the individuals within society, have of problem behavior. It asks the questions, "Why is some behavior considered bad? Why are some situations or conditions considered problems and why are some individuals labeled deviants?" And just as important, this approach asks, "What are the consequences to society and to the individual of being labeled bad, problem, or deviant?" When approaching social problems from this perspective, a number of new insights are possible. It becomes apparent that the attention sociologists give to social problems and the seriousness which we attach to problem behavior are not determined solely by the extent to which that behavior may damage the individuals involved or the degree to which it destroys the existing social order. Frequently, the major determining factor in defining a social problem is the attitude or perspective of most members of society.

For example, investigators using this approach in studying drug abuse might well inquire why society considers some uses of drugs deviant, and whether the user considers himself to be a deviant. They would be interested in the consequence of certain drugs, such as tranquilizers and sleeping pills, being defined as legitimate, and other drugs (sometimes no different chemically) being defined as improper. Does the housewife who feels that her regular use of tranquilizers is socially approved experience something different from the teenager who pops pills because his friends dare him to? The social-problems approach does not always lead to a clear recommendation for change or cure. However, it does call our attention to the fact that in order to understand the effect that social problems have on society, we must know something about how problem behavior is defined, both by society at large and by the individual engaged in the behavior.

In a rapidly changing society it is important to know how the values and orientations of members of society change and how these changes affect the general perception of those forms of behavior we call social problems. A review of the table of contents of this book will reveal some significant factors about social problems. Ten years ago, no book of readings in social problems would have had a section on social protest. Five years ago we would not have found a section on ecology and man's environment, and we can anticipate that five years from now a new book of readings will have topics that don't seem relevant today. This is because new problems that need attention are always emerging in the eyes of society. Some problems seem to persist. The study of crime persists at a rather constant rate, always seen as an important social problem. However, the definition and analysis of poverty as a social problem seems to go up and down with the state of our economy. During the depression years, poverty was seen as a major social problem. Then, during the Second World War and in the relative prosperity that followed, it lost its significance. In more recent years, with the "war on poverty" and various public outcries in this regard, it has become fashionable once again to consider poverty as a major social problem.

The decision to use popular magazines and other nonsociological sources for this book reveals our compatibility with the social-problems approach. These sources both reflect and contribute to society's definition of social problems. The role of the media in American society has become a topic of much concern in recent years. Whether the media simply reflect the values, and in our case the social problems, of modern society or whether they determine and direct these values is a question of significant sociological interest. We would suggest that it works both ways. Certainly the mass media, and specifically the national magazines, have a great deal of influence in determining the sorts of things that are seen by the public as important social problems. However, at the same time the media must be responsive to their readers and must, therefore, deal with the social problems which they feel the public thinks are important in their everyday life. The problems of ecology have become of widespread concern, largely because the media have called them to the attention of large segments of society. At the same time, we might argue that the problems of war still appear in the mass media because a large element of society is directly affected by it and is responsive to articles about it.

SOCIAL PROBLEMS AND SOCIAL CHANGE

In this book we take the position that the pace of change in our current society is unique to modern times. The changes experienced in the lifetime of any person reading this book will be vastly more significant and far-reaching than those confronted by his parents, or his parents' parents before him.

Industrialization has been a major force in western civilization for a hundred years now. The mechanization and automation of many dimensions of society have led many people to feel that the machines are taking over. Our ability to produce at a high rate and to accomplish such significant feats as landing on the moon, have led many to question why it is that this technological know-how seems only to create, rather than resolve, social problems.

One of the immediate effects of modernization or industrialization in American society has been a great reduction in the need for farm workers. Over a hundred years ago it was necessary for the large majority of the population to live in rural areas in order to provide the labor for producing farm goods, but with automation of farm work, only a small minority of the total population is needed on the farms. As a consequence, another major force of changing American society appears to be urbanization. The majority of the population in the United States now live in metropolitan areas. Here those traditional social problems—crime, racial tensions, unemployment—seem to be intensified. New problems, such as air pollution, traffic congestion, and the like, also emerge as a result of urbanization.

It is for these reasons that this book leans towards a social disorganization approach, but it also relies, for analysis, on certain dimensions of what we called the social-problems approach. A basic premise underlying our approach is that the structure of a society—its institutions, its values, and its norms—plays a major role in the extent and severity of, and reactions to, the social problems of that society. Moreover, in a rapidly changing society like American society, the disjunctions which can develop between institutions, attitudes, and norms can be a leading factor in contributing to social problems.

In taking this position we do not mean to imply that social problems are just something to observe or study with little chance for change. We recognize that when we discuss social problems we are discussing people's lives—and not infrequently the lives of people in misery, despair, and deprivation. For this reason our study of social problems takes on a new seriousness and a new challenge. We firmly believe that social problems can be solved, and that the first step towards finding solutions is an understanding of the nature of the problems, both in the minds of social scientists and of the public.

ORGANIZATION OF THE BOOK

There are any number of ways a book in social problems can be organized. The classification of social problems can take a variety of forms. We have chosen to move from problems affecting the life cycle of the individual, to ever larger categories until we finally come to world social problems. However, the student should never lose sight of the fact that any classification is artificial and that the problems of individuals may have worldwide consequences while world social problems may affect individuals.

In the first section we deal with the individual as he goes through his life cycle and how he confronts social problems that emerge in a complex, changing society. The second section considers the ways in which classes of persons or groups, as differentiated members of society, are affected by various social changes. Here we deal with race problems, problems of workers or the poor, and the problems of the criminal, and other persons who deviate from the formal law in our society. In the third section we deal with problems that are national in scope, which must be dealt with on a broad level. Here we have topics of ecology, social protest, and the like. In the final section we talk about international social problems and social change, such as widespread overpopulation. One factor that will become apparent as one goes through the book is that no classification scheme satisfactorily deals with the heterogeneity and complexity of the social problems dealt with in this book. There is no problem that is strictly individual or national or international. All problems have consequences both for individuals and for the society of which they are a part. Also it will become apparent that none of the social problems are unique or can be dealt with in a vacuum. For example, when we talk about the problems of the family, we are at the same time discussing the problems of urbanization and might also be dealing with problems of racial tension, poverty, or a number of other topics.

It is hoped that the perceptive student will see the analysis of social problems as a device whereby he listens and responds to the complexities of modern society. The student should not look for a series of individual and independent problems, but rather an integrated conglomerate of problems that can only be meaningfully understood when responded to as an interrelated whole.

PART ONE
TURMOIL IN THE LIFE CYCLE:
PROBLEMS OF INDIVIDUALS

TURMOIL IN THE LIFE CYCLE: PROBLEMS OF INDIVIDUALS

One very useful analytical tool that the sociologist has provided for the understanding of human social behavior is the concept of *role*. A good bit of sociological analysis is based on the assumption that man acts according to his perception of what is expected of him in social settings. These expectations are called *norms*. When they pertain to an individual because of a particular *position* he holds in the group or society we refer to them as role-norms, or just roles.

In American society, as is true in varying degrees in all societies, we tend to develop varying expectations (roles) for people in various age categories. To put it another way, people are assigned positions in accordance with their place in the life-cycle. We refer to persons as children, kids, youth, boys and girls, adults, senior citizens, and so on. These words are labels which we use to differentiate people within the society. Along with the labels come roles, or sets of expectations that are relevant to the persons within the categories.

This concept provides us with an excellent device for organizing our study of the social problems that the individual is confronted with in society. We will see in this section how the individual is affected by some social problems because of his position in the life-cycle. Every stage in the life of the individual seems to have the potential for problems of one sort or another.

As soon as the person moves out of childhood into adolescence he is confronted with a number of problems that relate to his role. First, because the society is changing so rapidly, the expectations that adults have for him, based on their own adolescence, are frequently not relevant to the demands that society places on him. Only three or four generations ago a father could be relatively certain that his son would follow the same general pattern that he did as a boy; now such an expectation does not even make sense to many in our society. The first two articles in this section deal with the generation gap. When Adelson argues that most of what we have been led to believe about the generation gap is, in fact, a myth, he is not saying that life is the same for youth today as it was a generation ago; rather, society is changing for all its members and notions of severe conflict between generations probably is exaggerated.

Of course, Adelson does not deny that in our society adolescence is a time of transition between childhood and adult life which is filled with ambiguities. When does a child become an adult? In many states, he can drive a car at sixteen, be drafted and vote at eighteen, but he cannot drink or sign a contract until he is twenty-one. The fact that some of these legal age restrictions are changing or vary from state to state adds even more to the ambiguity.

As the individual emerges from adolescence he is faced with a number of potential problems. To show the contrast in the types of problems which he faces, we have included articles on higher education, drugs, and the family. What is involved in getting into college? How important is it? Should he explore the drug scene? How dangerous is it? And the family. He is just about to leave one. What has it done for him? And what has it done to him? Should he start another family of his own? How will his family membership affect his ability to face other problems?

If we were following a chronological sequence in this section we come next to that long period in a person's life where his major role is that of employee, provider, and/or child bearer. We have chosen to deal with some of the problems of this age category in Part II, which will be concerned with the problems of the worker, the poor, the minorities, and so on.

However, in those years when the individual approaches retirement other problems are likely to bother him. The strains of a long life of competition and the stresses of continuous pressure to succeed frequently lead the individual to look for an escape. Many try alcohol, which has become a major social problem in our society. Others try suicide. After articles on these two subjects we end this section with an article on the final category in the cycle—old age.

1 / WHAT GENERATION GAP?

Joseph Adelson

Can the truth prevail against a false idea whose time has come?

The idea that there is a generation gap is not totally false, perhaps. But it is false enough, false in the sense of being overblown, oversimplified, sentimentalized. This may be too strong a way of putting it. Let us say, then, that the idea of a generation gap is at the least unexamined, one of those notions that seems so self-evident that we yield to it without taking thought, and without qualms about not taking thought.

Once we examine the idea, we find it is almost too slippery to hold. What do we mean by a generation gap? Do we mean widespread alienation between adolescents and their parents? Do we mean that the young have a different and distinctive political outlook? Are we speaking of differences in styles of pleasure-seeking: greater sexual freedom, or the marijuana culture? Or do we simply mean that the young and the old share the belief that there is a significant difference between them, whether or not there is?

These questions—and many others one might reasonably ask —are by no means easy to answer. Few of them can in fact be answered decisively. Nevertheless, enough information has been accumulated during the last few years to offer us some new understanding of the young. As we will see, this evidence contains some surprises; and persuades us to cast a very cold eye on the more

From *The New York Times Magazine*, January 18, 1970. © 1970 by The New York Times Company. Reprinted by permission.

simple-minded views about this young generation and its place in our society.

PARENTS AND CHILDREN

One definition of generational conflict locates it in rebellion against parental authority, or in the failure of parents and their adolescent youngsters to understand and communicate with each other. (In short, "The Graduate.") On this particular issue, there is, as it happens, abundant evidence, and all of it suggests strongly that there is no extensive degree of alienation between parents and their children. Vern Bengtson, one of the most careful scholars in this area, has collected data from more than 500 students enrolled in three Southern California colleges. About 80 per cent of them report generally close and friendly relationships with their parents; specifically, 79 per cent feel somewhat close or very close, 81 per cent regard communication as good, and 78 per cent feel that their parents understand them all or most of the time.

Essentially similar findings have emerged from Samuel Lubell's perceptive studies of college youth. He reports that only about 10 per cent of the students he interviewed were in serious discord with their parents, and there was in most of these cases a long history of family tension. Any clinician working with college-age students would agree; among the rebellious or alienated, we find that their troubles with their families go back a long way and surfaced well before the college years.

In some respects the findings of Bengtson and Lubell are not really surprising. What they do is bring us up to date, and tell us that a long-established line of findings on adolescence continues to be true. A few years ago my colleague Elizabeth Douvan and I studied 3,000 youngsters of 12 to 18, from all regions of the country and all socio-economic levels. We concluded that there were few signs of serious conflict between American adolescents and their parents; on the contrary, we found that it was more usual for their relationships to be amiable.

The recently published study by psychiatrist Daniel Offer—of a smaller group, but using more intensive methods of scrutiny— arrives at much the same conclusion. Incidentally, there is no support for the common belief that the adolescent is hostage to the influence of his friends and turns away from parental guidance. A number of studies, here and abroad, tell us that while peer opinion may carry some weight on trivial issues—taste, clothing and the like—on more central matters, such as career and college choice, it is parental opinion that counts.

Whatever the supposed generation gap may involve, it does not seem to include deep strains between the young and their parents. The idea of the adolescent's family milieu as a kind of *Götterdämmerung*, as the scene of a cataclysmic struggle between the forces of authority and rebellion, is exaggerated. As Lubell put it: "we found both much less authority and much less rebellion than popularly imagined."

POLITICS

Those who are convinced that there is a generation gap also tend to identify youth in general with radical or militantly liberal beliefs. Thus, the young are sometimes seen as a New Breed, impatient with the political pieties of the past, less subject to that fatigue and corruption of spirit characteristic of the older generation of voters.

There is indeed a generational element in politics; there always has been. But to identify the young with liberal or left militancy makes sense only from the perspective of the élite university campus. Once we look at the total population of the young a decidedly different picture emerges. We have, for example, a brilliant and revealing analysis of the 1968 election by the University of Michigan's Survey Research Center, based upon 1,600 interviews with a representative national sample of voters. Perhaps the most interesting finding was that the under-30 voter was distinctly overrepresented in the Wallace constituency, and that the Wallace movement outside the South drew proportionately more of its strength from younger than from older voters.

Some of the center's commentary on generational influences is worth quoting at length. "One of the most important yet hidden lines of cleavage split the younger generation itself. Although privileged young college students angry at Vietnam and shabby treatment of the Negro saw themselves as sallying forth to do battle against a corrupted and cynical older generation, a more head-on confrontation at the polls, if a less apparent one, was with their own age mates who had gone from high school off to the factory instead of college, and who were appalled by the collapse of patriotism and respect for the law that they saw about them. Outside of the election period, when verbal articulateness and leisure for political activism count most heavily, it was the college share of the younger generation—or at least its politicized vanguard—that was most prominent as a political force. At the polls, however, the game shifts to 'one man, one vote,' and this vanguard is numerically swamped even within its own generation."

To overemphasize the role of generational conflict in politics is to ignore or dismiss what we have learned over the years about the transmission of political sentiments in the great majority of cases— it seems to average about 75 per cent in most studies—children vote the same party their parents do; it has often been noted that party preference is transmitted to about the same degree as religious affiliation. Political attitudes are also acquired within the family, though generally less strongly than party affiliation; among studies on this matter there is hardly one which reports a negative relationship between parental attitudes and those of their children.

My own research during the last few years has dealt with the acquisition of political values during adolescence, and it is patently clear that the political outlook of the parents, particularly when it is strongly felt, tends to impress itself firmly on the politics of the child. Thus, the most conservative youngster we interviewed was the daughter of a leader of the John Birch Society; the most radical was the daughter of a man who had—in 1965—ceased paying income taxes to the Federal Government in protest against our involvement in Vietnam.

The strongest recent evidence on this subject seems to come from studies of the student radical. These studies make it evident that the "rebellious" student is, for the most part, not rebelling against the politics he learned at home. Radical activists are for the most part children of radical or liberal-left parents; in many instances, their parents are—overtly or tacitly—sympathetic to what their children are doing. (This is shown in the letters written to the press by parents of the students expelled by Columbia and Chicago; the rhetoric of these letters reveals how strong the bond of political sympathy is between the parents and their children. For instance, a letter from a group of Columbia parents states: "We are, of course, concerned about the individual fates of our sons and daughters, but more so with resisting such pressures against a student movement which has done so much to arouse the nation to the gross horrors and injustices prevalent in our country.")

VALUES

Are the young abandoning traditional convictions and moving toward new moral and ideological frameworks? We hear it said that the old emphasis on personal achievement is giving way to a greater concern with self-realization or with leisure and consumption; that a selfish materialism is being succeeded by a more humanistic outlook; that authority and hierarchy are no longer automatically accepted, and are replaced by more democratic forms of participation; that rationalism is under attack by proponents of sensual or mystical perspectives, and so on.

The most ambitious recent survey on this topic was sponsored by Fortune magazine. Fortune seems to believe that its findings demonstrate a generation gap and a departure from "traditional moral values" on the part of many of the educated young. A careful look at the survey suggests that it proves neither of these propositions, but only how badly statistics can deceive in a murky area.

The Fortune pollsters interviewed a representative sample of 18-to-24-year-olds, dividing them into a non-college group, a group of upward-mobile college youngsters interested in education for its vocational advantages, and a so-called "forerunner" group (largely students interested in education as self-discovery and majoring in the humanities and social sciences). Some substantial, though not surprising, differences are found among these groups—the "forerunners" are more liberal politically, less traditional in values, less enchanted about business careers (naturally) than the two other groups. But the findings tell us nothing about a *generation* gap, since the opinions of older people were not surveyed. Nor do they tell us anything about changes in values, since we do not have equivalent findings on earlier generations of the young.

What the findings do tell us (and this is concealed in the way the data are presented, so much so that I have had to recompute the statistics) is, first, that an overwhelming majority of the young —as many as 80 per cent—tend to be traditionalist in values; and, second, that there is a sharp division within the younger generation between, on the one hand, that distinct minority that chooses a liberal education and, on the other, both those who do not go to college and the majority of college students who are vocationally oriented. In brief, the prevailing pattern (of intra-generational cleavage) is quite similar to that which we find in politics.

The Fortune poll brings out one interesting thing: many of those interviewed—well over 80 per cent—report that they do not believe that there are great differences in values between themselves and their parents. This is supported by other investigations. Bengtson's direct comparison of college students demonstrates that they "shared the same general value orientations and personal life goals." He concludes that "both students and parents in this sample are overwhelmingly oriented toward the traditional middleclass values of family and career." From his careful study of normal middleclass high-school boys, Daniel Offer states flatly, "Our evidence indicates that both generations *share the same basic values*" (his italics).

Despite the impressive unanimity of these appraisals, the question of value change should remain an open one. It is hard to imagine that some changes are not taking place, in view of the vast social, economic and technological changes occurring in industrialized countries: the growth of large organizations, shifts in the occupational structure, the rapid diffusion of information, etc., etc. Yet the nature of these changes in values, if any, is by no means evident, and our understanding remains extremely limited.

We simply do not know which areas of values are changing, how rapidly the changes are taking place, which segments of the population they involve, how deeply they run, how stable any of the new values will turn out to be. Many apparent changes in "values" seem to be no more than changes in manners, or in rhetoric.

All in all, the most prudent assessment we can make, on the basis of the evidence we now have, is that no "value revolution" or anything remotely like it is taking place or is in prospect; and that if changes are occurring, they will do so through the gradual erosion, building and shifting of values.

PLEASURE

Let us limit ourselves to the two areas of pleasure where generational differences are often held to be present: sex and drugs. Is there a sexual revolution among the young? And has a drug culture established itself as a significant part of youth culture?

Announced about 10 to 15 years ago, the sexual revolution has yet to take place. Like the generation gap itself, it may be more apparent than real. Support for this statement is provided by the Institute for Sex Research at Indiana University, which has just completed a new study, begun in 1967, in the course of which 1,200 randomly selected college students were interviewed. Comparing the findings with those obtained in its study of 20 years ago, the institute reports increasing liberalism in sexual practices but stresses that these changes have been gradual. One of the study's authors states, "There remains a substantial commitment to what can only be called traditional values." Most close students of the sexual scene seem to agree that the trend toward greater permissiveness in the United States probably began back in the nineteen-twenties, and has been continuing since. Sexual attitudes and habits are becoming more liberal—slowly. We are becoming Scandinavians—gradually.

The sexual changes one notes on the advanced campuses are of two kinds. First, there is a greater readiness to establish quasi-marital pairings, many of which end in marriage; these are without question far more common than in the past, and are more often taken for granted. Second, there is a trend, among a very small but conspicuous number of students, toward extremely casual sexuality, sometimes undertaken in the name of sexual liberation. To the clinician, these casual relationships seem to be more miserable than not—compulsive, driven, shallow, often entered into in order to ward off depression or emotional isolation. The middle-class inhibitions persist, and the attempt at sexual freedom seems a desperate maneuver to overcome them. We have a long way to go before the sexually free are sexually free.

As to drugs, specifically marijuana: Here we have, without

much question, a sharp difference between the generations. It is a rare citizen over 30 who has had any experience with marijuana, and it is not nearly so rare among the young, particularly those in college. Still, the great majority of youngsters—almost 90 per cent —have had no experience with marijuana, not even to the degree of having tried it once, and, of course, far fewer use it regularly. Furthermore, a strong majority of the young do not believe marijuana should be legalized. What we have here, then, is both a generation gap and (as we have had before) a gap in attitude and experience within the younger generation.

It would be nice if we could keep our wits about us when we contemplate the implications of marijuana for our society. That is hard to do in the presence of hysteria on one side, among those who hold it to be an instrument of the devil, and transcendent rapture on the other, among those who see it as the vehicle and expression of a revolution in values and consciousness. In any case, the drug scene is too new and too fluid a phenomenon for us to foretell its ultimate place in the lives of the young. Drug use has grown rapidly. Will it continue to grow? Has it reached a plateau? Will it subside?

A more interesting question concerns the sociological and ideological factors involved in marijuana use. As marijuana has become more familiar, it has become less of a symbol of defiance and alienation. Lubell points out that just a few years ago the use of marijuana among college students was associated with a liberal or left political outlook; now it has become acceptable and even popular among the politically conservative. From what I have been able to learn, on some campuses and in some suburban high schools drug use is now most conspicuous among the *jeunesse dorée*—fraternity members and the like—where it succeeds or complements booze, and co-exists quite easily with political indifference or reaction and Philistine values. To put it another way, marijuana has not so much generated a new life style—as Timothy Leary and others had hoped—as it has accommodated itself to existing life styles.

Is there a generation gap? Yes, no, maybe. Quite clearly, the answer depends upon the specific issue we are talking about. But if we are talking about a fundamental lack of articulation between the generations, then the answer is—decisively—no. From one perspective, the notion of a generation gap is a form of pop sociology, one of those appealing and facile ideas which sweep through a self-conscious culture from time to time. The quickness with which the idea has taken hold in the popular culture—in advertising, television game shows and semi-serious pot-boilers—should be sufficient to warn us that its appeal lies in its superficiality. From another perspective, we might say that the generation gap is an illusion, somewhat like flying saucers. Note: not a delusion, an illusion. There *is* something there, but we err in our interpretation of what it is. There *is* something going on among the young, but we have misunderstood it. Let us turn now to the errors of interpretation which bedevil us when we ponder youth.

PARTS AND WHOLES

The most obvious conceptual error, and yet the most common, is to generalize from a narrow segment of the young to the entire younger generation. With some remarkable consistency, those who hold that there is a generation gap simply ignore the statements, beliefs and activities of the non-college young, and indeed of the ordinary, straight, unturned-on, nonactivist collegian. And the error goes even beyond this: on the university scene, the élite campus is taken to stand for all campuses; within the élite university, the politically engaged are taken to reflect student sentiment in general; and among the politically active, the radical fraction is thought to speak for activists as a whole.

It is not surprising to come across these confusions in the mass media, given their understandable passion for simplification of the complex, and their search for vivid spokesmen of strong positions. Thus, the typical TV special on the theme, "What Is Happening to Our Youth?", is likely to feature a panel consisting of (1) a ferocious black militant, (2) a feverish member of S.D.S., (3) a supercilious leader of the Young Americans for Freedom (busily imitating William Buckley), and (4), presumably to represent the remaining 90 per cent, a hopelessly muddled moderate. But we have much the same state of affairs in the quality magazines, where the essays on youth are given to sober yet essentially apocalyptic ruminations on the spirit of the young and the consequent imminent decline (or rebirth) of Western civilization.

Not too surprisingly, perhaps, the most likely writer of these essays is an academic intellectual, teaching humanities or the social sciences at an élite university. Hence he is exposed, in his office, in his classes, to far more than the usual number of radical or hippyesque students. (And he will live in a neighborhood where many of the young adolescents are preparing themselves for such roles.)

On top of this, he is, like the rest of us, subject to the common errors of social perception, one of which is to overestimate the size of crowds, another to be attracted by and linger upon the colorful and deviant. So he looks out of his office window and sees what seems to be a crowd of thousands engaging in a demonstration; or he walks along the campus, noting that every second male face is bearded. If he were to count—and he is not likely to count, since his mind is teeming with insights—he might find that the demonstration is in hundreds rather than thousands, or that the proportion of beards is nearer one in 10 than one in two. It is through these and similar processes that some of our most alert and penetrating minds have been led astray on the actualities of the young; that is why we have a leading intellectual writing, in a recent issue of a good magazine, that there are "millions" of activist students.

It is not surprising, then, that both the mass media and the intellectual essayists have been misled (and misleading) on the infinite variety of the young: the first are focused upon the glittering surface of social reality, the second upon the darker meanings behind that surface (an art brought to its highest state, and its highest pitch, by Norman Mailer). What is surprising, and most discouraging, is that a similar incompleteness of perception dominates the professional literature—that is, technical psychological and sociological accounts of adolescence and youth.

Having attended, to my sorrow, many convocations of experts on the young, I can attest that most of us are experts on atypical fractions of the young: on heavy drug users, or delinquents, or hippies, or the alienated, or dropouts, or the dissident—and, above all, on the more sprightly and articulate youngsters of the upper middle class. By and large, our discourse at these meetings, when it is not clinical, is a kind of gossip: the upper middle class talking to itself about itself. The examples run: my son, my colleague's daughter, my psychoanalytic patient, my neighbor's drug-using son, my Ivy League students. Most of us have never had a serious and extended conversation with a youngster from the working or lower-middle classes. In our knowledge of the young we are, to use Isaiah Berlin's phrase, hedgehogs, in that we know one thing, and know it well, know it deeply, when we also need to be foxes, who know many things less deeply.

What we know deeply are the visibly disturbed, and the more volatile, more conspicuous segments of the upper middle class. These are the youngsters with problems, or with *panache*—makers and shakers, shakers of the present, makers of the future. Their discontents and their creativity, we hear it said, produce the new forms and the new dynamics of our social system. Thus, they allow us to imagine the contours of a hopeful new order of things or, contrariwise, permit us visions of Armageddon.

Perhaps so, but before judging this matter, we would do well to recognize that our narrowness of vision has led us to a distorted view of adolescence and youth. We have become habituated to a conflict model of adolescence—the youngster at odds with the milieu and divided within himself. Now, adolescence is far from being a serene period of life. It is dominated by significant transitions, and like all transitional periods—from early childhood to middle age—it produces more than its share of inner and outer discord. Yet, we have become so committed to a view of the young based upon conflict, pathology and volatility—a view appropriate for some adolescents most of the time and for most some of the time—that we have no language or framework for handling conceptually either the sluggish conformity or the effectiveness of adaptation or the generational continuity which characterizes most youngsters most of the time.

YOUNG AND OLD, NEW AND OLD

Another common error is to exaggerate the differences between younger and older generations. Differences there are, and always have been. But the current tendency is to assume that anything new, any change in beliefs or habits, belongs to or derives from the country of the young.

This tendency is particularly evident in the realm of politics, especially on the left, where "young" and "new" are often taken to be synonymous. Is this really so? To be sure, the young serve as the shock troops of New Left action. But consider how much of the leadership is of an older generation; as one example, most of the leaders of the New Mobilization—Lens, Dellinger, Dowd and others—are in their forties and fifties. It is even more significant that the key ideologues of radical politics—such men as Marcuse, Chomsky, Paul Goodman—are of secure middle age and beyond. The young have, in fact, contributed little to radical thought, except perhaps to vulgarize it to a degree painful for those of us who can remember a time when that body of thought was intellectually subtle, rich and demanding.

For that matter, is New Left thought really new—that is, a product of the nineteen-sixties? I was dumfounded several weeks ago when I stumbled across a book review I had written in the nineteen-fifties, a commentary on books by Erich Fromm, Lionel Trilling and the then unknown Herbert Marcuse. My review suggested that these otherwise disparate authors were united in that they sensed and were responding to a crisis of liberalism. The optimistic, melioristic assumptions of liberalism seemed to be failing, unable to cope with the alienation and the atavistic revivals produced by technological civilization.

Thus, even in the sunny, sleepy nineteen-fifties a now-familiar critique of American society was already well-established. The seminal ideas, political and cultural, of current radical thought had been set down, in the writings of C. Wright Mills, Marcuse, Goodman and others, and from another flank, in the work of Norman O. Brown, Mailer and Allen Ginsberg. That sense of life out of control, of bureaucratic and technological things in the saddle, of malaise and restlessness were, in the nineteen-fifties, felt only dimly, as a kind of low-grade infection. In the middle and late nineteen-sixties, with the racial explosion in the cities and our involvement in Vietnam, our political and cultural crisis became, or seemed to become, acute.

What I am getting at is that there is no party of the young, no politics indigenous to or specific to the young, even on the radical left. The febrile politics of the day do not align the young against the old, not in any significant way. Rather, they reflect the ideological differences in a polarized nation.

What we have done is to misplace the emphasis, translating ideological conflict into generational conflict. We have done so, I believe, because it suits our various psychological purposes. On the left, one's weakness in numbers and political potency is masked by imagining hordes of radicalized youth, a wave of the future that will transform society. On the right, one can minimize the intense strains in the American polity by viewing it, and thus dismissing it, as merely a youth phenomenon—kid stuff. And for the troubled middle, it may be easier to contemplate a rift between the generations than to confront the depth and degree of our current social discord.

PRESENT AND FUTURE

A third error we make is to see the mood of the young—as we imagine that to be—as a forecast of longterm national tendencies. In our anxious scrutiny of youth, we attempt to divine the future, much as the ancients did in their perusal of the entrails of birds. Yet consider how radically the image of the American young has changed within as brief a period as a decade.

Ten years ago, we were distressed by the apparent apathy and conformism of the young, their seeming willingness, even eagerness, to be absorbed into suburban complacency. We were dismayed by the loss of that idealism, that amplitude of impulse we felt to be the proper mood of the young. By the early nineteen-sixties we were ready to believe that that lost idealism had been regained; the prevailing image then was of the Peace Corps volunteer, whose spirit of generous activism seemed so much in the American grain. And for the last few years we have been held by a view of youth fixed in despair and anger.

It should be evident that these rapid shifts in our idea of the young run parallel to changes in the American mood. As we moved from the quietude of the Eisenhower years, to the brief period of quickened hope in the Kennedy years, to our current era of bitter internal conflict dominated by a hateful war and a fateful racial crisis, so have our images of youth moved and changed. Yet, we were in each of these earlier periods as willing as we are today to view the then current mood of youth, as we saw it, as a precursor of the social future.

The young have always haunted the American imagination, and never more so than in the past two decades. The young have emerged as the dominant projective figures of our culture. Holden Caulfield, Franny Glass, the delinquents of the Blackboard Jungle, the beats and now the hippies and the young radicals—these are figures, essentially, of our interior landscape. They reflect and stand for some otherwise silent currents in American fantasy. They are the passive and gentle—Holden, Franny and now the flower children—who react to the hard circumstances of modern life by withdrawal and quiescence; or else they are the active and angry—the delinquents and now the radicals—who respond by an assault upon the system.

In these images, and in our tendency to identify ourselves with them, we can discover the alienation within all of us, old and young. We use the young to represent our despair, our violence, our often forlorn hopes for a better world. Thus, these images of adolescence tell us something, something true and something false, about the young; they may tell us even more about ourselves.

2 / THE YOUNG PEOPLE OF NORTH LONG BEACH

James Q. Wilson

North Long Beach, where I grew up, is one of the many communities in the Los Angeles basin that, blending imperceptibly into one another, seem to be neither city nor suburb. It is also a community that has reached maturity and begun to show its age. The period of rapid growth of the Thirties and Forties is at an end, and has

From *Harper's Magazine*, December, 1969. © 1969 by Minneapolis Star and Tribune Co., Inc. Reprinted by permission of author.

been for some time. Even in the Fifties, the population increased only by about 7,000 to a 1960 total of 48,000. An area of single-family houses, it has for many years seen little new construction of this sort; instead, the few remaining vacant lots, as well as the backyards of existing homes, are being filled in with small apartment buildings, two or three stories high, having little open space · and catering to older persons, young couples without children, or "singles." Long Beach was never the center of whatever youth culture Southern Californa may have—if any age-group in the city received special attention and concern, it was the old folks to be found near the public shuffleboard courts—and now with the population changes young people are even less at the center of gravity. North Long Beach has begun to change from being an outlying area in which child-rearing was the focus of life to a place out of which young couples move in search of larger or newer homes.

Today, as twenty years ago, the area is neither affluent nor squalid—it combines in a way unfamiliar to Easterners a suburban life-style (single-family homes, neat gardens) with a working-class and lower-middle-class population. Driving north on Atlantic Avenue from downtown Long Beach, one passes through Bixby Knolls, now, as in the past, a prosperous neighborhood bordering on the Virginia Country Club and with an attractive, off-the-street shopping center. North Long Beach begins abruptly as one passes under the Union Pacific railroad tracks and encounters, on each side of the street, small, semidetached stucco storefronts, painted various pastel shades and cluttered with a patchwork of neon signs. The street is broad, wider than many big-city thoroughfares, but the shops are almost all one-story and together they convey no clear sense of line, mass, or color. Things seem strangely out of scale and slightly out of focus—the stores are too low for the width of the road, and the muted green, beige, and pink colors offer no sharp contrast with the hazy, often smog-filled sky. Even the low-income public housing project on county land near the railroad tracks is distinctively Southern Californian. Though built over twenty years ago, it is set back off the main street and consists of one- and two-story buildings surrounded with grass and vegetation and painted the same yellow, green, and coral shades as private housing. It is into this area that most of the few Negro families in North Long Beach have moved, though many of the tenants are still white.

David Starr Jordan Senior High School, which I attended, first appears along Atlantic Avenue like an oasis. Towering palm trees border the well-kept park adjacent to the school, and the campus itself has tall eucalyptus trees that impart a sweetly pungent smell to the walks. In my student days, it was filled with children born in the Depression. For many, the bungalows of North Long Beach were their first non-farm homes, or at least their first taste of a city of any size. Though the war had just ended and many parents had saved a good deal of money from wages earned at the Douglas aircraft plant or in the Long Beach shipyards, there was not yet much to spend it on (the new postwar cars were eagerly awaited) and little inclination to hand it over to the kids. Many people spent what they had to pay off as much as they could on their house. Accordingly, there was little exotic clothing and few expensive hobbies—surfboards, for example, cost more than anybody I knew could afford. The young people were mostly Protestant and Midwestern, and all white.

Twenty years later, the young people look very much the same, only more prosperous. They are still Protestant, but now they are Californians, not Okies, Arkies, and Missourians. By 1968 eighteen black students had entered the high school, but a majority lived outside North Long Beach. Many, indeed, were transferred to Jordan High from other schools for disciplinary reasons, a system that may not augur well for the development of friendly inter-racial contacts among the students.

The young people, especially the girls, are better-dressed (and I think better-looking, though I can't trust my judgment on that) than in 1948, when I graduated. But their general style is very much the same—"really" or "real" is for them, as probably for all adolescents, still the standard, all-purpose adverb ("Gee, that's real great!") and "ya know" still serves as a kind of oral punctuation ("I think, ya know, he's all right, ya know?"). Big or difficult words are still avoided, even by bright students, because they convey ostentatious intellectuality; as one girl told me, "In class, I've gotta talk in words of one syllable, or the guys will think I'm a kiss-up" (*i.e.* teacher's pet).

Names have changed, at least for the girls. It is almost as if their parents, symbolizing the greater security and prosperity they felt as compared with *their* parents, wished to bestow first names that conveyed fashion and what they took to be urbanity. In the class of 1948, my yearbook tells me, girls' names were simple, straightforward—Patricia, Jo-Ann, Barbara, Shirley, Mary. Though there was one Darlene and a few other "stylish" names, they were the exception. Many boys had rural names—LaVerne, Dwayne, Dwight, Verlyn, Delbert, Berl, Virgil, Floyd. In the class of 1968, the girls had blossomed out with unusual names and unusual spellings of familiar names—no fewer than eight Sharons, six Cheryls, two Marlenes, two Sherrys, two Charlenes, and one each of Melodee, Jorjana, Candy, Joy, Cherry, Nanci, Carrolyn, Cyndi, and Darlene. Mary may be a grand old name, but it is no longer a very common one.

In a school where ethnic and class distinctions are either nonexistent or invisible, the social structure is organized around differences in behavior. There are distinct social groupings, complete with names, at Jordan High, though there is no agreement that they are hierarchically arranged, and little agreement as to the membership of each group. Most students, of course, belong to no particular group at all. Three that have names are the "soshes," the "surfers," and the "cruisers." "Sosh" is a word with a double meaning—perjorative for someone who is snobbish, aloof, or preoccupied with matters of dress and appearance, and descriptive for the well-dressed, personable young people who get elected to most of the student offices, are active in the clubs, and "support the school." They are great favorites of the teachers and the administrators, though they are also fearful of being thought "kiss-ups." Because the term has two meanings, no one with these attributes likes to apply it to himself, but for better or worse the obvious non-soshes use the label frequently and with respect to a clearly visible group.

"Surfers" may or may not be people who actually surf—indeed, most don't, though they all like the beach. The term applies not so much to what they do as to what they look like. Unlike the soshes', their hair is long (at the extreme, and there are a few cases at Jordan, the surfers fade into the hippies) and blond as a result of inheritance, sun, or chemicals. Compared to the soshes, they are more casual in dress and less deferential to teachers (though hardly rude). "Cruisers" (sometimes called "Northtowners") are the "rough" group oriented to automobiles and with little interest in studies. The boys wear their hair neither short (as do the soshes) nor long (as do the surfers) but in modest pompadours or otherwise waved. Their pants are tight, their shirts untidy (and, whenever they can get away with it, out of their pants), and their shoes run toward suede, sharp-toed, elevator-heel boots. Their girlfriends are called "hair girls" because they wear wigs or have their own hair arranged in fantastic creations rising precariously almost a foot above their heads and held in place with a hair spray that must have the adhesive power of epoxy cement. During compulsory physical education classes, all girls turn out for softball or other games dressed in regulation blue gym suits designed, no doubt intentionally, so as to make a Sophia Loren look like something out of Louisa May Alcott. The hair girls will be out, too, their towering creations waving unsteadily as they run about. A softball hit into one of those hairdos would have to be called a ground-rule double since it could not possibly be extracted in less than half an hour.

Cruisers cruise. The accepted routes are Atlantic Avenue and Bellflower Boulevard; the accepted cars are the ones that have been lowered, equipped with mag wheels (sometimes fake), and their windows decorated with a tasseled fringe and a hand-painted slogan ("Midnight Hour"); the accepted driving style is slowly, with the driver slumped down in his seat until only the top of his head shows and his hand draped casually out the window. Pinstriping, metallic paint, and other car fashions described by Tom Wolfe are no longer much in evidence around high schools (partly, no doubt, because customizing has become very expensive). And, sadly, the classic hot rods of the 1940s, with exposed, reworked engines, straight pipes, and minimal driver comfort are rare. Perhaps they have been taken over by adults whose nitro-methane fueled super-eliminators make a conventional hot rod look now like what it once emphatically was not—kid stuff. Or perhaps no one in North Long Beach knows how to make them anymore, or perhaps the parts are unavailable, or perhaps no one cares.

(For the benefit of middle-aged suburbanites anxious to close the generation gap, I should report seeing a customized Volkswagen driven by a young cruiser. It had a lowered front end, wide-oval racing tires on the rear, glistening paint, an extractor exhaust, and the word "Hessians" written in elegant script on the rear window. The beetle has been gilded.)

Casual observation of the campus conveys chiefly an impression of sameness—middle-class Wasp students preoccupied with social life, school activities, and class work. But the students themselves see differences where adults see similarities, and though the differences might be narrow indeed on a scale that included all teen-agers in the country, they are nonetheless important. I suspect the differences may be even more important today than twenty years ago, and that there are now fewer uniformities in behavior and manner. For example, in 1948 styles of dress were more or less standard (simple skirts, sweaters or blouses, and white Joyce shoes for girls; jeans or cords, and T-shirts and lettermen's sweaters for most boys); today, though scarcely radical by the standards of contemporary fashion, clothing is more varied, reflecting in part the freer choice that comes from prosperity and in part the emergence of more distinctive sub-groups with which students consciously identify.

Dress regulations have always been a major issue in the high school and a not infrequent cause of disciplinary action. The rules are set by a city-wide committee of students and teachers, subject to administrative approval, and revised annually. The effort to define what constitutes an acceptable mini-skirt has been abandoned as dress lengths have steadily risen, an inch or two ahead of the regulations every year. In resignation, the rule-makers have retreated into comfortable ambiguity, saying only that "skirts must be of reasonable length and appropriate for school wear." My close study of the situation suggests that the meaning of "reasonable" is not self-evident—some skirts come almost to the knee, some remain defiantly (and gloriously) at mid-thigh. For the boys, clothing must "avoid extremes," hair may come down to the collar but not below it, and sideburns and moustaches (but not beards) are all right. A few young men display long hair (thereby becoming surfers even if they don't know how to swim) but going beyond modest deviance is risky. As one football player and student officer told me, "The guys don't like hippies much. One of the guys walked up to a fella with hair down to his shoulders and just hauled off and hit him. A lot of guys will say something to the hippies, sort of challenge them, and if they answer back, then it can get rough."

One might suppose, to judge from the breathless accounts

given by a mass media fascinated by "youth culture," that teen-agers today thrive on individuality, independence, and fancifulness —each person "doing his own thing." Though this state of nature may prevail in some places, it is not found in North Long Beach, nor, I suspect, in most communities. Young people of course are always struggling to rebel against adult authority, but precisely because of that they tend to place even greater stock in the opinion of their peers. Teen-agers draw together, discovering themselves in the generalized opinion they form of each other—seeing them-selves reflected, as it were, in the eyes of their friends. What is surprising is not that their life tends to a certain uniformity in manners and dress, but that there is any heterogeneity at all.

The chief social values of the young people to whom I spoke (and whom I remember from two decades ago) are friendliness and, above all, "sincerity." Anything smacking of a pose, a "front," or "phoniness" is hotly rejected. The emphasis in Media Youth Culture on love, honesty, communication, and intense self-expression are not reactions *against* traditional youth values, but only extreme expressions *of* these values. Affluence, freedom, and rapid social change produce more exaggerated statements of the enduring concerns of young people (or, for that matter, most people) than a repudiation of those concerns. Of course, to a true hippie or young political radical, the Jordan High School student is at best a square—the embodiment of tradition, philistinism, and middle-class preoccupation with property, dating, and boosterism. Though in behavior and ideology the hippie and the square could not be more different, the animating impulse in both cases is sim-ilar—a deep concern with honesty in personal relations. For the "square," honesty is simply not as complex a value as for others.

Among surfer and sosh alike, as well as among the mass of unaffiliated students, the strongest criticism voiced about the be-havior or attitude of others is that it seemed "snobbish" or "phony" or that the individual was part of a "clique." The most popular students are not those one might imagine if one remem-bers the Hollywood musical comedies about campus life; they are not the socially aggressive "big men on campus." They are instead rather quiet persons who are socially at ease but who also embody in greatest degree the quality of being "sincere." The student-body president said little in meetings I attended of student leaders, but when he spoke, he was listened to respectfully—perhaps precisely because he did not chatter or try to be a wise guy and because he seemed to think carefully about what he wanted to say, and when he spoke he was neither flustered nor bombastic.

Still, I detect sharper cleavages among the social groupings of the students, sharper, that is, than I would have expected knowing merely that young people seek to find a place where they can belong and a circle they can join. I think that one new factor, almost unknown to my generation of students, helps explain these wider distinctions—drugs. There is no doubt whatever that at Jordan, as (according to the police) at all Long Beach high schools, illegal drugs (marijuana, barbiturates, amphetamines) are widely used. During the fall semester preceding my arrival on campus, twenty-six drug cases came to the attention of the school authorities. Every student I spoke to knew of persons who used drugs, several implied (without quite admitting) that they had used them, two or three told me they could make a purchase for me "within the hour" if I wanted. (I did not.)

Students were concerned about this and aware that certain social groupings were heavily populated with "dopies." (The term connotes more than it should. No one believes there are any addicts, or users of physiologically addicting drugs, among the students; drugs—"reds" and "whites"—are used much like alcohol, on weekends and at parties and occasionally at school.) Many kids are worried about drugs because of fears over health or acquiring a police record, and leery of groups or parties where the dopies gather. For the city as a whole, police arrests of juveniles in cases involving marijuana increased between 1962 and 1968 from 18 to 186; cases involving pills rose from 12 to over 650. For a student, being a user—or worse, being caught as a user—intensifies normal social cleavages.

For some boys, athletics is seen not only as fun but as an absorbing activity that increases one's chances of staying away from a social life involving dopies. One player told me that "if it hadn't been for football" he probably "would have wound up where the guys I used to hang around with are"—in trouble with the school and the police. On the other hand, the same young people reject as "phony" many of the materials they see in class designed to warn them of the dangers of drug use. One complained that "The stuff they show you in those movies about dirty old men hanging around school trying to push dope—that's all pretty stupid, that's not the way it is at all. Anybody who wants to buy drugs can get them easy."

Perhaps because social groupings are more sharply defined, perhaps for other reasons, most students complained that there was not enough "school spirit" and that many of the formal student organizations were "meaningless" or ineffective. "Nobody cares about the school," one girl said. "There are no cheers at the pep assemblies." Many students think student government is a "waste of time" (only a third of the students voted in the last election), and most of those in student government worry about the same thing—organizations seem weak, "spirit" is flagging.

If the football team could have a winning season, this all might change, but it has not for some time, mainly, it appears, because it is playing over its head in a league composed of several larger schools with more and bigger talent to draw on. But nobody is convinced that a losing record in football is the whole reason. One girl (labeled by others a surfer though she herself, as everybody else, refused to accept any label) said that students want to be "more individual" not "try to act just like the soshes," but then complained of the absence of school spirit. I asked her whether more intense individualism was incompatible with school spirit; she puzzled over it a moment and then said she guessed that was right.

The formal student organizations cut across the informal social groupings, and that may be one reason for their weakness. More than thirty clubs exist in a student body of 2,200, chiefly to serve social, vocational, or hobby interests. The Shutterbugs enjoy camera, the Rooks play chess, the Thespians participate in drama, the Girls' Rifle Team does whatever girls do with rifles. There are chapters of Future Teachers of America and Future Medical Leaders of America. Music produces the most organizations, partly because many grow directly out of elective classes—the Concert Band, the Orchestra, the Marching Band, the Military Band, the String Quartet, A Capella, the Girls' Choir, the Mixed Chorus, the Choraliers, the Straw Hatters. An important way in which the community reaches into the school is through the sponsorship of student organizations by business and civic associations—the Kiwanis sponsors the Key Club, Rotary sponsors Interact.

Because the formal organizations crosscut, rather than coincide with, informal groupings, their vitality is compromised (except those which pursue a clear activity, such as the music organizations). Social organizations are not, and under school rules cannot be, exclusive as to membership, and thus a number of unofficial, "secret" organizations flourish. These are mainly fraternities and sororities that have no (and want no) approved adult sponsor, and thus are illegal. The administration struggles against them, but with little success. Students differ as to the importance of the secret organizations; some members feel they have declined in recent years but all members compare them favorably to the official clubs with open memberships, no hazing, adult sponsors and, thus, no fun.

One official organization that has both a large number of followers and considerable respect is Campus Life, a quasi-religious group begun by members of the Youth for Christ movement. It holds a number of dances during the year and in addition has education programs featuring, for example, films about LSD or other controversial subjects. The popularity of Campus Life is one current indication of an enduring feature of community and school—the extraordinary importance of churches. The area from the first had many storefront Protestant sects and the more successful of these have become large, active organizations. The local Brethren church, for example, has a huge physical plant, including a school, and runs a number of well-attended youth activities. Mormons for decades have accounted for a sizable fraction of the student population, and Baptists, Methodists, and Presbyterians are also numerous. It is difficult to assess the religious significance of the strong and clear church affiliations, but their social and institutional importance are unmistakable.

The most striking aspect of organizational life, however, is the complete absence of any group devoted to questions of public policy, world affairs, or community issues. Only one club, Cosmopolitan, touches matters external to the school (it organizes and raises money for an exchange-student program that brings one foreign student to campus each year and sends one Jordanite abroad). Twenty or twenty-five years ago, in the years of slowly fading optimism following the second world war, the World Friendship Club was an active organization, sponsoring an annual World Friendship Day and meeting regularly to study international events with heavy emphasis, as I recall, on the Chinese government of Chiang Kai-shek and especially on the views of Madame Chiang. Neither the club nor the day remains, and no new policy area has generated any substitutes.

I asked various groups of students what questions other than personal or campus matters concerned them, but other than one boy who mentioned the draft, I got no clear answers. To be sure, if I had asked them whether they were interested in, say, civil rights or the Vietnam war, many would have said they were. And most issues of this sort are discussed, often heatedly, in their classes. But what is impressive is that no general question, couched in broad terms, elicited any strong feelings or active, spontaneous concern. The issues which they did volunteer were wholly campus-oriented—the students had argued with the principal over the date of the senior prom, there was some indignation about a fence that had been erected between the school and the adjacent park (not, it seems to keep the kids in but to keep "undesirables" out), and some complaints about the tight control the administration was believed to exercise over the contents of the student newspaper. Some students noted wistfully that another high school in the city had an underground newspaper but almost in the same breath said they did not like the recent efforts of a group of older men, perhaps college students, to distribute such a paper on the Jordan campus.

In an era of "aroused" youth preoccupied with "relevance," why should the young people of North Long Beach be neither aroused nor relevant? It is easy, too easy, to think of explanations, some plausible but none convincing. The students are "middle-class," they are Wasps, they live in a "sheltered community," there are few Jewish students on campus, North Long Beach is not a "central city," they are all part of Southern California and probably "just another crop of young backlashers." And of course their parents were not radical; no Jordan student could be a "red diaper baby." Some explanations, especially the last one, have partial significance but none satisfies me. What is perhaps equally important, none would even be intelligible to the persons described. To them, almost everybody is middle-class; extremes of wealth or poverty are outside their experience. Some may know what "Wasp" means, but the term is still an Eastern invention, largely marketed in the East. Long Beach is, to them, neither sheltered nor "non-central"—to them, it is highly "central." ("We've got everything around us here," one said. "The beach, the mountains, LA, Hollywood, Disneyland. It's really great.") As for the idea that families have a tradition of liberalism or radicalism, they can scarcely imagine it. And they would be embarrassed to hear anyone speak of the influence of Jewish culture on social change— it's "not nice" to speak of a person's religion, you "shouldn't generalize" about other people, and besides the Jews are supposed to be just like everyone else.

The most important fact about these students is not their class, ethnicity, religion, or location; the most important thing about them is their age. They are sixteen years old, give or take a year or two. They are coming to grips with problems of identity, sex, career, and adult authority. Their responses to these central concerns produce the social groupings we see—the soshes, with their ready acceptance of adult values, especially the virtues of work, service, neatness, neighborliness; the cruisers, with their rejection of those values, their open pursuit of girls as objects of conquest, their contempt for studies that signifies either rebellion or despair; the surfers, who are reevaluating standards, suspending judgments, and above all resisting a premature commitment to the adult world or any abandonment of values of individuality, which they greatly prize. When one is sixteen, the larger world does not touch one, except in crisis or because one's parents make involvement in that world a central adult value. In a profound sense, community or world issues are irrelevant to the focal concerns of the students, and not vice versa.

Now, as when I was in that world, young people have great natural idealism, but the objects of that idealism are principally personal relations (friendship, the team, the "crush") or else distant and lofty goals (religiosity, human brotherhood in some ultimate sense, world peace). There is rarely any middle ground (again, except when circumstances provide it) of public policy toward which one acts or about which one thinks with much intensity. When an issue from the middle range intrudes, an effort is made to translate it into simpler human values. One student leader spoke critically of the demonstrations on college campuses because they showed a "lack of respect for other people"; another (in a classroom discussion) was critical of de Gaulle's policies toward the United States because he had displayed neither gratitude nor fairness; a third, in a class report on pornography, concluded that censorship wouldn't work but that we must be careful, as parents, to inculcate "the right moral values" in our children.

There is less aversion to classroom discussion of controversial issues than when I attended Jordan but the same tendency to evaluate or resolve those issues by reaffirming traditional values. It would have been most unlikely that, twenty years ago, a girl would have given an illustrated report on pornography, much less gather material for that report by attending (with her brother) a skin flick and patronizing a downtown dirty book store. Had the discussion occurred, the boys in the back of the room would have nervously snickered over the (rather mild) illustrations and concluded that the girl must not be "nice" and thus fair game. There were no snickers, nervous or otherwise, the discussion was matter-of-fact (and rather quickly branched off to include student use of marijuana and drugs), and the girl was obviously "nice." The teacher played almost no role in the uninhibited discussion that followed but despite this, a general agreement on the importance of morality and family training was quickly reached. At this point, several girls spoke disapprovingly of the looseness of the "younger generation," by which they meant their ten-year-old kid brothers. "They are learning too much, too soon," one said. "You'd be amazed at the words and things they know *already!* It wasn't like that for *me.*"

* * *

Jordan High School, like North Long Beach, has not changed in any fundamental way. New buildings of green and pink stucco have replaced the wooden bungalows in which I attended class, but the social structure and the values of the people are essentially the same, modified, perhaps, by the influence of higher incomes and the settled sense of being a "Californian" rather than a migrant. So striking is the continuity one finds in North Long Beach that one is tempted to describe it under a pseudonym, and then let the reader guess where it is actually located. Many will suppose, even as I might have supposed, that it is an isolated backwater of the nation—a small town in Iowa, perhaps, or a suburb of Omaha.

But it is not: it is near the center of one of the most populous, affluent, mobile, media-conscious areas in the United States, part of a state where Robert F. Kennedy and Eugene McCarthy met head-on in a bitter, closely watched primary election, and very near the place where, in August of 1965, the "black revolt" is thought to have begun. At one nearby university, two Black Panthers were recently shot and killed; at two others, a fraction of the student body has been in open revolt.

The Jordan students are aware of the turmoil but not seized by it. How it has affected them will probably not be apparent for years. Already, of course, the older teachers lament that the "work ethic" has been eroded: "They just don't seem to work as hard in class as they used to," one told me. "There's no real discipline problem, but it seems as if they want to be entertained more, they want to know what they'll get out of it if they do an assignment." Another veteran teacher agreed, but thought the reason was not in broad social changes or in student values, but in the school itself: "Increasingly, the emphasis here is on college preparation, but when you get right down to how many actually go to a four-year college, the answer is, damned few. For the rest, we're not preparing them for much of anything. Some shouldn't even be here— they ought to be out learning a trade, but the law says we have to keep them here until they're sixteen."

It is hard to evaluate such comments. Men in their fifties are bound to see young people somewhat differently than the same men in their thirties. At the end of one's career, students may not seem as bright, or as hard-working, or as exciting as they did when one first started teaching. But there is another possibility: the great increase in the proportion of students going on to college, even if only to City College, as a result of both parental pressure and their own assessment of career needs, has undoubtedly placed great strains on the normal social processes of the high school. The new definition of success—college and a "good" job, rather than immediate marriage and "any" job—represents simultaneously a school norm, an adult expectation, and an adolescent hope. The normal (and normally minor) symptoms of youthful rebellion against those adult expectations that seem excessive, unreal, or unrelated to their own needs and opportunities may have been intensified by these newer and more demanding expectations which have made high school seem less "fun," less responsive to adolescent interests, and more a system to be beaten by doing what is necessary but doing it without zeal. Even the elusive school spirit that students find so lacking may be in part the victim of a process that has made the high school less an end in itself and more a means to a larger and more equivocal end—career success.

Underlying the continuity of manner and style, there may thus be deeper changes at work. But it is unlikely they arise from what, in our intense preoccupation with the immediate crises of race and peace, we imagine—not from the issues and fashions of the moment, but from a fundamental restructuring of the ways in which one enters society and the labor force, and thus of ways in which one grows up.

3 / THE RIGHT TO COLLEGE

Maurice R. Berube

The Nixon Administration has ordered a major retreat in providing educational opportunities for the poor. In his State of the Union message, President Nixon carefully excluded education as part of the "range of opportunities for all Americans" to "fulfill the American dream." Instead, the President emphasized voting rights, employment and ownership as the triad of government priorities to end poverty. In the name of economy, the President pledged that his Administration would scuttle "pending programs" even though they may "benefit some of the people" because "their net effect would result in price increases for all the people."

From *Commonweal*, April 3, 1970. Reprinted with permission of Commonweal Publishing Co., Inc.

One of these "pending programs" would attempt to guarantee a college education to all Americans. For some time now, the President, Secretary of Health, Education and Welfare, Robert Finch, and Commissioner of Education, James Allen, have had such a program before them. This program, first commissioned by President Johnson in the last months of his Administration, recommends a system of universal higher education. According to the designers of this program, an unwilling President Nixon has been forced to consider a national universal higher education policy. And he has rejected this "pending program"—a legacy of Johnson's Great Society—as too costly.

In October of 1968, an amendment to the Higher Education Act of 1965, sponsored by Democrats, Senator Ralph Yarborough and Representative James Scheuer, established the groundwork for a national policy on free higher education. Known as the "508 study," it instructs that "on or before December 31, 1969, the President shall submit to Congress proposals relative to the feasibility of making available a post-secondary education to all Americans who qualify and seek it." In short, a universal higher education law.

Plainly embarrassed by this Democratic maneuver, the incoming Republican President went through the motions of fulfilling the mandate. After a long delay, Office of Education specialists and education consultants from research institutes argued out the semblance of a national higher education policy in a series of small white papers. The Democratic holdovers in the Office of Education, with some outside support, favored a spending program, at least as a long-range goal, whereas Nixon representatives in the Office took a more conservative approach.

Key issues were the role of the Federal government and aid directly to the pupil or to the institution. Following the lead of Clark Kerr's and Harry Rivlin's private studies, most of the papers opted for a spending program that would be institution-oriented with Federal cost-of-education supplements. Under the cost-of-education principle the Federal government would reimburse the college for the education of those students who are poor. Although Commissioner Allen favored such a spending program, the White House did not. As a result, the President technically failed to present the recommendation of the "508 study" by the required deadline. Those who worked on the study suspect that he will make some passing reference in a later education message to fulfill the intent of the law. But for all practical purposes the "508 study" lies buried deep on the Presidential desk.

Instead, President Nixon proposed an Educational Opportunity Act which constitutes a mild effort to placate demands that the poor be given a free college education. Mainly, the President has amended but one small current Federal program—that of Federal loans—so that only the poor can now qualify for student loans. By themselves, these student loans act more as a deterrent than an incentive for college; they are burdensome to repay and only the most ambitious seek them out. Nixon's proposal came on the heels of a recommendation to completely overhaul all current Federal programs, in response to the second report of the Carnegie Commission on Equality in Higher Education chaired by Clark Kerr. Although stopping short of a free, open admissions policy, the Kerr group advanced Federal reforms that would enable all high school students, who so wished, to be in college by 1970; and all students, including those with severe learning disabilities, to be in some college by the end of the century. The disparity between Nixon's tepid proposal and the Carnegie plan indicates the severe educational lag of the government.

The national attitude towards education as an antidote to poverty was not so previously jaundiced. Both the Kennedy and Johnson Administrations embodied education as a major theme of their poverty programs: nearly every domestic reform program included some educational training. And President Johnson and Vice President Humphrey displayed a reverence for education that only a former schoolteacher and a former college professor could possess, by sponsoring more educational legislation than had been enacted in the previous 190-odd years of the Republic.

Moreover, President Johnson had let it be known through his Special Assistant for Education, Douglas Cater, that he privately favored 14 years of free schooling—beyond High School into Junior College. In addition to these public rumblings Johnson made some significant private soundings on the cost of such a venture. In late 1966, a series of highly confidential studies on universal higher education were completed for the President. Since Johnson considered assuming the tuition costs of every student, his consultants priced direct Federal financing of two college years for all students at some $400 million dollars—an amount far from exorbitant. Currently higher education expenditures total $18-$19 billion of a national education bill of some $58.5 billion. When one considers that our Gross National Product of $932 billion will, in the next decade, by President Nixon's own estimates, increase some 50 per cent, such a system of free higher education does not appear too expensive.

What prevented Johnson from passing a universal higher education law, of course, was his escalation of the Vietnam war, which consumed most of the Federal budget. Even with an end to the war, however, it is extremely unlikely Nixon would divert monies toward expanded higher education opportunities. What funds have already been earmarked will go towards a clean waters program and welfare reform. Clearly, President Nixon is concerned with "managing" the existent Federal investment rather than incurring fresh obligations.

Johnson, however, broke no new ground. Traditionalist that he was—his great desire to emulate Roosevelt led him only so far as to propose a Great Society that would make good the unfinished business of the New and Fair Deals—Johnson followed in his Democratic predecessor's footsteps. What Johnson advocated echoed the seminal report of President Truman's 1947 Commission on Higher Education. The report concluded that the nation must "make education through the fourteenth grade available in the same way that high school education is now available." The Commission, composed of representatives of the education establishment, interpreted the "critical need" of higher education for all "in the light of the social role" of colleges and universities. And it was "obvious" to the members of Truman's Commission "that free and universal access to education, in terms of the interest, ability and need of the student, must be a major goal in American education." Twenty years later Johnson would merely reinforce the same concept.

But, most important, the Commission clearly enunciated a *right* to college. Education, the report intoned, was not only the "biggest and the most hopeful of the Nation's enterprises," it was the "foundation of democratic liberties." Moreover, education was a "birthright." This, the Commission report reassured, was nothing less than part and parcel of the "democratic creed" that "assumes (education) to be their (Americans') birthright: an equal chance with all others to make the most of their native abilities."

What prompted the Commission report was the experience of the GI Bill of Rights—the nearest equivalent to universal higher education. The GI Bill gave rise to mass education and to the more potent questions such opportunities raised. The Truman Commission grappled with the problems of deciding who should go to college. Their answer was framed in the egalitarian American tradition: everyone. They offered a series of recommendations that optimistically would result in having all students, who so wished, in some college by 1960. One generation and four Presidents later we are still considering that proposition.

Two developments have since changed the character of the debate over who should go to college. The emergence of a post-industrial state after World War II with a service economy that generates nearly two-thirds of its jobs in white collar fields has made college education a *sine qua non* for economic advancement. The result is that a majority of our college-age population attends some form of higher institution; the typical American possesses approximately 13 years of schooling. Consequently, some college becomes increasingly necessary as a credential for employment.

And the nature of the college and university has quietly shifted from private to public. As the costs of college education increase, these institutions have more and more relied on Federal beneficence. Federal monies account for over a fourth of all higher education expenses. And for our leading "private" universities, such as Princeton and Columbia, Federal outlays account for as much as 50 to 80 per cent of the costs of operating these universities. It is difficult, under these circumstances, to conceive of Princeton, for example, as a "private" university. And as Federal support increases, according to all expectations, the distinction between private and public universities will be further blurred.

The Federal government, therefore, is under a moral and social imperative to provide equality of educational opportunity to all—not only to assist the education of the affluent youngster at Princeton, who can pay, but the black student from a Chicago ghetto who cannot. Thus, the need for a college background in today's market and the changing character of most of our system of higher education into a "public" rather than a "private" system, reinforces the egalitarian concept of college as a "birthright."

But, can we afford to send to college all those who want to go? Certainly not without strong Federal support. If one can base policy on the Gallup Poll's report that 97 per cent of all parents want their children in college, and that these children go on to college, the costs would more than double—from the current $18 billion to educate 6 million students to well over $40 billion to educate upwards of 9 million students. And the amount would increase as more students went to college. Even under a modified system of universal higher education as recommended in the "508 study" the costs would be substantial. Nevertheless, the Federal government has the means to pay *all* higher education costs.

Initially, an open admissions policy would not be too great a burden. The open admissions plan for next year at the City University of New York's nine senior and seven community colleges would add some 9,000 students to the already 180,000-member student body—not too dramatic an increase. But, only 10 per cent of the students in the senior colleges and 26 per cent in the junior colleges are black and Puerto Rican in a city where well over half the public school population is black and Puerto Rican. In time, open admissions will mean more money. Still, California has managed to offer college to all who desire it in the state since 1960— the first open admissions plan in the nation—without undue financial strain.

Enlightened educators have argued for a progressive increase in Federal aid as the only solution to the problems of higher education. They have hoped that Washington would double its current investment by the mid-70s—to account for one-half the total cost of higher education—and that by the end of the century, the Federal government would be paying all of the bills. "If this nation's needs for higher education are to be met in the years to come, the Federal government will have to accept the principal part of the consequent financial burden," Carnegie Foundation head Alan Pifer has stated. "And, judging from the statements of those representing higher education, this is what they think and want, as contrasted with an earlier period when there was considerable doubt."

However these educators may welcome Federal aid, they are not so enthusiastic over a national open admissions plan. "We may see the decline of our great colleges and universities," fears Martin Meyerson, President of the State University of New York, "as admissions become broader under a variety of pressures." The cause for alarm over the lowering of academic standards, however, has little justification. The consequences of the GI Bill were not a devaluation of the academy. It is not only difficult to imagine that universal higher education will mean the death of the university but the evidence does not support such a calamitous view.

Many educators equate education standards, more often than not, with selective admissions. Only since World War II and the rise of mass education, have colleges strengthened their admissions requirements. Since then, college administrators of both public and private universities have felt, correctly, that they were in a seller's market. Consequently, they introduced the theory of selective admissions: out of the mass of applicants one could pick and choose an academic elite. College administrators then made it increasingly difficult for a high school student to get into college. For example, in order for a poor youngster, last year, from New York City to qualify for admission to City College he had to obtain an 85 per cent scholastic average in his high school combined with a high test score from a specially designed Scholastic Aptitude Test. In 1924 that high school average requirement was only 72 per cent; in 1936, 78 per cent. It is the poor, particularly the black and Puerto Rican poor, who suffer most from selective admissions. Whereas an institution such as City University, like other public universities, served well the depression immigrant poor—through a modest admissions policy—it has (until recently) held back the black and Puerto Rican poor through a more stringent admissions policy.

The assumptions of selective admissions are deceptively simple. Once one considers the inability to educate all who apply —on the grounds that the educational plant is lacking—then the job is to choose those applicants most likely to succeed in college. So admissions policies are generally predicted on high school performance plus additional aptitude tests that would serve to verify that performance. This circular reasoning served admission people well: One expects students admitted to succeed in college, these expectations influence that success, and that success confirms one's expectations.

However, the doctrine of selective admissions has been far from infallible. Recent national studies on student achievement show a student's college performance to be an extension of his high school performance; so that one can expect any high school graduate to survive college. Significantly, a fourth of the students sampled did less well than expected and ten per cent did better.

Another important study of "high risk" students, by Professor Robert Williams, of all the current programs for students who are poor, showed that these students were as likely to make it in college as their more affluent counterparts. Williams estimated that at least half of the nation's colleges and universities operated some form of program for children of the poor. (None, however, made strenuous effort to recruit students with severe learning problems.) And the ingredients for academic success of these students in these programs transcended traditional admission requirements. Among the criteria, Professor Williams suggested, were such elusive qualities of student learning-potential as "minimal perception of self-worth," emotional toughness, intense motivation to improve one's life and success in some activity other than scholastic which requires sustained effort. And special remedial programs, such as the SEEK tutorial program operating in New York, would help those students from the ghetto with serious academic deficiencies. In short, there is every reason to believe that a national open admissions policy would not lower educational standards, would not mean a revolving door experience for the poor and would not destroy the university.

What is most pernicious about the selective admissions myth is that it pervades even our policy of more liberal universal higher education. Good students are steered into the four-year academic colleges and poor students into the more vocationally-oriented community colleges. The proliferation of community colleges, at the expense of the regular academic college, has managed, in effect, to create a tracked system of higher education. And this track system further impoverishes the disadvantaged. Studies of the California system show that less money is spent on the education of the poorer community college student than the more affluent senior college student. Moreover, the desire for social mobility of the poor is more hindered than helped by the community college. They are more likely programmed into para-professional and white collar jobs that have little chance of advancement. All in the name of selective admissions.

A key demand of the black students in last year's CUNY protest was for admission of all black high school students into the senior colleges. Thus, the tracked system would be avoided. It is this particular request that has made educators and politicians anxious over open admissions.

Nevertheless, it is difficult to comprehend the rationale for continuing selective admissions through a track system. Prospective college students should be free to attend the college of their choice, regardless of their academic records. Historically, college was the preserve of a leisure class, without particular academic merit. College faculties would educate the sons and daughters of the rich into good citizens without concern over their academic potential. The poor, alas, were something else. In order to qualify for a college education they had to show merit. Thus, in the 19th century, American college presidents devised the scholarship scheme— for bright poor youngsters—as a means of entering the privileged academic groves. But the not-so-bright poor were never to be so fortunate as to join this Calvinistic elect. These attitudes persevere today.

Yet there is no reason why poor not-so-bright students should not be entitled to an academic college education. (New York's Governor Nelson Rockefeller has often admitted he was a mediocre student and that he graduated from Dartmouth only because his name was Rockefeller.) The meritocratic conception of education only superficially appears egalitarian. In reality it resembles most the harsh Calvinism of our Puritan forebears, which sanctified the *status quo*: the gifted and well-to-do who succeed possess an inner grace, whereas the less gifted and less affluent who fail were so destined. By not helping the least able, meritocracy merely sanctions the results of a race that was fixed to begin with.

That the poor—including the least intellectually gifted— should have the option to exercise their right to college should not be construed as but a more subtle appeal to meritocracy. What David Bazelon extols as a "new class," based on education rather than property, has dubious value. As Professor S. M. Miller and Ivar Berg clearly point out, this "new class"—a "credentials society"—is but a programmed distortion whereby hiring is based on academic credentials which, in turn, militate against job performance. Berg's studies show, for example, that many over-educated employees are less efficient, less productive and less personally fulfilled than those employees who have little comparable academic background but come up through the ranks. The classic example Berg cites of overqualification is of the editorial secretary with a college degree, who rarely is advanced to the editorial position she wanted in the first place.

This criticism of the credentials society raises some profound questions. For one thing, formal education does not present a necessarily elevated processing for many. It is doubtful whether either many talented people—or not so talented—could flourish under academic auspices, no matter what educational reform could be accomplished. The counter-culture, the current phrase replacing the old "avant garde," certainly does not thrive in average formal settings; one is hard-pressed to conjure up images of Allen Ginsberg with a Ph.D. in English Literature. This example can be multiplied in other areas.

Equally important, the economy is still sufficiently fluid to avoid the rigid stratification of meritocracy. The only job category —professional technocrats—requiring specialized academic preparation remains at a rather stable ten per cent or so of the work force. Still, the relation between education and income is great, so that one cannot disregard the economic value of college. And last year nearly 60 per cent of college students were the first in their families to go to college, attesting to their regard for the social mobility implicit in a degree. Up to now, college has been, in the main, an alternative the poor—except for the brightest among them—could not pursue.

The arguments for a national policy of free higher education for all are overwhelming. Moreover, the nation has sufficient resources and growth prospects to pay for such a policy. But, the Federal government must take the lead in making the rhetoric of equality a reality. So far, a policy that was contemplated a generation ago has faltered. And President Nixon has signaled another step backward in his preoccupation with "developing better ways of managing what we have." For all those Americans who do not have—and who will need a college education to have—the President's words do not offer hope.

4 / THE DRUG EXPLOSION

Joel Fort

If you pick 20 adults at random, the odds are that 15 of them drink moderately, two are problem drinkers and one is a desperate alcoholic. Two who use alcohol are also using marijuana, a couple are taking tranquilizers on doctors' orders and one or two have been popping barbiturates to relieve insomnia and are perilously close to addiction. Three or four have taken amphetamines to stay awake or to lose weight and nearly all of them drink caffeine, another stimulant. Ten or 12 of this group of 20 continue to smoke tobacco even after the medical hazards of that habit have been amply documented. One has probably taken acid or mescaline. The children of some have sniffed glue or carbon tet for kicks (thereby risking brain and liver damage), more smoke pot and some have had an LSD trip. The drug culture, as the newspapers call it, doesn't just belong to the kids; everyone's in it together.

The hard figures on drug use in America today are dramatic. Taking our society's favorite drugs in order of their popularity, alcohol heads the list—and has ever since Colonial times. Just 20

From *Playboy*, September 1972. Copyright © 1972 by Playboy. Reprinted by permission of Playboy and the author.

years after the Pilgrims landed, William Bradford was fretting in his diaries about the number of drunks running around Plymouth; and in the three centuries since, the problem has only grown with the population, quite in spite of religious disapproval, temperance movements and even a constitutional amendment. In 1970, in fact, 23,400 highway fatalities were traceable to alcohol. That is 64 every day: almost three every hour.

Warning: The Surgeon General has determined that cigarette smoking is dangerous to your health. But the warnings are recent and a cultural habit as widespread as smoking is not easily changed. Among the 51,300,000 Americans who still smoke, 250,000 can be expected to die from it this year. And the prospects are for more of the same—250,000 deaths every year until the end of this century.

If there is one drug problem today that remains practically invisible, it's pill taking. Chiefly through television, we've grown accustomed to the notion that the only way to deal with those hammers pounding in our heads, lightning bolts shooting into our spines and gremlins bowling in our stomachs is to take a pill; and in the past decade or so, we have extended that practice to include a considerable variety of psychological ailments as well. Today 35,000,000 Americans use sedatives, stimulants or tranquilizers, mostly obtained legally through their doctors. Despite this medical supervision, between 500,000 and 1,000,000 of these people have become abusers. Manufacturers, meanwhile, continue to produce such pills abundantly and with apparent enthusiasm, turning out roughly 80,000 pounds of amphetamines and 1,000,000 pounds of barbiturates in 1970 alone. Some have bizarre distribution routes: One respectable firm was discovered by the House Select Committee on Crime to be shipping to a golf hole in Tijuana, from which the product returned to the United States and entered the black market. Perhaps 100,000 young people who are introduced to amphetamine-based drugs in this way graduate to methamphetamine (speed), which is injected into the veins like heroin and can cause rapid mind deterioration, while chronic abuse produces severe symptoms of paranoid psychosis. Some meth freaks graduate easily to heroin, seemingly the quickest way to soothe a frantic speed trip.

Unlike alcohol, tobacco or speed, marijuana apparently has no permanent and only a few transitory side effects—yet in many states, the penalties for simple possession are severe. But all the legal sanctions against it have had about the same effect that Prohibition had on our drinking habits. When Harry Anslinger first convinced Congress in the mid-Thirties that pot was an evil killer weed, it was being used almost exclusively by Mexican-Americans and blacks. But it has flourished under oppression: In the past five years, it has spread throughout the middle class, and right now some 20,000,000 to 30,000,000 people have tried it, with perhaps 10,000,000 being regular users.

Psychedelic-hallucinogenic drugs, credited for a brief generation of star-wandering rock music and bright melting poster art, are generally less popular now than they were a few years ago. Nonetheless, it's estimated that 1,000,000 Americans have tried LSD, mescaline or similar psychedelics. The number of regular psychedelic users is relatively small in comparison with drinkers or grass smokers, but there are still enough of them—and they still manage to have enough bad trips—to keep acid-rescue telephone services alive and busy in almost every major city.

There are at least 200,000 (and perhaps as many as 400,000) junkies in the nation today, making heroin addiction one of the smallest yet most sensationalized of our drug problems. Recently, the heroin habit has been changing its nature: Where most addicts used to be poor and black, now a large percentage come from the white middle class. More depressing: Younger children are becoming involved. New York City has had a rash of heroin-overdose deaths of teenagers.

Some doctors are predicting a heroin epidemic. Others, such as Dr. Helen Nowlis of the U.S. Office of Education and Professor Samuel Pearlman of New York's Inter-University Drug Survey Council, insist that students are very aware of the perils of heroin and most want nothing to do with it. What is undeniable is that many children who should know better are playing around with heroin needles.

There is no consistent antidrug movement; but there is a strong ideological conflict over which drugs are socially acceptable and which are not. On one side is the booze-and-trank-using group; on the other side is the pot-and-psychedelic-using group. Conventional wisdom classifies the first group as mostly older and conservative, the second as primarily young and radical. But the lines, if they really exist, are being crossed: Some pot users are past 40, some of the young are conservative and use drugs more commonly associated with the older generation. Barbiturates and amphetamines, on the other hand, are not characterized by any identifiable patterns. LSD, which reached the peak of its popularity in most colleges around 1968 and has been declining ever since, is just beginning to be a fad at some Southern universities; while at Swarthmore a student told *The New York Times* that "the jocks are getting into drugs and all the freaks are going to alcohol." Meanwhile, conflict continues to flourish on all levels: When the mayor's office of the District of Columbia released a recent report on drug abuse in the capital, it was rumored that one member of the committee that had drafted the report lit a joint during the press conference and smoked it in front of the reporters to dramatize his opposition to the study's anti-marijuana bias.

None of this is as new as most commentators seems to think. Drug taking in America goes back to the Indians' tobacco farms, their occasional use of deliriants such as Jimson weed and the religious use of peyote and magic mushrooms. The first Pilgrims brought in ample rum and made it an integral part of the slave trade; alcohol excesses, some historians think, were actually widespread in England by the 18th Century. In the second half of the 19th Century, along with the Civil War, came a wave of morphine addiction and, soon after, patent medicines consisting mainly of alcohol often spiked with opium derivatives began hooking some of their many users. There was even a Hashish Club in New York City in the 1850s where writers and artists met to turn on and recount their visions to one another, while scholarly Fitz Hugh Ludlow was quite legally (there was no anti-pot law then) gathering the experiences for his famous *The Hasheesh Eater*. Around the turn of the century, a Harvard psychologist named not Timothy Leary but William James was dosing himself with nitrous oxide and discovering religious significance in the experiences so gained.

Nor is this peculiarly American. The earliest brewery, found in Egypt, is dated at 3700 B.C. and there is evidence that people used alcohol as far back as the Stone Age. Some paleolithic tribes in the Near East even buried their dead with marijuana plants, evidently with religious intent. Around the world, people continue to chew, smoke and drink every plant and shrub that alters their consciousness, provides temporary escape or increases their pleasure: There are more than 200,000,000 Cannabis (marijuana) users in the world today, for instance, and we have only a fraction of them in the United States.

What is unique about the American drug scene are (1) the accelerated rate at which changes are occurring, (2) the controversy over the use of drugs and (3) the increasing lack of discrimination shown by many in their choice of intoxicants and the amounts used. The main factor is the accelerated rate of change, which is also true of all other areas of our life these days and is creating the phenomenon known as future shock. But this cultural mutation, even without the dizzying speed at which it is occurring, would have to create problems in a society that is still flirting heavily with puritanism and still tends to believe that all behavior is molded by punishment. The reaction of people in power to drugs, both those that are truly dangerous and those that are merely annoying to their prejudices, has been the same: Make the drug takers uncomfortable. When this doesn't work, the next step is more punishment. Harsher laws. Longer sentences. More narcotics agents. And when this in turn doesn't work, the next move is further escalation, and so on. But it's a solution that has created more problems than it has solved. Moreover, it hasn't worked.

The fallacy of the punishment theory is best illustrated by the heroin problem, which is small in terms of the number of individuals involved. A free society of 200,000,000 could easily tolerate and nullify the negative effects of our 200,000 junkies. Instead, they have been criminalized, thereby driving the price of their fix up from a few cents to $50 or more a day. Since few can afford that price, most are forced to steal or become prostitutes—and to earn $50 per day from underworld fences, a man must steal at least $100 worth of property. One hundred dollars times 200,000 addicts is $20,000,000 per day that gets stolen from the rest of us, and that is 7.3 billion dollars per year. Anybody in a large city with an apartment window facing a fire escape has learned the individual application of that figure. Alcohol prohibition produced even more expensive by-products in terms of the black market in that drug, the creation of organized crime and the foundation of the narcotics traffic. Not only did alcohol and pot prohibition increase the use of those drugs but the pot laws have caused countless harmless citizens to spend long unproductive periods behind bars in the company of professional criminals.

As society moves toward grudging admission that indiscriminate criminalization in this area just does not work, sporadic efforts are being made toward drug-abuse prevention through education. This, obviously, is part of the answer, but efforts so far have been shoddy. When evaluators employed by the National Coordinating Council on Drug Education examined over 100 educational films about drugs, they found 36 of them inaccurate. Mrs. Sue Boe, assistant vice-president of consumer affairs for the Pharmaceutical Manufacturers Association, commented recently that children frequently know more about drugs than their teachers (although neither know as much as they should), and Dr. Gelolo McHugh, formerly of Duke University, after giving a drug-information quiz to 60,000 citizens, commented that correct answers were no more frequent than chance; the subjects could have done as well closing their eyes and choosing at random. It is no surprise, in this context, that students at San Mateo High School in California, asked what celebrity they would trust as narrator of an anti-LSD film, overwhelmingly answered, "Nobody."

Intercepting drug shipments from abroad is held out as a panacea by some. This motivated President Nixon's ill-fated Operation Intercept, which clogged the crossover points from Mexico three years ago, infuriated the people and government of that nation and finally had to be abandoned, as marijuana use continued to rise. If some method is ever found to stop the heroin shipments from Southeast Asia, Turkey and Mexico, which feed most of our junkie market at present, without resolving the root causes, the already-high prices will probably escalate further, a handful of addicts will die and most of them will steal more than ever to pay for $100 or $250 fixes.

Something obviously is wrong in our attempts to adjust to the global drug village—to face up to the arrival of marijuana habits from Mexico, speed and acid and downers from the laboratory, hashish cultism from Arabia, opiates from the Orient, peyote from our Indians, magic mushrooms from the ancient Aztecs.

It is hard to affix blame on anyone in particular. Senator Frank Moss recently suggested that we should investigate whether the hypnotic repetitions in the aspirin and other drug commercials on TV are conditioning us to seek a drug whenever we have a problem. This may be true, but people were getting stoned long before TV. Bert Donaldson, director of programs for emotionally disturbed children in Michigan, commented that many students are "actually bored to death in their classes"; others point to the boredom of much of our work in this industrialized world. ("Guys are always stoned," a Dodge auto-plant worker told *Time* magazine. "Either they're taking pills to keep awake or they're zonked on a joint they had on a break.") Considering the interminable Vietnam war, increasing air and water pollution, the continuing threat of a thermonuclear holocaust and the dehumanizing effect of our bureaucracies, there is much cause for people to feel nervous and to take something to calm down or to get away from it all.

The sinister fact is not that most citizens are taking drugs; people have always done that, although never as many or as much. The real terror implicit in our current drug culture is that so many, incredulous about official pronouncements, are experimenting, sometimes lethally, with very dangerous ones.

If the attempt to stop people from using all psychoactive drugs is hopeless, society nevertheless can and should try to persuade its members to use fewer drugs and safer ones. Libertarians from Jefferson and Mill to the present have emphasized that government has no business trying to enforce its notions of morality via police power—and there is something absurd and repulsive about a martini-guzzling bureaucrat imprisoning a pot user. Ideally, government and such powerful paragovernmental institutions as the schools, churches, labor unions and businessmen's organizations should be using their influence to provide positive alternatives and to genuinely enlighten people instead of trying to get them to march to a particular morality; but the times often seem less ideal than ever. If we were more committed to actually solving the problem than to whipping the people who have it, we could have been seriously and creatively looking for real solutions for over a generation. But instead we have tried to beat one another into submission with drug laws that have no parallel in the free world and can only be duplicated in totalitarian societies.

5 / THE BRUTALITY
OF
MODERN FAMILIES

Richard Sennett

In the past ten years many middle-class children have tried to break out of the communities, the schools and the homes that their parents had spent so much of their own lives creating. If any one feeling can be said to run through the diverse groups and life styles of the youth movement, it is a feeling that these middle-class communities of the parents were like pens, like cages keeping the young from being free and alive. The source of the feeling lies in the perception that while these middle-class environments are secure and orderly regimes, people suffocate there for lack of the new, the unexpected, the diverse in their lives.

There is an irony in this accusation for it seems to run counter to widely held beliefs that, far from being more secure, the lives of metropolitans have become almost intolerably complex, wildly out of control. Yet what the kids have touched on in an oblique way is that what Lewis Mumford calls the "technics" of city life—the means by which people communicate with each other, work together or exchange services with each other, aided by machines and complex bureaucratic rules—are a cornucopia of tools with which metropolitan man is brutalizing his social relations into ever more simple, ever more controllable, ever less anarchic forms. In the process, the civilizing possibilities that a metropolis uniquely can offer are disappearing. The possibilities for unexpected and unplanned social encounter, the coexistence of diverse communities, the eccentricity and human variety that flourish when masses of people live without rules together—all these urbane qualities of community are on the wane. It is this urbanity the young are searching for but cannot find.

* * *

ON HALSTEAD STREET

Let us take a tour down Halstead Street, the center of Chicago's great immigrant ghetto, around 1900. The street was 22 miles long, most of it teeming with people. Were we to start at its northern end and move south, we would see that most of these people were "foreigners," but at any given point different kinds of foreigners, all mixed together. A native might tell us that a certain few blocks were Greek or Polish or Irish, but were one actually to look at particular houses or apartment buildings, one would find the ethnic groups jumbled together. Even on the Chinese blocks of the street—for the Chinese are supposed at this time to have been the most closed of ethnic societies—there would be numerous families from Ireland or eastern Europe.

The functioning of all these groups on Halstead Street would appear hopelessly tangled to modern observers. The apartments would be mixed in with the stores, the streets themselves crowded with vendors and brokers of all kinds; even factories, as we moved to the southern end of Halstead Street, would be intermixed with bars, brothels, synagogues, churches and apartment buildings. In the midst of this jumble, there were some hidden threads of a structured social existence.

Were we to follow one of the residents of Halstead Street through a typical day, the experience would be something like this: up at six in the morning, a long walk or street-car ride to the factory and then ten or 11 hours of grueling work. With this much of his day we would be familiar. But when the whistle to stop work blew at six in the evening, his life would take on a dimension that is perhaps not immediately recognizable. The path back home from the factory might be broken by a hour's relaxation at a tavern or coffeehouse. Halstead Street was crammed in 1900 with little cafés where men would come after work to let the tension drain out, talking to friends or reading a newspaper. Dinner would usually be at home, but after dinner the man, sometimes with his wife, would be out of the house again, attending a union meeting, caring for a sick member of a mutual-aid society to which he belonged or just visiting the apartment of friends. Occasionally, when the family needed some special help, there would be a glass of beer shared with the local political boss and a plea for assistance—a soft job for an infirm relative, help with a naturalization form, some influence in getting a friend out of jail. Religious responsibilities also pulled the man and woman out of the house, particularly if they were Jewish or practicing Catholics. Synagogues and churches had to be built in this strange city, and the money and organization to build them could come only from the little men who were their members.

The life of a child on Halstead Street in 1900 would also seem odd to us, not to say frightening. The child of ten or 11 would be awakened early in the morning, scrubbed and sent off to school. Until three in the afternoon he would sit at a high desk reciting and memorizing. This experience is not strange to us, but again, his life after school would be. For if he did not come home to work, and many did not, he would be out on Halstead Street selling or hawking in the stall of someone much older, who sold and cajoled the passing traffic just as he did. It is amazing to see in old photographs of Halstead Street the young and old, shoulder to shoulder in these stalls, shouting out the prices and the virtues of their wares. Many youths would, with the tacit consent of their parents, enter into the more profitable after-school activity of stealing—we read, for instance, in the letters of one Polish family of great religious piety, of the honor accorded to a little son who had stolen a large slab of beef from a butcher on the corner. Life was very hard, and everyone had to fight for his needs with whatever weapons were at hand.

This life on Halstead Street required an urbanity of outlook, and multiple, often conflicting points of social contact, for these desperately poor people to survive. They *had* to make this diversity in their lives, for no one or two or three institutions in which they lived could provide all their needs. The family depended on political favors, the escape valve of the coffee shops and bars, the inculcation of discipline of the *shuls* and churches and so forth. The political machines tended in turn to grow along personal lines, to interact with the shifting politics of church and synagogue. This necessary anarchy took the individuals of the city outside the ethnic "subcultures" that supposedly were snugly encasing them. Polish people who belonged to steel unions often came into conflict with Polish people who had joined the police. It is the mark of a sophisticated life style that loyalties become crossed in conflicting forms, and this sophistication was the essence of these poor people's lives.

This condition has been carefully described by the great Chicago urbanist, Louis Wirth, in his essay "Urbanism as a Way of Life." He tried to show how the city of necessity broke apart the self-contained qualities of the various ethnic groups. The groups were not like little villages massed together in one spot on the map; rather they penetrated into each other, so that the daily life of an individual was a journey through various kinds of group life, each one different in its function and character from the others.

The subtlety of this idea can be seen by comparing a city subculture, as Wirth observed it, to the structure of village culture from which the ethnic groups came. In the small towns of southern Italy, in the *shtetl* of eastern Europe or the settlements of Anatolia, one finds what Robert Redfield has called a "village ethic": the accessibility of all village activities to all members of the village community. The village ethic is a web of cohesion: there are no disconnected or isolated social regions because, though different people might hold different rank or perform specialized activities, the character of the separate activities is known to everyone, and the differences add up to one organic whole. What made areas like Halstead Street in Chicago, New York's Lower East Side or London's East End seem so different to writers like Wirth was that the separate activities, or the different groups, depended on one another but were not harmoniously related. Each piece of the city mosaic had a distinct character, but the pieces were free of each other, they were not organically bound, they did not dovetail neatly. Individuals had to enter into a number of social regions in the course of daily life, even though the regions were not fluently organized and may even have been warring.

*   *   *

When I first began to do research on the structure of city family life, I encountered over and over a popular stereotype: the idea that city conditions somehow contribute to the instability of the home. Evidently, the assumption is that the diversity of the city threatens the security and attachment family members feel for each other. Especially as suburban community life has come to dominate cities, there has grown up a mythological family image of affluent homes where Dad drinks too much, the kids are unloved and turn to drugs, divorce is rampant and breakdowns are routine. The good old rural families, by contrast, were supposedly loving and secure.

The trouble with this popular image is that it simply isn't true. Talcott Parsons has amassed evidence to show that the rate of divorce and desertion was much higher "in the good old days" at the turn of the century than it is now. William Goode has taken the idea a step further by showing how divorce is *less* frequent in affluent homes than in working-class homes. There may still be a great deal of unrest and tension in these suburban families, but it cannot be allied to their structural instability. In fact, we shall see, it is the juncture of great formal stability with deep and unresolved tension that now marks these families.

The idea of the city weakening the family has also come to express itself in the popular perversions of the Moynihan report on the family lives in the black ghettos. The phenomenon this document actually describes is the impact of unemployment on family structure. It has been misread, however, as a description of how northern city life has broken apart the black family, and, in its most distorted form, as a sign that there is something too "weak" in black culture to enable it to withstand the terrors of the city. What Moynihan describes occurs wherever unemployment or intermittent employment is a long-term family experience; one therefore finds a much higher rate of female-headed households, with shifting male partners and "illegitimate" children, among persecuted rural Catholics in Northern Ireland than among the blacks of New York City. But the myth remains: somehow it is the city that is the destroyer.

There is an important history to this stereotype of the city's threat to the home. At the turn of the century, the bulk of the population of American cities was working-class, people whose origins and urban experience was of a piece with the residents of Halstead Street. But there was a numerically smaller group of middle-class families in cities like Chicago whose family patterns were very different, much closer to the narrowness of the life of the affluent middle class in today's metropolitan areas. In *Families Against the City* I explored the lives of one such middle-class community and what the history of these people revealed was that the common stereotype of the city's impact on the family has to be reversed for middle-class homes. For the disorder and vigor of city life in the first decade of this century frightened middle-class families, but, unlike working-class people, they had the means to do something about their fears. They drew in upon themselves: there was little visiting outside the confines of home; voluntary groups like churches and political clubs claimed few bourgeois participants; in America, unlike France or Germany, the urban middle class shunned public forms of social life like cafés and banquet halls. The home became for these early middle-class city dwellers a sanctuary against the confusions of the outside world.

FAMILY INTENSITY

That kind of family isolation has abated in modern times, particularly when a family is in crisis. But there was something about such urban middle-class families at the opening of the twentieth century that has survived over time. These families possessed a character that now typifies families in middle-class suburbs as well as the middle-class islands within the central city; it is a quality of living that unites newly middle-class families whose parents were immigrants with the native-born urban middle-class families that have always lived in large cities. This characteristic of family life is the intensity of family relations. It links the variety of groups and backgrounds of people lumped together as middle-class, and the reach of this phenomenon extends beyond the city proper into the suburb and the town.

What is meant by an "intense" family life? There are, I think, a state of mind and a style of living that define the family intensity now found in many if not most segments of the urban population. The state of mind is that family members believe the actions and feelings that transpire in the family are in fact a microcosm of the whole range of "meaningful" actions and feelings in the world at large. The belief is, as one middle-class mother in Queens explained to an interviewer recently, that nothing "really important" in human relationships occurs that cannot be experienced within the boundaries of the home. People who think in this way can therefore conceive of no reason for making social forays or social contacts that cannot be ultimately reconciled or absorbed in family life.

The style of living that makes for an intense family life is the reduction of family members to levels of equality. This characteristic is much more pronounced in American urban families than in European ones. The feeling consists, most vulgarly, in fathers wanting to be "pals" to their sons and mothers wanting to be sisters to their daughters; there is a feeling of failure and dishonor if the parents are excluded from the circle of youth, as though they were tarnished by being adult. A good family of this sort is a family whose members talk to each other as equals, where the children presume to the lessons of experience and the parents try to forget them. That the dignity of all the family members might lie exactly in mutual respect for separateness and uniqueness is not conceived; dignity is conceived to lie in treating everyone equally. This brings the family members into a closer relation to each other —for there are taken to be, ideally, no unbridgeable gaps.

Both the state of mind and the life style have become in fact structures for limiting the sophistication and tolerance of the people who live in such homes.

The conviction that a family is the whole social arena in microcosm stifles parents and children both in an obvious and in a subtle way. Clearly, no band of four or five people represents the full spectrum of attitudes and human traits to be found in the wider society. The family as a world of its own can therefore become highly exclusive. Studies of intense family attitudes toward strangers reveal that the outsiders are judged to be "real," to be important and dealt with, only to the extent to which they reflect the particular attitudes and personalities found within a family circle. The most striking form of this can be seen in situations where middle-class neighborhoods have been successfully integrated racially. The black families have been accepted to the extent that people feel they are after all "just like us," or as a respondent in one study put it: "You wouldn't know from the way the Jones family acts they were Negroes." Accepting someone ineradicably different is not what occurs under these conditions.

CONFLICT IS A "NO-NO"

The subtle way in which families, feeling themselves a microcosm of the society, become self-limiting has to do with the base of stability on which such families rest. This base is the existence, or the belief in the existence, of long-term trust. For families to believe they are all-important there has to be the conviction that no betrayal and breakup will occur. People do not concentrate all their energies in one place and simultaneously believe it may one day shatter or betray them. Yet long-term situations of trust and reliability are rare in the larger social world. Not only in work but also in a variety of human affairs there are experiences of power and significance that cannot depend on a mutual commitment or trust for a long period. An intense family must refuse to grant worth to that which is shifting, insecure or treacherous, and yet this is exactly what the diversity in society is built of.

When people in a family believe they must treat each other as equal in condition, the same self-blinding, the same limitation, occurs. A recent project made psychiatric interviews in homes of "normal," "just average" families in a modest suburb outside a large city. Over and over again in these interviews adults expressed a sense of loss, sometimes amounting to feelings of annihilation, in the things in their lives they had wanted to do and could afford to do but refrained from doing for fear of leaving out the children. These sacrifices were not dictated by money; they were much more intimate, small-scale, yet important things: establishing a quiet spot in the day after work when a man and his wife were alone together, taking trips or vacations alone, eating dinner after the children were put to bed. In another frame, fathers spoke again and again of how they had failed their sons by not being able to understand them. When the interviewers asked what they meant, the response usually came as a version of "he doesn't open up to me the way he does to his friends." Such burdens are acquired, so many daily chances for diversity and change of routine are denied, out of the belief in the rightness of treating children as much as equals as possible, especially in early and middle adolescence.

In one way, the belief in the family as a microcosm of the world leads to this will to believe the family members all alike, all "pals." For if the family is a whole world, then somehow the conditions of friendship and comradeship must be established within its borders, and this can only be done by treating all the family members as comrades who can understand each other on the same grounds.

* * *

SUBURBAN CLOSENESS

The vehicle for replacing the sophistication of an older urban life by the suffocation in the family today is the growth of middle-class suburbs in this country. The shrinking of diverse community life into the family is the hidden history of suburban places—which seem so empty of secrets; this history makes sense of their simplicity and their great appeal to Americans.

The classic pattern of industrial city-suburb arrangements up to the Second World War was the pattern still extant in Turin or Paris. Cities were arranged in rings of socio-economic wealth, with the factories at the outskirts of town, workers' suburbs or quarters next to them and then increasingly more affluent belts of housing as one moved closer to the center of the city. There were exceptions to this pattern, to be sure, like Boston or Lyons, but the pattern seemed to apply to most of the great urban centers in the United States; New York, Philadelphia and Chicago showed in general such a pattern at the opening of the present century.

When the flight to the suburbs first began in massive numbers after the Second World War, it was commonly thought that its causes were related to the depression and to the population dislocation of the war. But this explanation is simply inadequate to explain the persistence of the event over the course of time.

Nor, in the United States, can the movement to the suburbs be explained by the growing presence of Negroes in the urban centers after the Second World War. For one thing, these Negroes seldom moved close to areas where young middle-class people had lived; those poorer people whose neighborhoods were gradually taken over by Negroes did not move to far-lying suburbs but relocated only slightly farther away from the urban core. There are some exceptions to this latter pattern; there are some people in outer Queens who moved to avoid blacks, but few in Darien, Connecticut, did.

The historical circumstances of depression, war, land value and racial fear all have played a role, but they are offshoots of a more central change in the last decades that has led to the strength of suburban life. This deeper, more hidden element is a new attitude about the conduct of family life within and without the city.

A variety of recent books on suburbs, like Herbert Gans' *The Levittowners* or John Seeley's *Crestwood Heights*, reveal that people who now live in suburbs value their home settings because they feel that closer family ties are more possible there than in the city center. The closeness is not so much a material one—after all, families in city apartments are extremely close physically. Rather, as is now being learned, it is the simplification of the social environment in the suburbs that accounts for the belief that close family life will be more possible there than in the confusion of the city.

In most American suburbs, physical space has been rigidly divided into homogeneous areas: there are wide swatches of housing separated from swatches of commercial development concentrated in that unique institution, the shopping center; schools are similarly isolated, usually in a parklike setting. Within the housing sectors themselves, homes have been built at homogeneous socioeconomic levels. When critics of planning reproach developers for constructing the environment in this way, the developers reply truthfully that people want to live with people just like themselves; people think diversity in housing will be bad for social as well as economic reasons. In the new communal order made possible by affluence, the desire of people is for a functionally separated, internally homogeneous environment.

HOMOGENEOUS ZONES

I believe this homogeneous-zones idea in suburbs is a brutalizing community process, in contrast to the urban situation that preceded it in time. For the homogeneous zones of function in a suburb prohibit an overlay of different activities in the same place; each place has its own predefined function. What therefore results is a limitation on the chance combination of new situations, of unexpected events, of unlikely meetings between people that create diversity and a sense of complexity in individual lives. People have a vision of human variety and of the possibility of living in a different and better way only when they are challenged by situations they have not encountered before, when they step beyond being actors in a preordained, unchanging routine. This element of surprise is how human growth is different from the simple passage of time in a life; but the suburb is a settlement fitted only to muffle the unknown, by separating the zones of human activity into neat compartments.

This prohibition of diversity in the arrangement of suburban areas permits, instead, the intensity of family relations to gather full force. It is a means for creating that sense of long-term order and continuity on which family intensity must be based. In a stable family, where long-term trust between pretend-equals exists, the "intrusions" of the outside must be diminished, and such is the genius of the suburban mode. The hidden fear behind this family life in the suburbs is that the strength of the family bond might be weakened if the individual family members were exposed to a richer social condition, readily accessible outside the house.

When the suburbs began to grow rapidly after the Second World War, some observers, such as David Riesman, were moved to criticize them for an aimlessness and emptiness in communal relations. But there was and is a peculiar kind of social bond made possible by this very emptiness, this lack of confusion. The bond is a common determination to remain inviolate, to ensure the family's security and sanctity through exclusionary measures of race, religion, class.

Involved here was a new event in the idea of a "neighborhood," for such a place became much more definable in becoming more homogeneous. Social scientists used to spend a great deal of time fighting with each other about the meaning of "neighborhood" in cities, one of the principal points being that there was such a multiplicity of social contact that individuals could not be neatly categorized by where they lived. Now they can. The growth of intensive family life in the suburb has brought into being a metropolitan region where each neighborhood is all too identifiable in socioeconomic, racial and ethnic terms. Now people really are getting to know who their neighbors are: they are just like themselves.

This kind of family living in the suburbs surely is a little strange. Isn't the preference for suburbia as a setting for family life in reality an admission, tacit and unspoken to be sure, that the parents do not feel confident of their own human strengths to guide the child in the midst of an environment richer and more difficult than that of the neat lawns and tidy supermarkets of the suburbs? If a close, tight-knit family emerges because the other elements of the adult and child world are made purposely weak, if parents assume their children will be better human beings for being shielded or deprived of society outside the home and homelike schools, surely the family life that results is a forced and unnatural intimacy.

Of course there are many similar criticisms one could make of suburbs, all centered in some way on the fact that suburbanites are people who are afraid to live in a world they cannot control. This society of fear, this society willing to be dull and sterile in order that it not be confused or overwhelmed, has become as well a model for the rebuilding of inner-city spaces. It is often said that the differences are disappearing between the suburbs and such central-city developments as Lefrak City in New York or the urban renewal projects of inner Boston or the South Shore of Chicago. It would be more accurate to say that these inner-city, middle-class communities are becoming suburbanized in a historical sense:

rigidly planned usage of space, an emphasis on security and warding off intrusions from the outside—in short, a simplification of the contacts and the environment in which the family lives. In the name of establishing the "decencies" of life as regnant, the scope of human variety and freedom of expression is drastically reduced. The emotions shaping the rebuilding of inner-city living-places run much deeper than protection from the blacks or from crime; the blacks and the criminals are a symbolic cover under which the family can turn inward, and the family members withdraw from dealing with the complexities of people unlike themselves.

6 / SUICIDE
AND
CIVIL RIGHTS

Arthur J. Snider

Ernest Hemingway shot himself to death, some people believe, because he was depressed about many things, including a conviction he could never write again. Friends had said the action was justified because it was consistent with his philosophy that a man can be destroyed but should never be defeated.

Those who have set fire to themselves and have been burned to death in protest of Russian oppression in Czechoslovakia or the Vietnam war have been similarly defended.

The ethical issue of whether a person has a right to kill himself is being discussed in professional circles. Dr. Paul W. Pretzel of the Suicide Prevention Center, Los Angeles, says suicide is never rational and should always be discouraged. Dr. Thomes S.

From *Science Digest*, January 1970. Reprinted with permission of *Science Digest*, © The Hearst Corporation.

Szasz of Syracuse, professor of psychiatry at the State University of New York, agrees that it should be discouraged but adds that if that fails then the patient has a right to take his life.

"Only a patient has a right to decide whether what he is about to do is rational," Szasz says "No psychiatrist has the right to sit in judgment on another person's rationality."

In reviewing 36,000 patients who have contacted the suicide center in the last 10 years, Pretzel says he could not find one with a justifiable cause.

"I've seen many suicidal people who felt their situation was desperate," he says, "but when you work with them you find the suicidal condition was the result of a depression. Depression can have the effect of limiting a person's ability to see alternatives. It imprisons him in a certain set pattern of thought that is a dead end. If the depression is treated other alternatives become apparent. It has been my experience that people can cope with an awful lot if they can avoid a depression."

Szasz contends that an individual has "an unqualified constitutional right to be dangerous to himself—whether it be to take up smoking, have an abortion, or commit suicide.

"Certainly he should be discouraged, just as a friend should be discouraged from buying bad stock or marrying the wrong woman," says Szasz. "But I object strenuously to the use of 'rational' because it involves the judgment of one person by another. It is obvious that an intelligent person might conclude that another person's behavior with respect to marriage, divorce, economics, suicide and so forth is stupid. But that does not give him the right of coercion or the psychiatrist the right to call the police or commit him to an institution."

Pretzel points out that mutually contradictory desires to live or die, to be rescued or abandoned, are part of suicide. Thus one can never assume that a statement, "I want to die," accurately expresses a patient's state of mind. In most cases these words may actually be communicating a need for help.

"The professional person who simply accepts at face value the literal meaning of a depressed person's suicidal threat is naive," says Pretzel.

While hospitalization of a suicidal patient who is not psychotic may violate his civil rights, it provides a safer environment than his own home. There are many examples of highly suicidal individuals who carried out their plans after being released from custody through exercise of their civil rights.

7 / OLD MYTHS
AND NEW FACTS
ABOUT ALCOHOLISM

In the past, an alcoholic usually got censure instead of help; today he is viewed as the victim of a disease. The change came about through renewed efforts to understand his complex problem. And with greater understanding has come the opportunity to clear away the cloud of misconception that obscured the true nature of alcoholism—and condemned him in the first place.

Each of the following statements in heavy black type is a common misconception about alcoholism. After each statement, we supply the medical facts.

Most alcoholics are on skid row

No. Though the word "alcoholic" sometimes brings to mind a reeling, rheumy-eyed derelict, few alcoholics actually fit the description. According to recent calculations, 95 to 97 per cent of our alcoholic population are *not* found staggering down dingy streets or huddled in dark doorways, but leading responsible lives in respectable communities. As a group, they're indistinguishable, representing both sexes, a variety of ages, and every race, creed, and calling. As individuals, most of them meet the criteria of middle-class America; they're married, have nice homes, raise a couple of kids or more, live with their families, and go to work or keep house. In numbers, they add up to an estimated nine million.

Alcoholics can stop drinking if they really want to

The alcoholic has gained an undeserved reputation for being a weak-willed person who drinks because he likes to. In the light of what is known about alcoholism, the strength of his resolve has little to do with the compulsion to drink, and he would crave alcohol even if he disliked the taste of liquor.

According to leading authorities on the subject, alcoholism is a form of drug addiction and, like other forms, involves changes in the chemistry of the body that lead to physical dependence. On withdrawal, the alcoholic becomes subject to real, not imagined, pain. Depending on how advanced his case is, he can be subjected to a nightmarish range of discomfort such as: extreme nervousness, night "sweats," leg and arm cramps, stomach pains, nausea, dizziness, uncontrollable trembling, hallucinations, convulsive seizures similar to epileptic attacks, and delirium tremens which can be fatal if untreated. Considering that relief comes with alcohol, one can readily understand why an alcoholic would be unable to simply "stop drinking" without help.

An equally difficult problem is the alcoholic's psychological dependence. He feels an overwhelming *need* to drink in order to cope with his problems, even though he knows that his drinking may have destructive consequences on his health, job, arrest record, marriage, and family.

Alcoholics don't want to be helped

While authorities concede that the alcoholic seems to be singularly help-resistant, they do not interpret this as a sign that he doesn't want help. They attribute it instead to an underlying tendency to deny his condition by failing, or refusing, to recognize alcoholism in himself. Many more alcoholics, they say, would seek help if the stigma attached to the disease were removed, and the alcoholic could openly admit to his problem without risking scorn and reproof.

Authorities also agree that at some level of understanding all alcoholics are aware of the destruction in their lives. In many cases, alcoholics become help resistant because they've been subtly (or not so subtly) rejected by people who should have helped them in the past, or because efforts to help them have not been particularly well tailored to their needs.

Women rarely become alcoholics

Current statistics indicate that nearly two million women are alcoholics, dispelling the notion that an alcoholic woman is a rarity. And while these statistics show that four or five times as many men as women are alcoholics, not all authorities are convinced the reading is dependable. Some, in fact, maintain that the incidence of alcoholism may well be just as high among women as it is among men, but that intensified efforts to protect female problem drinkers against exposure lowers the probability of detection. Also, men usually feel less need, and have less opportunity, to drink unobserved, making it more difficult for them to keep alcohol addiction a secret.

Alcoholics drink to escape reality

It isn't so. Saying that an alcoholic drinks to escape reality implies that he sets out to drink himself into a state of oblivion, where his problems can't reach him. Actually, what he's looking for is a way to cope with, not to escape from, reality. If he looks for it in drinking, it's because alcohol has an anesthetic effect and dulls the sensibilities. By depressing the brain's nerve centers it not only takes the edge off physical pain, fatigue, and emotional stress, but seems to cancel out inhibiting personal characteristics—self-consciousness and timidity, for example—that might otherwise act as a barrier in dealing with everyday tensions and situations. His motive in drinking, in other words, is not basically different from that of the estimated 86 million Americans who drink and don't have any problem with it.

Heavy drinkers are alcoholics

Not necessarily. Many authorities feel two main distinctions can be made between heavy drinking and alcoholic drinking. First, the alcoholic builds up a tolerance to alcohol, which means that his capacity for alcohol increases and it constantly takes more alcohol to have an effect on him. In the heavy drinker, the same amount of alcohol generally produces the same effect: if he drinks more than he usually does, he is affected more. Second, someone who is a heavy drinker and not alcoholic can choose where, when, how much, and with whom he drinks; he can drink or not, as he likes. In short, he has control over his drinking. With the alcoholic, it's the other way around.

Some experts, however, feel such definitions may be too narrow. Dr. Morris E. Chafetz, director of the new National Institute on Alcohol Abuse and Alcoholism, says "Alcohol abuse, in one sense, is present any time a person becomes drunk. And repeated episodes of intoxication or heavy drinking which impairs health— or the consistent use of alcohol as a coping mechanism in dealing with the problems of life to a degree of serious interference with an individual's effectiveness on the job, at home, in the community, or behind the wheel of a car—is alcohol abuse, and may raise the strong suggestion of alcoholism."

Alcoholism strikes without warning

Not really. Experts consider the prodromal, or early, stage of alcoholism a time of warning before the actual onset of the disease. It is a period when a person continues to function, at least outwardly, as he always has, but displays signs of psychological dependence on alcohol, such as the following:

- He tends to drink on "signal": before starting the day's work, with lunch, after dinner, at bedtime; when he's bored, when he's keyed up, when he's tired, when he's upset, when he's elated.

- He always drinks more than his companions, often more than he intended, and a great deal more than he used to.

- He can't have a good time without drinking; it's a "must" for picnics on the beach, golf, fishing, card-playing, attending football games, and the like.

- He doesn't sip his drinks, but gulps them down.

- He indulges in some solitary drinking, often on the sly.

There is, in addition, one important warning sign that is significant in itself. It's called a "blackout."

A blackout is not the same as "passing out"; the person doesn't lose consciousness, and he behaves in what appears to be a normal manner while he's drinking. He may not even have had more than two or three drinks, although "blackouts" are usually produced by heavy drinking. Afterward, the drinker has no recollection of episodes following his drinking, or even that they took place.

It takes years of heavy drinking to become an alcoholic

Not always. Once a person's drinking has gone out of control and is creating problems in the different areas of his life, he is said to have become addicted to alcohol and in the acute stage of alcoholism. Generally, it takes an average of ten years of heavy drinking to reach that point. But there's no rule about it. For some individuals, the disease begins with the very first drink. With others, it takes three to five years of what experts consider moderate drinking. And there are people who drank heavily for 20 and 30 years before they showed signs of addiction, while others have been drinking as much and as long with no apparent ill effects.

Only a certain type of person can become an alcoholic

Researchers used to think so, too, and tried to paint a personality picture of addiction-prone individuals by studying the behavior and characteristics of chronic alcoholics. In doing so, they noted many striking similarities. The subjects were, for example, typically sensitive, easily frustrated, unable to cope with anxiety or tension, and tended toward feelings of depression and inferiority; many showed signs of emotional immaturity, hostility, guilt, and sexual problems.

But the theory simply could not stand up to scientific scrutiny, mainly because no set of characteristics could be assembled that would apply to them all. Furthermore, it could not be determined if the traits they exhibited were an inherent part of their personality, or had developed as a result of their addiction. Most authorities, in fact, are inclined to say there is no such thing as an "alcoholic personality," and any type of person is a candidate.

Alcohol is the sole cause of alcoholism

Obviously, no one can become an alcoholic without the use of alcohol. But authorities regard it as an *agent*, and not the cause of alcoholism. If it were the cause, they say, everyone who drinks would become addicted to it. Which isn't, of course, the case.

What actually does cause alcoholism is still a mystery, although several unproven theories recently have been advanced. It has been suggested, for example, that there is a basic physical difference in the way alcohol is disposed of in the body of an alcoholic. Another theory is that alcoholism is caused by a glandular malfunction, and nutritional deficiency is also suspect. Some say the disease is due to an abnormal emotional background, while others attribute it to serious psychiatric illness.

The informed concensus is that psychological, physical, social, and cultural conditions all contribute to alcohol addiction. However, most authorities do not discount the possibility that a single underlying cause, sometimes referred to as the X-factor, may be at the root of the problem.

A person can't inherit alcoholism

No evidence has been unearthed to specifically relate alcoholism to heredity, but there is a substantial amount of research that indicates alcoholism does run in families. Children of alcoholic parents, for example, are considered by authorities to be extremely high-risk individuals. And while their greater susceptibility might be accounted for by an unfavorable home atmosphere, learned attitudes regarding drinking, and imitation of adult behavior, some experts feel that the discovery of a direct genetic connection—either as a predisposition to alcoholism or an immunity to it—is not as remote as most people think.

Alcohol doesn't cause cirrhosis of the liver

It's long been known that only a small percentage of alcoholics—an estimated ten per cent—succumb to cirrhosis of the liver. If alcohol were the cause of cirrhosis, the reasoning once went, a much greater percentage of alcoholics would get this disease. Most medical authorities assumed that the true cause of the prevalence of cirrhosis of the liver in alcoholics (eight times more frequent) was malnutrition, caused by the inclination to drink rather than eat. But now they're not sure.

Cirrhosis of the liver means scarring of the liver, and recent studies have shown that even small doses of alcohol unquestionably cause scar tissue in the liver. Other studies confirm that when people with advanced cirrhosis of the liver stop drinking, their condition shows striking improvement. As for the theory that malnutrition is the cause of this disease in alcoholics, studies say that it's simply not so.

"For the first time," says Dr. Frank A. Seixas, medical director of the National Council on Alcoholism, "we're getting medical evidence which confirms the observations doctors have made—and dodged—for years: alcoholism and cirrhosis are very closely linked."

Alcoholism is an allergy

Former alcoholics sometimes refer to their addiction as an "allergy," but do not use the word in its scientific sense. What they mean is that they react to alcohol differently.

It is possible, of course, for an individual to be allergic to any of the ingredients used in the distilling process, as well as to the alcohol itself. But if he were, his allergy wouldn't manifest itself as alcoholism. In such cases, the sensitivity would more likely produce symptoms similar to those that occur in other allergies, such as sneezing in hay fever or hives in food allergy. Also, allergies do not ordinarily lead to a craving for the substance that causes them *after* the reaction.

Alcoholism can't be cured

To be technical about it, an alcoholic can't be "cured." It would mean restoring him to a condition that enables him to drink in a controlled manner, and the majority of experts agree that, because alcoholism is a lifelong addiction, this usually can't be done. But the illness can be interrupted, and he can recover through abstinence and treatment.

Modern methods of treating alcoholism include: *medication,* which is used to ease the discomforts of withdrawal, to treat any medical complications that may be present, and sometimes to induce an aversion to alcohol; *counseling* or *therapy,* which consists of treating the psychological or emotional aspects of the problem; and *Alcoholics Anonymous,* a worldwide fellowship of nearly half a million people who succumbed to alcoholism and now share their own experiences in the hope of drawing strength and inspiration to solve their common problems.

Reports of success from various sources range from 15 to 80 per cent, but the method employed seems to be less of a determining factor in recovery than early treatment, the patient's earnest desire to get well, and the support of those close to him.

8 / WHERE WE PUT THE AGED

David H. Pryor

Almost one million Americans, a large silent minority, are in 20,000 nursing homes. They've been sent there to die, in a half-way house somewhere between society and the cemetery. We've had the idea that if we could funnel more money into the nursing home industry, the quality of care would rise. We've been wrong: the patient has taken the backseat to profits. This is where government erred: it treated nursing home care as a housing, not a health program.

A few months ago, an *Associated Press* series of articles on the nursing home industry disclosed that:

- Physician care for the nursing home patient is so scarce that it is a national scandal;

- One-seventh of drug prescriptions to nursing patients are administered wrong, and drugs are commonly used to make patients "easier to handle";

- The average food-cost per patient in many nursing homes today is less than $1 per day;

- In a Topeka, Kansas home three-fourths of the patients checked had not been seen by a doctor in six months, and in Minnesota, the average amount of physician care per patient in 100 nursing homes was 2-½ minutes per week;

- The National Fire Prevention Association shows nursing homes at the top of unsafe places to live.

A *New York Daily News* reporter, hired as a nurse's aide, found the food in several New York homes abominable, filthy rooms, roaches in glasses, dirt in water pitchers and indescribable conditions in bathrooms.

From *The New Republic*, April 25, 1970. Reprinted by permission of *The New Republic*, © 1970, Harrison-Blaine of New Jersey, Inc.

From other news reports we learn that a nursing home administrator may well have as his only qualifications that he was a junk dealer; that tough federal regulations have been much slower reaching the nursing homes than federal dollars; that 87 nursing homes that failed to meet federal standards were paid $380,000 in the last half of 1968; that in Wisconsin, a 317-bed home went without regular state inspections for almost three years, although a 1967 check resulted in a four-page list of violations.

It will be recalled that 32 persons recently died at Marietta, Ohio, in a "good" nursing home which had been allowed to operate with "deficiencies."

A maze of pyramiding new government programs such as Medicare and Medicaid, new methods of financing nursing homes, new formulas adopted by Social Security and welfare agencies to reimburse the proprietors of nursing homes, together with a lack of interest in both the enactment and enforcement of tough regulations which protect the patient—all this adds up to booming profits for the owners, and explosive and rising costs for the patient, their relatives and the American taxpayer. A Wall Street executive states that "in the nursing home business—there is no way to lose." Some 70 nursing home chains have been established in recent months which now sell their stock to the public. Mutual fund companies own approximately six million shares of these stocks. Nursing home securities are referred to as "the hottest stock on Wall Street." *Business Week* entitles an article, "Nursing Homes Offer an Investment Lure." The same publication elsewhere explains a novel financing plan whereby several nursing home chains induced doctors to find patients for them by selling a major interest in each home to a group of local physicians.

Only 10 per cent of our nursing homes are non-profit institutions, and these as a general rule are operated by communities, locally supported hospitals, churches, religious organizations, or fraternal groups. Those who are entering the nursing-home-for-profit business, according to many of the prospectuses now on file with the Securities and Exchange Commission, are generally builders, contractors, restaurant operators, fast buck entrepreneurs.

The price per bed in these homes is zooming upwards at an alarming rate—$700 a month is not uncommon. In addition to the basic room and board fee, there are often "extras," which are not known until the first statement arrives.

I became interested in this scandal several years back while serving as a freshman legislator in the Arkansas House of Representatives. At each legislative session we found ourselves voting additional welfare payments for the local nursing home industry. We were told that the additional money would be spent for additional care. We never discovered what additional care or services would be improved or how the patient would benefit.

Coming to Washington, I spent four weekends as a volunteer worker at nursing homes in the area. I saw loneliness, despair, anxiety,—and boredom—total, absolute boredom. The only relief comes when the attendant brings a meal into the room. In one room of 14 beds, the proprietor woke an elderly lady, asked her how she was feeling and then told me that this particular patient had had a "slight heart attack" early in the day, but that they did not make a practice of calling the doctor on Sunday. In another home, as I was clipping the toenails of an 80-year-old veteran, he told me not to let the attendant see me do this as they charged $7 when they did it. I saw toothless patients served big slabs of cold meat, which they were incapable of cutting into bite-size portions. In a home of 80 patients, there was only one attendant on duty. In the hall I saw four helpless people in wheelchairs, three of whom were sitting in their own excretion. The attendant told me, "We just don't have enough help and the owners don't pay us enough to live on."

"Who shaves your older men?" I asked one proprietor. "About every three days, when they catch up with their other work, that is the job for the maintenance crew," was his reply. "How much does it cost to have a patient here?" I asked an attendant in a Maryland home. "It depends on their income," she said.

A friend of mine in Connecticut recently visited four nursing homes in his area with the idea of placing his father in an extended care facility. He saw "attendants ignore one old woman's call for help; I saw one owner talk in an insultingly derogatory way about a patient, in front of that very patient; I saw incredible filth and signs of neglect; and I heard things that seemed to me to evidence a callousness and crudity that I certainly would not want any parents of mine exposed to. The owner of the home said to me, 'Look, your father is getting old and he is hard to handle, right? You bring him right here, maybe in a few weeks you can take him home on a Sunday afternoon, but the first thing you've got to show these old people is who's boss.' The brochure the owner handed me refers to 'pleasant home atmosphere.' "

Several myths have been successfully sold to the American public. One of them is that all nursing homes or homes for the aged are strictly licensed, duly inspected, and that a "health team" is physically present at all times, or at least nearby to serve the patients. It's not true. Another myth is that if an institution states that it is "approved for Medicaid and Medicare," then it is a home which provides good service to the patient. That's also untrue. There is no control over the nursing home industry, though two out of three patients in nursing homes and homes for the aged in our country are kept there through some federal or federally assisted program. One chain nursing home owner said in a recent newspaper article that 85 cents of each dollar that flowed into his business came from government sources.

The taxpayers are paying $2 billion a year to the nursing home industry. All controls over where this money goes and what it buys are fragmented, self-frustrating, and ineffectual. Both the Medicaid and Medicare agencies in the Department of Health, Education and Welfare issue standards for nursing homes participating in their respective programs; neither agency enforces its standards. In the case of Medicaid, which is a state-administered program, nursing homes are certified for participation by state agencies. Certification is often on the basis of surveys and reports by county agencies. The federal administrative agency, the Social and Rehabilitative Service, has virtually no control over the quality or frequency of these surveys and does not even receive information on the number of homes certified by the states. If a patient or his family writes to his representative in Congress to complain of conditions in a Medicaid nursing home, the complaint is usually referred to HEW for investigation. HEW in turn refers it to the state agency and from there to the county agency, which probably is responsible for permitting the condition to exist in the first place. The patient has nowhere to turn. No one is in charge.

The Social Security Administration must approve nursing homes for participation in Medicare as extended care facilities. Here too, the standards, which in many respects are vague, are actually applied by state and county agencies. Reports are sent to the regional offices of the Social Security Administration where the certifications are signed, with little or no knowledge of actual conditions in the homes. Social Security officials have no information on the qualifications of surveyors doing Medicare inspections.

The tremendous sum which federal programs are pouring into nursing home care is profoundly affecting the development and growth of the industry. The infusion of dollars has stimulated a building boom in nursing homes which is completely out of hand. Congress has appropriated funds to assist state and regional planning agencies in their efforts to rationalize the numbers, types and distribution of new health facilities; to curtail waste and duplication; and to provide our communities with a balanced complex of facilities which can deliver modern medical care in an effective and economical way. At the same time, Congress has frustrated those aims by enticing investment capital into the industry on a huge scale, with a virtual guarantee of business and profits.

The Securities and Exchange Commission is charged with serving the investor public. Let me then put to the SEC some questions the public needs to have answered: Are the nursing homes listed as properties of a particular company good or bad, are they properly staffed, do they give good care? Are some of these newly formed public companies simply devices for paper transfer of ownership and inflating the capitalization of the properties? Are the SEC and HEW working together to assess the burgeoning growth of public investment in nursing home chains? They are not. No one is protecting the public, no one is protecting the tax dollars, and no one is protecting the patients.

PART TWO
TROUBLED GROUPS IN
MODERN SOCIETY

TROUBLED GROUPS IN
MODERN SOCIETY

Perhaps no other problem in American society has received more attention from the public than those problems related to race. From the time of slavery the problems of racial differences have been seen as a major social problem in our society. If we are convinced that social problems consist of situations which the public defines as problem areas, and in regard to which they would like to see changes take place, it may be difficult to understand why the problems of race have not diminished. There are a number of explanations for this. First, some may say that the problems have been reduced. Negroes can vote, they have better schools, and so on. However, this argument does not explain why some of the most serious race riots have occurred in the last five or ten years. It ignores the fact that in many areas of American society, while everyone's standard of living may be going up, economic differentials between the races are increasing.

Even more important in explaining why we have not reduced this social problem is the fact that being aware of a social problem and even desiring to do something about it are simply not enough to bring about a change. Often there is little agreement as to what form a solution should take. Some argue that equality should be the goal, others freedom, but just as many would like to solve the problem by keeping the minorities content and quiet, "in their place." A few, like Hitler, would even propose genocide as a solution.

Once it is recognized that both the problem and its solution have many dimensions, it is easy to understand that some social problems persist over long periods of time. Those who felt that the remedy for racial conflict was to get the races together, so that they would come to understand each other, failed to take into consideration, among other things, the fact that many persons in influential positions within society profit from the oppressed position of the racial and ethnic minorities. It seems fair to suggest that the first step toward relieving a social problem of this magnitude would be to change the basic structure of society that makes an oppressed class profitable for others.

Three articles on race are included in this section to give a picture of the variety of forms that racism can take in our society.

In studying the problems of the poor we find many of the same situations as with the study of racial and ethnic minorities. As we know, these minorities make up a disproportionate number of the poor. In searching for an understanding of the problems of the poor, we must look at more than the poor themselves, or the question of how they, as individuals, got that way. More important, we must look at the society that has created poverty in the midst of affluence.

The analysis of the problems of the poor which is considered in Articles 12 and 13 is closely related to the problems of work and the worker. However, we must not be led to believe that the possibility of being poor is the only problem of the worker. The problems of the blue collar worker, who is making an excellent salary compared with twenty years ago, is carefully considered in the *Time* article in this section.

Traditionally crime and the criminal have been thought of as a social problem. No one would suggest that persons who commit violent acts or seriously violate the law in other ways do not constitute a problem for society. However, it is interesting to note that today we are beginning to see that some of the methods used to deal with social problems have become social problems in themselves. Some would suggest that our whole system of "justice" from the police to the prisons and the probation system have become more of a problem than crime itself. Without taking sides on such an argument, we can see that both are problem areas. The *Time* article on prisons helps to show this.

A relatively new area in the sociological study of crime as a social problem deals with what have been called crimes without victims: homosexuality, prostitution, drug addiction, and so on. These are interesting social problems for a number of reasons. First, there is by no means complete agreement that these are crimes or that they should even be considered social problems. There are some who claim that the addict, the homosexual, and the prostitute should be treated as sick persons, not as criminals. Others violently disagree and claim that neither the "sick" or the "criminal" label is appropriate and that persons in these categories should simply be treated as different, or, better, not treated at all. Legally the prostitute, the homosexual, and the drug user are all law violators and thus criminals. However, there are some moves afoot to change some of the laws. Legislation has been introduced in California which would make any sexual behavior between consenting adults legal (thus making many forms of homosexuality and prostitution legal). In other actions there have been attempts to make the selling, not the using of drugs, the only offense.

As you read the articles in this section, ask yourself how differences in the definition of the problem behavior would affect any analysis or strategy for change. Also, as you consider each type of "problem person," ask yourself how that person may reflect a "troubled society."

A. MINORITIES

9 / THE RACIAL PALLOR OF CAIRO

G. Louis Heath

Cairo, a town of 8,500, 45 per cent black, stands at the confluence of the Ohio and Mississippi Rivers. This is the southernmost point of Illinois and in Cairo prejudice is often translated into action. Intense enmity between white and black has been a historical constant here; confrontation and violence have frequently cracked the veneer of community order, particularly since World War II. Recently, hostilities have escalated. Fire bombings and snipings are common occurrences, and several buildings have been burned to the ground (if a destroyed business has hired Negroes, the suspicion is that the arsonists were white). A few blacks have been wounded, and at least one has been killed. There are incessant threats, implicit or overt, mostly from whites. Considerable numbers of machine guns and other weapons have been sold to both blacks and whites.

Black militancy is the current spark to Cairo's traditional powder keg. The blacks, particularly the younger ones who have not been assimilated into the ante-bellum Southern mores (Cairo lies south of Richmond), are challenging established authority relationships, whereby whites proclaim decisions and "nigras" shuffle off to church to stifle their hatred of "the Man" by praying to the Lord. Blacks, organized in the United Front, are now assertively asking for a greater role in city government, more Negro policemen and jobs in the businesses which they until recently patronized, but now boycott. They are defying white paternalism as fervidly as they once chopped cotton.

From *The Nation*, December 22, 1969. Reprinted by permission.

As late as the summer of 1966, Negroes in the three southern Illinois counties, Alexander, Pulaski and Massac, were chained to low-paying cotton-chopping jobs by the seasonal withdrawal of welfare payments. Each spring the Alexander County office of the Illinois Public Aid Commission notified Cairo Negroes who received aid to dependent children that payments were to be terminated because seasonal labor was available. The labor was in the cotton fields of southern Illinois, southwestern Kentucky and southeastern Missouri, from May to September at 50¢ an hour. William H. Robinson, a black member of the Illinois Advisory Committee to the U.S. Commission on Civil Rights, reported in 1966: "There is evidence of collusion between the large farmers of the three states, the public aid department, and the Illinois State Employment Service to keep the Negroes in a form of slavery by paying them slave wages. When workers return to welfare rolls after the cotton-picking season, they are put on general assistance which pays less than regular welfare payments." The Illinois Advisory Committee's findings stimulated a larger investigation and the practice has been abolished.

The white community has been unable to deal with the new black militancy on any rational level. Their major response, following a black civil disturbance in July 1967, has been to organize a white vigilante group, the White Hats, allegedly "to protect our families, our homes, and our property," but actually to defend ingrained values and practices against the onslaught of the new movement. The present State's attorney for Alexander County, Peyton Berbling, was one of the organizers and even served as an officer. The group is now defunct, but the fact that a man who was once an agent of a terrorist organization could become the foremost representative of the law in Cairo says much about the quality of its justice. The White Hats armed 600 citizens, and drilled conspicuously in the downtown park, wearing white pith helmets. They were deputized as sheriff's deputies and deputy coroners. Cairo businessman Philip D. Marsden once claimed, "I could get my dog deputized in this town." The White Hats periodically participated in target practice and crisis alerts.

The White Hats disbanded last spring under pressure from the state government, particularly from Lieut. Gov. Paul Simon. The Apprehension of Horse Thieves and Other Felons Act, the legislation granting legal status to vigilante groups, was repealed at the same time. But a new group, United Citizens for Community Action (UCCA), has sprung up, and the Negro community views it as the same thing. One can even hear Negro children near the all-black Pyramid Courts housing project jumping rope and singing: "Where have all the White Hats gone? Not far away. Where have all the White Hats gone? They have gone underground to the UCCA."

The United Citizens practice a modern-day vigilantism. Equipped with two-way radios, they cruise the Negro district at night, sometimes with shotguns and rifles protruding from car windows. Both blacks and whites monitor civilian band radio in the evenings. (Preston Ewing, Jr., president of the local NAACP chapter, was until recently a radio and TV repair shop owner.) The messages remind one of the tactics of warfare: "We're close to Niggertown now. The guns are in the back. Our station will be about 100 yards behind Niggertown." "O.K., I'm coming down Walnut now. I'm staying here on this side of the tracks, so if any make any move out of Niggertown, I can handle it." Other conversation focuses upon contingency tactics: "We can roll a string of boxcars in behind Pyramid Courts for cover, if we need 'em. Cuz the city cut down all the brush between the tracks and the Courts, there won't be no cover outside. We can pin 'em down inside." (On one occasion the blacks of Pyramid Courts cornered a guerrilla band of whites on a nearby levee.) This sort of dialogue is not unusual on citizen band radio in Cairo.

The black community organized the United Front in response to the vigilante threat. It also is armed, but it has sought to de-emphasize weapons, realizing that it would be the weaker side in any showdown. Thus, when an AWOL Cairo soldier mysteriously "hung himself" in the local jail and an elderly black man was beaten to death, the blacks didn't make major issues of their suspicions, fearing a mass reprisal upon Pyramid Courts, residence for 2,000 of Cairo's 3,800 Negroes. Instead, the United Front has decided that the way to improve the Negro's position in the town is to wield as much economic power as possible. Accordingly, it declared a boycott of white business. It has been honored by all the blacks, who now buy at a black cooperative store established just north of Cairo or go 38 miles to Cape Girardeau, Mo. For some white merchants business has dropped by two-thirds. "Hell," griped a motel owner, "I'd be out of business if it weren't for the state police and newsmen staying here. I'm losing a lot of money." A real estate man claimed he had sold only two houses since last January. "Me and my family, we're moving to Florida. It's got to be better there. My God, what do they want? They're on aid. They don't work." " I'm losing $150 a day," complained another businessman. "I'm a small businessman and that's too much to lose."

Refusal to patronize local business works a drastic effect upon Cairo, which is in a depression. Of eighty-six Illinois communities with populations ranging from 5,000 to 10,000, Cairo ranks first in family units earning less than $3,000 a year, the income level defined by the federal government as the minimum for subsistence. Some 44 per cent of Cairo's families are below it. Cairo is second among the eighty-six towns in substandard housing: 45.8 per cent of all families reside in such dwellings. Since 1960 only nine new houses have been built and more than 200 have been torn down. There has been no public housing construction since 1927. Cairo is third in unemployment with a 9.4 per cent rate. For Blacks, the rate is twice as high and runs to 20 per cent for the Negro males. Cairo is part of the Alexander-Pulaski Counties' depressed area, where Senator McGovern's Select Committee on Nutrition and Human Needs found considerable hunger and malnutrition. Cairo and Alexander County rate at or near the top for Illinois in high school dropouts, premature births, infant mortality, disease, aid to dependent children and old age pensions.

Part of Cairo's problem is a great loss of population; it has shrunk to one-third of its 1920 figure. Those who leave are disproportionately the young, the potential leadership, which Cairo desperately needs if it is not to become a ghost town. Many whites display bumper stickers proclaiming "Cairo—Love It or Leave It." The young, black and white, have taken the bitter advice, emigrating to St. Louis and Chicago, abandoning Cairo to become "an ugly sepulchre, a grave uncheered by any gleam of promise," as Charles Dickens described it during his visit in 1842.

The tax base has diminished with the population decline, but the percentage of the population on welfare has not—in fact, it has increased. The minuscule population influx has been composed primarily of poor whites from Kentucky, Missouri and Tennessee, who contribute little to the tax base. They compete with blacks for low-paying jobs; many have become resentful welfare recipients. Their presence heightens racial tension.

Father Gerald Montroy, since 1968 representative in Cairo of the Belleville, Ill., Catholic Diocese (all of southern Illinois), referred to by Cairo whites as the "white nigger"; and Rev. Charles Koen, a black leader of the United Front, have advised the state government that major violence lurks just below the ruffled surface. (The Reverend Koen was a controversial leader of the Black Liberators in St. Louis and East St. Louis in 1967 and 1968. The press has referred to him as an "extreme militant.") They have requested Governor Ogilvie to intervene with a long-term scheme for peace, rather than to continue treating the symptoms of basic problems as though they were isolated emergencies. They have even asked the Governor to declare Cairo a disaster area, but Ogilvie thought that unnecessary.

However, when the Cairo merchants began to feel the pinch of the boycott (six had liens on their businesses), President Nixon declared the part of Southern Illinois which includes Cairo an economic disaster area, thereby making federal small business loans easily obtainable. This action, whether or not so intended, effectively undercuts the boycott.

The Governor has dispatched the Illinois National Guard to Cairo on two occasions, but only a temporary cessation of hostilities has been achieved. He has looked the other way throughout much of the trouble. Lieut. Gov. Paul Simon has evinced more concern; he has visited Cairo, and has offered to serve as negotiator. But the United Citizens will have no truck with "outside interference" and "emotional sensationalism" on the part of politicians. The United Front, on the other hand, insists that the Governor or Lieutenant Governor act as negotiator in talks designed to end hostilities. To satisfy Negro demands after the disruptions in the summer of 1967, the white leadership made a "good faith" agreement; but it later reneged and destroyed any trust that may have existed between blacks and whites. Now the Front wants a binding agreement, signed by the parties to the dispute and by a high-ranking state official, preferably the Governor.

Cairo blacks have suffered numerous frustrations in their attempts to secure access to places of public accommodation. They sought to integrate the city swimming pool in 1962, gaining entry by force. After three weeks of unwilling integration (actually a series of sit-ins, demonstrations, cracked heads and arrests), the city officials closed the pool, saying it was not making enough money, and later selling it to a private concern for $1. Today the pool remains closed.

The blacks also attempted in 1962 to integrate a skating rink, owned by Billy Thistlewood, then a member of the local police force. Thistlewood furnished local whites with clubs and chains to repel the intrusion. In 1967, Negro leaders asked that they be permitted to convert into a youth and community center a chicken processing plant that had folded. The city contended that it wanted to keep the factory available for new industry, but the building, after more than two years, stands vacant and unattended. Even the Cairo Little League is segregated; doctors persist in segregating their waiting rooms, and dentists refuse to treat Negro welfare recipients.

When the Cairo schools were integrated during the winter of 1967, four schools were abandoned (they were all-Negro ones; integration generally meant moving blacks into white schools). Black leaders asked the school board for use of the gymnasium in one of these abandoned premises as an activities center. The board refused the request, saying they had long-term plans for the property. "Fine," Negro leaders agreed, "let us use it until the plans are completed." The response was forthcoming within a few days when a bulldozer appeared on the scene and converted the gymnasium into a pile of rubble. City officials erected in its place two basketball goals, which stand at virtually the same locations as did the goals in the old gymnasium. Of the three remaining schools requested by black leaders, two were bulldozed to the ground (although white leaders claimed one of them was to become a medical center) and the other was sold to an all-white group to house a private school, Camelot Parochial. Camelot "serves the better, white children," according to school administrator, Rev. Larry Potts, the fundamentalist Baptist preacher who in 1968 clubbed to death with a baseball bat a 72-year-old Negro, Marshall Morris. Potts was never indicted. He contended that Morris was assaulting his wife in their home. He testified before an Illinois House of Representatives Special Investigating Committee that black militants put Morris up to the attack.

Potts believes the public schools have declined as a result of integration. "The first year after integration, it was chaos. A lot of parents pulled their children out of school then. Many of us felt we ought to give them another chance. The second year was even worse. So many parents just felt they couldn't send their children back again." Mrs. Freida Rose, who has enrolled her child at Camelot, but still retains her position as a board member for the public schools, noted: "We tried integration. But when the Negro children came into the schools, it was terrible. They wrote dirty words on the walls and used such terrible language that we just couldn't take it any more. It isn't that they're Negro. It's just that their morals are so atrocious. I guess they must learn it at home."

Black students in the Cairo public schools have been the target of systematic discrimination. Counselors advise Negro students to drop out of school. A frequent reason cited is that a student is too old for his grade level. Actually, many of the students encouraged to leave school are from families most active in the United Front. Teachers and administrators discourage Negro students from participating in the senior class trip, although all students raise funds for the trip. One student was expelled because he had allegedly been "too playful" with a white girl, and two were evicted from a school assembly for clenching their fists in the "black power" salute.

Racial confrontation has fixed a ghostly pallor on Cairo. Although located on a rich alluvial fan at the confluence of two great arteries of transport and commerce, potentially greater than Chicago (and at one time larger and more prosperous), the city is impoverished in 1969 because a rigid and paranoid social structure will not permit the rational use of resources, both human and physical.

The white leaders, believing God and the Bible to be on their side, would rather attack the boycott and the black militants than seek to eradicate the poverty and deprivation which victimize many of both races. A United Front resolution points out: "The real enemy of the poor people of Cairo, the black ones and the white ones, is the government (in Springfield and Cairo) which permits the poor to remain poor at the edge of an affluent society." The situation in Cairo is a classic one of wealthy elites, bound into a ruling clique, pitting one impoverished group against another. The white leaders know that if they can interpret every issue as a racial one, they will never lose an election (the population is 55 per cent white). They fear any organization that cuts across the racial barrier. The Illinois Migrant Council met great opposition when it initiated its adult education program for underemployed seasonal farm workers. The assistant program director was badly beaten and the area

coordinator was fired upon. The white leaders know that when impoverished whites and blacks study together, they are only one step
from joint political action, and they fear collective militancy even
more than black militancy. Black power can be contained in Cairo
because it is not sufficient to win political office, but the voices of
the impoverished (at least half the population), demanding change
through the ballot box, could not be ignored.

A coalition of poor blacks and whites is not an immediate possibility. The polarization of the races in Cairo is, in fact, so great
that it is difficult for black and white even to discuss their problems.
White police Captain W. H. Thompson claims, "I have never seen
so much hatred in my life as in this town." A truck driver snarls,
"When the niggers learn that if they start cutting on a white man
for no reason at all, they're going to get their head blown off, they'll
start leaving white people alone." A shopkeeper insists: "We got
the dumbest goddam niggers in the country." The Reverend Potts,
who regularly preaches on "Communism in Cairo," is the leading
advocate of the "devil theory" espoused by most white citizens. He
throws up his hands in disgust. "There's a criminal element in
Cairo. There's a militant element that has come and gone back and
forth from East St. Louis." A housewife confides: "We want to help
the nigras, but these cruddy black 'Castro guerrillas' just keep on
agitating. These things take time." This thinking in stereotypes,
this imputing of the basest motives to a whole group, creates a
sociological climate of intolerance. The most minor incident can set
off violence.

The blacks in Cairo have refused to turn inward the antagonism
they feel toward whites. There has been some militant preying upon
moderate blacks who do not agree with the activist strategy, even
one killing, but it has not been much, given the intensity of
feelings. The *Cairo News*, published by the blacks, moralizes:
"The one lesson we hope the White Hats have learned is that there
is a new black man, woman, and child in Cairo. They all stand ten
feet tall and they can smell a sick racist miles away and long before
they can begin to deceive the blacks."

The blacks have sought full participation in civic life by initiating legal challenges to discriminatory practices. For example, the
United Front challenged a proclamation, issued under the authority
of a Cairo City Ordinance, banning picketing in the corporate limits.

The Front won with the legal assistance of Robert Lansden, a lawyer and one of the few white liberals in Cairo, who took the case to federal court in Danville, Ill. Lansden also handled cases for Cairo blacks in 1949 and 1952, winning on both occasions. For his efforts, his home has been fire bombed and garbage has been strewn on his lawn. One neighbor, after suffering an accidental fire bombing of his porch, erected on his roof a neon arrow pointing toward Lansden's place. David Baldwin, president of the United Front, feels the boycott would be successful without picketing, but that the activity sustains in all blacks a sense of involvement that is essential to the black movement in Cairo.

Through the United Front, the blacks have discovered what it means to be a constructive agent of change (and when destructive, generally in self-defense). They no longer accept Cairo's archaic, plantation system of values. But the white community, isolated by its collective illusion about what blacks are like, has hypnotized itself into believing that the "niggers" really do not mean all those things about "Black Power" and "black dignity." How long this fantasy will last is difficult to say, but the violence will continue until it ends.

10 / THE ERA OF DUMMIES AND DARKIES

Stephen Fay

It is not surprising, though it is certainly significant, that the three best remembered black film stars of the first half of the century are Buckwheat, Farina and Mickey Mouse. While it could hardly be contested that Buckwheat and Farina, those endearing ragamuffins

From *Commonweal*, October 30, 1970. Reprinted by permission of Commonweal Publishing Co., Inc.

of the "Our Gang" series, were popular black screen personalities, some might challenge the legitimacy of including Walt Disney's renowned rodent in the thin ranks of Negro film stars on the grounds that Mickey, (though black), was not human. Indeed he was not human—a characteristic which makes him eminently qualified for membership in any grouping of Negro screen actors, none of whom was human.

There has been, and there still is, an odious trend in the American cinema to avoid depicting the black man as a human being. This "inhuman" tendency has brought about cinematic efforts in which the black man has been portrayed as anything from an imbecile to an Albert Schweitzer, but with painfully few exceptions a living, feasible black human being has not been on the American screen. The treatment of the Negro in American movies has been an incredible, outrageous business. Yet, the sometimes racist, sometimes silly attitude of Hollywood towards the blacks has undergone a fascinating evolution.

The Negro arrived on the American screen in 1910 when Vitagraph Studios released the first film version of Harriet Beecher Stowe's classic of condescending honkyism, *Uncle Tom's Cabin*. The attitude of the movie makers toward the slump-shouldered, tongue-lolling blacks in this primitive flicker was made clear by the words they used to advertise their wares:

It will be the real thing in every
respect—real ice, real bloodhounds,
real actors and real Negroes!

These innocent and unsophisticated days of calling a spade a spade were short-lived. With the release of D. W. Griffith's *Birth of a Nation* in 1915, a blow was struck for white supremacy with such frankness that future attempts to demonstrate this principle were doomed to be anti-climactic. For one thing, the Ku Klux Klansmen are depicted as severe, but nevertheless just, preservers of the law in the chaotic, antebellum South. The folk-image of the black man as a walking phallus is personified in Gus, an emancipated slave whose one aim in life is to rape the ivory-skinned, golden-haired daughter of his former master. He nearly succeeds in getting her between the sheets when the noble band capture Gus and hang him.

Though the Ku Klux Klan's popularity has diminished in most responsible circles, the mythology about the black man, particularly in regard to his alleged lust for white flesh, is still accepted as truth by people who should know better. One such person is William Styron who perpetuated this bit of mythological cockamania in his Pulitzer Prize-winning novel, *The Confessions of Nat Turner.* The portrayal of the black man in *Birth of a Nation* was not merely libelous; considering the fact that the "Negroes" in the film were actually white actors playing blackface, the film comes off as a blatant fraud.

Still, these early films were experimental and uncertain. It was not until the early twenties that the experience and judgment of film-makers crystalized into a recognizable form: comedy. These were the films of a more naive era, when audiences could laugh at the confusion of Willie Best without feeling guilty, or see something of their grandmothers in Louise Beavers without consulting their analysts. In the light-hearted realm of comedy of the twenties and thirties, one can discern two distinct types of screen blacks: the Dummies and the Darkies.

Every ethnic group of the screen had its archetypal personality back then, i.e., Edgar Kennedy: the ultimate Irish cop; Richard Loo: the consummate rat-fink Nip of the war films; Elisha Cook Jr.: the supreme squealer. In the black cinema, the archetypal Dummy was the marvelous Mantan Moreland. Don't be too hasty in claiming you've never heard of Mantan Moreland. Remember that slight, saucer-eyed, shiny-skinned black man who has always played the part of either a night-watchman in a cemetery (into which the Three Stooges invariably stumbled), or the porter in the sleeping car of a train on which Abbot and Costello were traveling. The scenes featuring the Dummy were unfailingly similar: while inspecting the darkest corner of the cemetery, or while sweeping up a dimly-lit corridor of the train in the wee hours, the Dummy would hear a suspicious sound. His eyes would widen to impossible hugeness, his ears perk up and his mouth tightens into a grimace of nameless terror. Then . . . slowly he turns, his features quivering involuntarily, and he finally wheels about to confront . . . Lawdamercy! a mud-caked Oliver Hardy, or a horribly reddened Huntz Hall who has just emerged from a vat of catsup. The Dummy's reaction to all this? Boinnng! A magnificent double-take, his cap magically leaps from his head, his eyes start from their sockets and he whispers down to his legs which are quivering like so much Jello: "Feets, get goin'!" With a final yelp he races away and dives through a window or races down the road (hurried along by a speeded-up camera) and disappears over the horizon.

Everyone laughed, but it was not with a malicious laughter that audiences regarded the Dummy's antics; it was with the innocently cruel mirth of children. Similar innocence, though one might call it ignorance, was demonstrated by film-makers in their character-ization of the second type of black funnymen of the twenties and thirties, the Darkie.

An excellent argument could be made for the case that the single, all-consuming ambition of the screen Darkie was to teach Shirley Temple how to dance. The ultimate exponent of Darkie-ism was "Bojangles Robinson," whose combination of shuckin' and jivin' humor and light feet would have touched the heart of Stephen Foster.

As mentioned, the Darkie's happier hours were spent with the dimpled child prodigy of the good ship Lollipop. In *Bright Eyes* and *Little Miss Broadway* black butlers taught Shirley the merits of singing a cheerful song when she felt low; in *The Little Colonel* the Negro house-servant tutored her in the joys of tap-dancing up the stairs.

As the years passed, the Darkie reluctantly shuffled off the screen. But he would not be forgotten. He had performed great services for his white masters: in *Birth of the Blues* he taught Bing Crosby how to play the clarinet. His terpsichorean influence on Shirley Temple cannot be over-emphasized. He was more dedicated than Lassie: he even returned from his cinematic grave in the fifties to give Danny Kaye a new lease on life in *The Five Pennies*.

The black man of the screen had to stay at home with the women and children during World War II while John Wayne and Errol Flynn were making the world safe for democracy. As every-one knew, fighting the war was men's work, so the Negro of the films was temporarily out of work. But after Superman had foiled the last, desperate, secret invasion plans of the Nazis, and Dana Andrews and Frederic March had returned from the front, a new black phenomenon appeared on the screen. The Negro of the postwar films was the product of a startling discovery in Hollywood: the word leaked out that the Emancipation Proclamation had been ratified. Further, rumor had it that some blacks (and not just the uppity ones) were a bit discontented with their status in the United States.

For a fleeting moment on the American screen the racially "aware" film came to the fore. Among these gems were *Pinky, Lost Boundaries*, and *Band of Angels*. All of these films, and others of the genre, were disasters. They supposed they could depict the problems and concerns of the Negro in white America, but in so trying they left out one essential detail: the Negroes. In *Pinky* Jeanne Crain played the part of the social-climbing black girl; in *Lost Boundaries* it was Mel Ferrer (talk about ethnic versatility: he portrayed a sulky Jew in *The Sun Also Rises*); in *Band of Angels* Yvonne de Carlo went blackface.

Though the above mentioned films were box-office flops and generally worthless, the treatment of the American Negro hit the most memorable low with the brief fling moviemakers took at producing black sexploitation films. *I Passed For White*, was the ultimate insult in this area, and it eminently deserved to be awarded a libel suit from the NAACP.

Things were looking pretty grim for the screen Negro of the late fifties. They were losing what little ground they had: the Three Stooges had a corner on the Dummy market; Gene Kelly could dance circles around the docile Darkie; and there was no way on earth moviemakers could return the Negro to the cinematic cotton fields and watermelon patches. Hope was finally found in the massive frame of folklore's epitome of black power, John Henry.

A score of films were released in the late fifties and early sixties in which (somewhere in the lower ranks of the cast) a muscular, taciturn black man could be found. The feature spot for the John Henry in these movies always involved some incredible feat of strength or physical prowess. In *The Devil At Four O'Clock* he hefted a sagging bridge which was about to tumble into a gorge so that the less powerful white people could scurry across. Then he died. In *The Dirty Dozen* he did in most of the Nazi general staff to save his white comrades. Then he died. In *Dark of the Sun* he wiped out a nest of feisty cut-throats and rescued his white co-star from certain doom. Then he died.

The John Henry genre was a popular one, but it, unfortunately, died out (literally).

And Then . . .

Like the Tin Woodsman and Scarecrow of *The Wizard of Oz*, the black man of filmdom longed for a heart and a mind. A new image was needed. As civil rights legislation passed in Congress, so too was equality demanded for the Negro of the screen. The film world responded to this urging with a singular lack of temperance and judgment, creating the most astonishing, breath-taking screen phenomenon since the day Colin Clive unveiled the first Frankenstein monster: Sidney Poitier, alias Super Spade.

A Super Spade is a perfectly incredible amalgam of the best parts of Socrates, Abe Lincoln, Popeye, Sherlock Holmes and Jesus. His overwhelming virtue is not that he possesses more zip and joy than Rootie Kazootie, nor even that he is more wise and perceptive than the Shadow; everyone loves Super Spade because he is not too black. His features are not too Negroid, his skin is not too dark.

A Super Spade performs more miraculous missions of mercy in a single day than any white man could effect in twenty years. In one of the first films of this genre, *Lilies of the Field*, Poitier rescues a band of needy nuns from financial disaster, assists an impoverished padre in his struggle against demon rum, single-handedly constructs a chapel out of sticks and cow dung, then quietly slips off, leaving the grateful objects of his benevolence wondering (as did the Lone Ranger's beneficiaries): "Who was that man?"

In *To Sir With Love* Super Spade transforms a wretched classroom of greasy pachucos and aspiring whores into young ladies and gentlemen of refinement. By his good example alone he revamps the entire British educational system. He further demonstrated, in his spare time, that he could box like Joe Palooka, dance like Rudolph Nuryev, and cook like Julia Child.

Super Spade hits his peak in *Guess Who's Coming to Dinner*. In this abominable effort he is not only dashing, handsome, sexy and articulate—he is the greatest doctor in the history of medicine. He has garnered more awards and Nobel Prizes than you could fit into Fibber McGee's closet.

Superlatives cannot do justice to Super Spade, much as film-makers can seemingly do no justice to the black man. Arguments to the contrary become untenable in light of the most recent addition to the continuing adventures of Super Spade, *The Lost Man*. In this timely delight Sidney Poitier portrays a black militant (about as successfully as Knucklehead Smiff could portray William F. Buckley). In fact, to our great relief, Sidney turns out to be a Robin Hood of the ghettos, not really black, not really a militant.

More recent films are sufficiently dismal to warrant my belief that these movies are crummy and due to get crummier. *Putney Swope* (which came out last summer) billed itself as something different. In fact, it is in the billing itself that one may find a grand insight as to just how "different" *Putney Swope* is. The newspaper and theater ads for *Putney Swope* featured a black hand earnestly flipping the bird. And though the film had some really funny bits, it was essentially comprised of vengeful vignettes in which blacks flipped the metaphorical bird to whitey. The black man is shown beating white America at its own games, but who cares? Why should blacks want to play at white man's games? This whole effort, which reaches a horrid low with the Black Miss America Contest, is a drag and a waste of time.

A real treat was *Change of Mind*, which sought to illustrate the difficulties of adjustment faced by a white man whose brain was planted in a black man's body. Or did it concern the problems of a black man with a white man's brain? The resolution to this enigma is the same as that provided for the great Cert's controversy: he was two men in one! However, everyone in the film hated both of the men he was and, in the end, he left in disgust (which is what the audience had been doing since the opening credits).

The movie I really had hopes for was *Cotton Comes to Harlem*. The product of an articulate black staff of writers, directors and actors, it seemed that at last the black man would be fairly represented. But *Cotton* was the same old hodge-podge of natural-rhythm and "nigger jokes." There was a small compensation: for every nigger joke there was a honky joke; for every black junkie there was a corrupt white cop. *Cotton* suggests a kind of equality that is less than encouraging: we are all murderers, boobs and creeps.

Thus, under the banner of up from knavery the black man of the films has evolved. Though in 1935 Charles Bickford could kick his black coolie in the teeth with his hobnail boots, in *The Plains-man*, the 1968 remake of that film would tolerate no such cruelty. The black man has been awarded a mind and a heart (though both of these "advances" have been made with unpalatable clumsiness). Yet the Negro of the American films has always been, and still is, a fraud, a joke, or an insult. After sixty years of trial and error (and mostly error) the black man depicted on the screen remains unreal and consistently comes up lacking. What does he lack? Need we ask? He got no *soul*.

And herein lies a possible resolution to half a century of foolish-ness. What is needed in the film world is segregation. A recent ray of hope entitled, *Nothing But a Man*, endorses this suggestion, as it was made entirely by a black film staff. For who but a Negro can portray a Negro, and who should coach him but a black man, and who should mobilize him but a black screen-writer? Will this emerging trend last? Will this one bit of rationality and sanity survive, or will the executives of Hollywood continue to serve a more aware audience the same vapid plate of warmed-over black-face?

11 / THE GREAT AMERICAN WHITE WASH

Vine Deloria, Jr.

One reason the Indian people have not been heard from until re-cently is that we have been completely covered up by movie Indians. Western movies have dominated the public's conception of what Indians are. It is not all bad when one thinks about the handsome Jay Silverheels bailing the Lone Ranger out of a jam, or Ed Ames

Reprinted with permission of The Macmillan Company from *We Talk, You Listen*, by Vine Deloria, Jr. Copyright © 1970 by Vine Deloria, Jr.

rescuing Daniel Boone with some clever Indian trick. But the other mythologies of the movies have blocked out any idea that there might be real Indians with real problems.

Traditional movie stereotypes pictured the Black as a happy watermelon-eating darky whose sole contribution to American society was his indiscriminate substitution of the "d" sound for "th." Thus a Black always said "dis" and "dat," as in "lift dat bale." (The "d" sound carried over and was used by White gangsters to indicate disfavor with their situation, as in "dis is de end, ya rat.") The important thing was to indicate that Blacks were like lisping children not yet competent to undertake the rigors of economic opportunities and voting.

Where the Black had been handicapped by his use of the "d," the Mexican suffered from the use of the double "e." This marked them off as a group worth watching. Mexicans, according to the movie stereotype, always said "theenk," "peenk," and later "feenk." Many advertisements today still continue this stereotype.

Even so, these groups were much better off than Indians. Indians were always devoid of any English whatsoever. They were only allowed to speak when an important message had to be transmitted on the screen. For example, "Many pony soldiers die" was meant to indicate that Indians were going to attack the peaceful settlers who happened to have broken their 300th treaty moments before. Other than that, Indian linguistic ability was limited to "ugh" and "kemo sabe" (which means "honky" in some obscure Indian language).

The next movie step was to acknowledge that there was a great American dream to which any child could aspire. As projected in the early World War II movies, the last reel was devoted to a stirring proclamation that we were going to win the war and it showed factories producing airplanes, people building ships, and men marching in uniform to the transports. There was a quick pan of a black face before the scene shifted to scenes of orchards, rivers, Mount Rushmore, and the Liberty Bell as we found out what we were fighting for.

By projecting an image of everyone working hard to win the war, the doctrine was spread that America was just one big happy family and that there really weren't any differences so long as we had to win the war.

It was a rare movie in the 1940s that actually showed a Black or a Mexican as a bona fide fighting man. When they did appear it was in the role of cooks or orderlies serving Whites. In most cases this was a fairly accurate statement of their situation, particularly with respect to the Navy.

However, World War II movies were entirely different for Indians. Each platoon of red-blooded White American boys was equipped with its own set of Indians. When the platoon got into trouble and was surrounded, its communications cut off except for one slender line to regimental headquarters, and that line tapped by myriads of Germans, Japanese or Italians, the stage was set for the dramatic episode of the Indians.

John Wayne, Randolph Scott, Sonny Tufts, or Tyrone Power would smile broadly as he played his ace. From nowhere, a Navajo, Commanche, Cherokee, or Sioux would appear, take the telephone, and in some short and inscrutible phraseology communicate such a plentitude of knowledge to his fellow tribesman (fortunately situated at the general's right hand) that fighting units thousands of miles away would instantly perceive the situation and rescue the platoon. The Indian would disappear as mysteriously as he had come, only to reappear the next week in a different battle to perform his esoteric rites. Anyone watching war movies during the '40s would have been convinced that without Indian telephone operators the war would have been lost in spite of John Wayne.

The typing spoke of a primitive gimmick, and it was the strangeness of Indians that made them visible in these movies, not their humanity. With the Korean War era and movies made during the middle '50s, other minority groups began to appear and Indians were pushed into the background. This era was the heyday of the "All-American Platoon." It was the ultimate conception of intergroup relations. The "All-American Platoon" was a "one each": One Black, one Mexican, one Indian, one farm boy from Iowa, one Southerner who hated Blacks, one boy from Brooklyn, one Polish boy from the urban slums of the Midwest, one Jewish intellectual, and one college boy. Every possible stereotype was included and it resulted in a portrayal of Indians as another species of human being for the first time in moving pictures.

The platoon was always commanded by a veteran of grizzled countenance. The whole story consisted of killing the members of the platoon until only the veteran and the college boy were left.

The Southerner and the Black would die in each other's arms singing *Dixie*. The Jewish intellectual and the Indian formed some kind of attachment and were curiously the last ones killed. When the smoke cleared, the college boy, with a prestige wound in the shoulder, returned to his girl, and the veteran checked out another platoon in anticipation of taking the same hill in the next movie.

While other groups have managed to make great strides since those days, Indians have remained the primitive unknown quantity. Dialogue has reverted back to the monosyllabic grunt and even pictures that attempt to present the Indian side of the story depend upon unintelligible noises to present their message. The only exception to this rule is a line famed for its durability over the years. If you fall asleep during the Late Show and suddenly awaken to the words "Go in peace, my son," it is either an Indian chief bidding his son goodby as the boy heads for college or a Roman Catholic priest forgiving Paul Newman or Steve McQueen for killing a hundred men in the preceding reel.

In recent years the TV documentary has arisen to present the story of Indian people and they are singularly the same. A reporter and television crew hasten to either the Navajo or Pine Ridge reservation, quickly shoot reels on poverty conditions, and return East blithely thinking that they have captured the essence of Indian life. In spite of the best intentions, the eternal yearning to present an exciting story of a strange people overcomes, and the endless cycle of poverty-oriented films continues.

This type of approach continually categorizes the Indian as an incompetent boob who can't seem to get along and who is hopelessly mired in a poverty of his own making. Hidden beneath these documentaries is the message that Indians really WANT to live this way. No one has yet filmed the incredible progress that is being made by the Makah tribe, the Quinaults, Red Lake Chippewas, Gila River Pima-Maricopas, and others. Documentaries project the feeling that reservations should be eliminated because the conditions are so bad. There is no effort to present the bright side of Indian life.

With the rise of ethnic studies programs and courses in minority-group history, the situation has become worse. People who support these programs assume that by communicating the best aspects of a group they have somehow solved the major problems of that group in its relations with the rest of society. By emphasizing that black is beautiful or that Indians have contributed the names of rivers to the road map, many people feel that they have done justice to the group concerned.

One interpretation of Indian history that has arisen in the past several years is that all of the Indian war chiefs were patriots defending their lands. This is the "patriotic chief" interpretation of history. Fundamentally it is a good theory in that it places a more equal balance to interpreting certain Indian wars as wars of resistance. It gets away from the tendency, seen earlier in this century, to classify all Indian warriors as renegades who were treacherous and would have been renegades had there been no Whites to fight. The patriot chiefs interpretation also conveniently overlooks the fact that every significant Indian leader of the previous century was eventually done in by his own people in one way or another. Sitting Bull was killed by Indian police working for the government. Geronimo was captured by an army led by Apache scouts who sided with the United States.

If the weak points of each minority group's history are to be covered over by a sweetness-and-light interpretation based on what we would like to think happened rather than what did happen, we doom ourselves to decades of further racial strife. Most of the study programs today emphasize the goodness that is inherent in the different minority communities, instead of trying to present a balanced story.

There are basically two schools of interpretation running through all of these efforts as the demand for Black, Red and Brown pride dominates the programs. One theory derives from the "All-American Platoon" concept of a decade ago. Under this theory members of the respective racial minority groups had an important role in the great events of American history. Crispus Attucks, a Black, almost single-handedly started the Revolutionary War, while Eli Parker, the Seneca Indian general, won the Civil War and would have concluded it sooner had not there been so many stupid Whites abroad in those days. This is the "cameo" theory of history. It takes a basic "manifest destiny" White interpretation of history and lovingly plugs a few feathers, woolly heads and sombreros into the famous events of American history. No one tries to explain what an Indian is who was helping the Whites destroy his own people, since we are now all Americans and have these great events in common.

The absurdity of the cameo school of ethnic pride is self-apparent. Little Mexican children are taught that there were some good Mexicans at the Alamo. They can therefore be happy that Mexicans have been involved in the significant events of Texas history. Little is said about the Mexicans on the other side of the Alamo. The result is a denial of a substantial Mexican heritage by creating the feeling that "we all did it together." If this trend continues I would not be surprised to discover that Columbus had a Cherokee on board when he set sail from Spain in search of the Indies.

The other basic school of interpretation is a projection backward of the material blessings of the White middle class. It seeks to identify where all the material wealth originated and finds that each minority group *contributed* something. It can therefore be called the contribution school. Under this conception we should all love Indians because they contributed corn, squash, potatoes, tobacco, coffee, rubber, and other agricultural products. In like manner, Blacks and Mexicans are credited with Carver's work on the peanut, blood transfusion and tacos and tamales.

The danger with both of these types of ethnic studies theories is that they present an unrealistic account of the role of minority groups in American history. Certainly there is more to the story of the American Indian than providing cocoa and popcorn for Columbus' landing party. When the clashes of history are smoothed over in favor of a mushy togetherness feeling, then people begin to wonder what has happened in the recent past that has created the conditions of today.

Under present conceptions of ethnic studies there can be no lasting benefit either to minority groups or to society at large. The pride that can be built into children and youth by acknowledgment of the validity of their group certainly cannot be built by simply transferring symbols and interpretations arising in White cultural history into an Indian, Black or Mexican setting. The result will be to make the minority groups bear the White man's burden by using his symbols and stereotypes as if they were their own.

The problem of stereotyping is not so much a racial problem as it is a problem of limited knowledge and perspective. Even though minority groups have suffered in the past by ridiculous characterizations of themselves by White society, they must not fall into the same trap by simply reversing the process that has stereotyped them.

Minority groups must thrust through the rhetorical blockade by creating within themselves a sense of "peoplehood." This ultimately means the creation of a new history and not mere amendments to the historical interpretations of White America.

B. THE POOR

12 / APPALACHIA: AGAIN THE FORGOTTEN LAND

Peter Schrag

Once again Appalachia is becoming America's forgotten land. Seven years and more than seven billion federal dollars after John F. Kennedy brought the region to national attention, grand solutions have soured into new problems, the exploitation of land and people continues, and even the best and most hopeful efforts are jeopardized by a war 10,000 miles away and by ugly political machines all too close to home.

Because of the work of a handful of dedicated people—VISTA workers, Appalachian volunteers, and local residents—some hope has returned with the mounting welfare checks, and some sense of the possible is growing even in the most remote creeks and hollows. But now the programs that have been most effective—many of them aimed at giving the poor a measure of choice and control—are threatened by the politicians' response to local commercial pressures and by the rapacious demands of the strip-mine operators. Efforts at regional development are being directed by distant planners and small-town chambers of commerce, while individuals trying to organize the poor are called agitators and Communists, and are driven from the region under agreements between state politicians and national poverty officials who have become politically too weak to resist.

Appalachia, the original American frontier, extends from southern Pennsylvania to northern Alabama, covering 182,000 square miles of land rich in coal, timber, sandstone, natural gas, water, and some of the most magnificent scenery on the continent. In 1966, nearly 100 million tons of coal worth close to $400 million were mined in Kentucky alone. Where the strip mines have spared the hillsides, the folded mountains, covered by white oak, pine, walnut, beech, and other trees, extend in all directions to the blue-gray horizon. But in the half-abandoned coal camps that adjoin the sulphur-polluted creeks, on the streets of the little towns, and in the welfare offices, the poverty of the people stands in brutal contrast to the wealth of the land. Along the winding roads, the rotting carcasses of abandoned automobiles lie alongside smoldering coal dumps and the decaying tipples of exhausted mines, and in the brown and yellow streams, once rich with fish, the sad trash of poverty accumulates in rusty piles.

Appalachia, now growing its third welfare generation, has counties where more than a third of the population is unemployed, where the government check—social security, welfare, aid to dependent children—is the prime source of income, and where some men are so far from their last job that it cannot properly be said that they have a trade at all. Here the average adult has a sixth-grade education, three-fourths of the children who start school drop out before they complete the twelfth grade, and the statistics of human pathology—tuberculosis, silicosis, infant mortality—are so high that they do not belong in the Western world at all.

Everything has eroded: The best of the resources flow forever downstream and toward the industrial cities of the North. Heavy rains wash the topsoil from the hills and turn the rivers into muddy torrents, the coal fires the mills of the North and the generators of the TVA (which is the prime buyer of Appalachian fuel), while the most skilled and ambitious of the young leave the hills and hollows to find work in Cleveland, Chicago, or Detroit. "We've been the great pool of manpower for the Northeast," said a poverty worker in eastern Tennessee. "And the pool has been turned on and off at will. The rest of the country gets automobiles and the gadgets of affluence. All this region gets is silicosis."

Appalachia's coal regions enjoyed a brief, uncertain moment of prosperity during and immediately after World War II, when the war economy and the pressure of John L. Lewis's United Mine

Workers brought decent wages, hospitals, and pension plans. But when the war boom ended, many of the mines closed, leaving the survivors of a single-product economy without resources or useful skills. The coal industry ultimately returned to prosperity with a rising demand for fuel, but it did so as a highly efficient, mechanized enterprise. Using modern equipment, 140,000 men can now dig more coal than 700,000 did twenty years ago. And while many of the deep mines continue to operate, frequently under enlightened management, a substantial part of the industry is now stripping the mountains, cutting or blasting away the topsoil and vegetation—which spills down the slopes—to get at the coal beneath. Each year the strip mines of Kentucky scar some 12,000 acres of land, leaving the bare cliffs of the high wall above and the sliding spoil banks on the hills below.

The legal basis for this damage rests in the so-called broad form deed: Before strip mining became prevalent, thousands of mountaineers sold their mineral rights to coal and land companies for a few cents an acre, entitling the companies to remove minerals and holding them harmless for any damage except that incurred through malice. The courts have held that this immunity extends even to the uprooting of graves and the destruction of the homes and gardens that are occasionally covered by slides. Under the broad form deed, said a mountaineer, "they've dug up the dead and buried the living." Although several states have enacted strip-mine laws requiring operators to restore the land, and although many companies are diligently trying to comply, enforcement is often difficult or ineffective.

In West Virginia, a new statute now entitles property owners to collect triple damages from the coal companies, but in the mountains of eastern Kentucky that state's law has had little effect. Kentucky's new governor, Louie B. Nunn, received support from the strip-mine interests in the 1967 election, and it is unlikely that he will be overzealous in enforcing or strengthening it. Under his predecessor, Edward T. Breathitt, state officials experimented with techniques of restoring the hillsides, but even they admitted privately that where the slopes are steep, there is no possible way of eliminating slides and reclaiming the land. In the mountains of eastern Kentucky, the only effective hope for conservation appears to be the elimination of the strip mine altogether. (Last month, the day Breathitt's term expired, he approved a set of tough regulations, limiting strip mines to slopes of less than 28 degrees; if those regulations stand, they will severely restrict strip mining and will represent a major victory for conservation in the region.)

In this sad economy of food stamps and subsistence, the coal company is no longer the great employer—and hence the paternalistic provider—it used to be. Gone are the days when the company owned the buildings, ran the store, and furnished the services, and even the most naïve have now abandoned the hope that some day "the mines will open up again." What remains is the condition of dependency: Through a half-century of rural industrialization, the once-independent mountaineer was reduced to reliance on a single enterprise, and, when it no longer required his labor, to nothing except the dole. The public payroll, and most notably the public schools, now furnish the prime source of employment. In Appalachia, schools mean jobs for bus drivers, clerks, lunchroom employees, coaches, and teachers, and hence they represent the most important source of political power at hand. In the isolated mountain counties, where kinship and tribal loyalties overshadow the abstractions of political ethics, the school superintendent is often a political boss who controls contracts for insurance, construction, and fuel, appointment to other offices, and employment in the system.

In Breathitt County, Kentucky, for example, Marie Turner or her husband have held the school superintendency for more than forty years, and thus they also control most of the other offices the county has to offer. There are similar machines in other areas, and although many people feel that people like the Turners have been benevolent bosses—Breathitt County, someone said, would have fallen apart without the Turners—they have been bosses nevertheless. At a time when Appalachia was out of the national consciousness and the mountaineer was a figure for mythology and amusement, the Turners did what they could for their people. The *quid pro quo* was patronage and power.

The American romance with the happy hillbilly came to an end in the early Sixties. Prompted by Mr. Kennedy's concern with Appalachian poverty—which he saw first hand in the 1960 West

Virginia primary—Americans began to discover the misery behind the moonshine. Television crews and magazine writers swarmed to the hills in such numbers that one Kentucky motel owner began to conduct photographic safaris to hollows that he promised "ain't been worked yet." While bands of hungry, desperate miners roamed the coal regions dynamiting trains and bridges, Congress passed the Manpower Development and Training Act, the Appalachia Redevelopment Act, and a variety of other measures designed to bring the heretofore invisible poor some share of the affluence that most Americans took for granted.

Although the federal poverty program was aimed at all indigent Americans, Appalachia came to symbolize, along with the urban ghetto, the most pressing item on the nation's social agenda. As a consequence, special funds have been appropriated for the construction of Appalachian highways, water facilities, and hospitals; the distribution of surplus food has been augmented through a food stamp program which enables the poor to purchase more groceries than their welfare checks would otherwise permit; unemployed fathers have been given jobs, at $1.25 an hour, in a "work experience and training" program (they are generally called "happy pappies"); young men and women have been enrolled in the Job Corps and the Neighborhood Youth Corps; vocational education has received increased support, and large sums have been made available for the education of the disadvantaged, which, in the mountain counties, means almost everybody.

To anyone visiting Appalachia now, these programs have clearly had an effect: new roads and vocational schools are under construction or already in use; the happy pappies have planted trees on hillsides that had been covered by stripmine spoil banks; medical facilities are more accessible; the school dropout rate has been reduced (partly because federal funds are keyed to enrollment); and there appear to be fewer obvious signs of malnutrition than there were three years ago. In some families, the money earned by adolescents in the Youth Corps has become the most important source of income. It has also become a source of pride and respect. "After those kids received their first pay check," said Don Roarke, the director of a four-county Youth Corps in eastern Kentucky, "they were dressed better, they held their heads higher. You could see the difference." At the same time, the graduates of many vocational programs are finding jobs as heavy-machine operators and mine technicians, a few of them in the mountains, others in Northern cities.

For many more, however, the existing programs serve only to hide the misery: The new highways are beginning to make it possible to cross large portions of Appalachia without seeing a tarpaper shack or a coal dump, the food stamps run out before the end of the month, and the schools, though far better than they used to be, still remain a blind alley, graduating children who are approximately two years behind the national average on standardized tests. "The bare gut essentials are now being met," said Tom Gish, the editor of the Whitesburg, Kentucky, *Mountain Eagle*, who is undoubtedly the most outspoken and dedicated journalist in the region. "By and large people are getting fed and getting coal for the winter. If you go back to the early Sixties when there was mass hunger and violence, then you can say there's been improvement. Peace has been restored."

But the peace is shaky, and the economy remains dependent on the federal government. President Johnson's recent declaration that "the dole is dead" was, to say it mildly, premature. Poverty remains endemic: Median family income in eastern Kentucky is $3,505, and Gish predicts that if poverty funds are reduced there will be more violence. In the county seats, the prosperous get roads and water lines and sewers, but only a few miles away the privies stand alongside the dirty creeks from which people draw their water, rain turns the unpaved roads into muddy ruts, and the youngsters can't go to school because they have no shoes.

The prime beneficiaries of government funds appear to be the swelling banks, which are afraid to invest their deposits in anything but government bonds; the small businesses; and the politicians. For all their ignorance and isolation, the economic and political interests of Appalachia have a highly developed knack for using outside help to perpetuate the existing structure and the conditions of dependency. In Perry County, Kentucky, a political enemy of a former county school superintendent used his influence as director of a poverty project to help elect a new school board and oust the superintendent; the new administration then rewarded him with the directorship of another federally financed program administered by the schools. In other areas, the directors of happy pappy programs discourage their charges from participating in community action groups that threaten local political machines, and in almost every community the traditions of nepotism are so powerful that many people still regard the poverty program as a source of employment rather than as a means of upgrading the skills of human beings and the social health of the community. "Jobs are coveted so much, and loyalties to kin are so strong," said a poverty worker in Kentucky, "that it's pretty hard to persuade anyone that you have to pick people on merit."

Although some training programs have brought new skills and confidence, and although many children who had once gone hungry through the school day are now receiving hot lunches (sometimes even in the most remote one-room schools), many school officials have refused to appoint outsiders, preferring to promote politically faithful employees to the uncertainties of new blood and new ideas. In one community, a group of men who were enrolled for training in construction and maintenance composed a letter to Washington:

We were in the building and maintainence class under MDTA that took up on April 10 and ended September 29. They told us each day we would have 2 hours of electricity, pluming, carpentry and painting but for the most of it all we did was paint school buildings and repair and cover the roofs of the schools. When some of the men bucked on painting so much they was told if they didnt like it they could leave. To start we was told the government would buy around a thousand dollars of lumber a month for us to work with we unloaded plenty new lumber and racked it up on the racks. For awhile we used some then we was told we could buy it for 25 cents a foot and then they said it wasnt for sale but it still got missing. In electricity all we had were 9 days, on our certificate of training it says we got 320 hours. They just didnt care much if we learned a thing or not we was just putting in time. Now we are in worse shape than when we started and we got knocked off the food stamps for 30 days. We didnt get the training they said or the permanent jobs they promised at the start. The only jobs we have heard about are temporary and a long way off. A man with a family in school cant just leave out at the promise of a job.

Given these conditions, the most promising idea for Appalachia has been community action—training individuals to organize local groups for social improvement, community welfare, and self-help. As originally conceived, the Community Action Program (CAP) of the Office of Economic Opportunity was to include "maximum feasible participation" of the poor: Community action agencies were, if possible, to be free from domination by local politicians. In some areas of Appalachia, the program worked effectively, despite the suspicions of county officials: Community centers have been built, small marketing cooperatives (selling quilts and other local products) have been organized, and new leadership has developed. In the eastern Kentucky counties of Leslie, Knott, Letcher, and Perry, a four-county Community Action Program (LKLP), which includes poor people as well as sympathetic county judges, has established a network of depots to inform people of their welfare rights, of new training programs, and of the availability of medical facilities. Among other things, LKLP operated a transportation system to bring the sick from the hollows to the area clinics, it is training local people in welfare work and social service, and it has prompted a number of projects to clear the region of decaying bridges and abandoned coal tipples.

Despite such successes, however—and there are others—many CAP agencies have been captured by established interests or abandoned after local battles destroyed embryonic organizations before they had a chance to function. Many of those that survive must straddle an uncertain line between ineffectiveness and the dangerous course of challenging the established order. Recent Congressional action, moreover, indicates that control for all local CAP agencies will be given to local elected officials, thus making CAP—in Appalachia, at least—the biggest potential pork barrel since the invention of rivers and harbors.

Because of the limitations of the Community Action Program, some of the most effective community work has been done by VISTA (Volunteers in Service to America—the domestic Peace Corps); by the Appalachian Committee to Save the Land and People, which has been fighting the strip mines; by the long-standing Council of the Southern Mountains; and by the Appalachian Volunteers, a private organization which originated among students at Berea College, but which is now fully autonomous. Originally, the Appalachian Volunteers (AVs) concentrated on the repair of school-houses, the distribution of books—more than a million were collected and placed in mountain schools—and on other community work. The AVs and VISTAs, who often work together, have moved into isolated mountain communities—places named Marrowbone and Cave Ridge, Clover Fork and Horse Creek—have come to know the inhabitants, and are helping to create new organizations and a new sense of confidence: adult education groups, nursery schools, community centers, craft shops, and, most significantly, a belief that choices are available and collective action possible. "These are the first people," said a woman in the mountains, "who promised to do something and then did."

What they have done, among other things, is to arouse the suspicions and fears of the established interests. In the past year, the AVs have become increasingly involved in the strip-mine issue and in tax reform, helping to organize protests, transport people to meetings, and warn affected property owners when the strip-mine bulldozers were coming. In their zealousness, some have talked, none too privately, about overturning local political structures and establishing some vague new order; a few were poorly trained or offensive in dress or manners. As a consequence, they have been labeled Communists and agitators (though many are natives of the region), and they are now threatened with the suspension of all federal support.

The precipitating incident took place in the summer of 1967 when a small Pike County, Kentucky, farmer named Jink Ray, supported by his neighbors (and, later, by Appalachian Volunteers), stood in front of the bulldozers of the Puritan Coal Company, which had come to strip his land. Within a few days the matter had become a regional *cause célèbre* and threatened to develop into a mountain shoot-out. Under the new Kentucky strip-mine law, Governor Breathitt lifted the company's permit, ordering the state's Department of National Resources to determine whether the slopes to be mined exceed the statutory limits. Two weeks later, after several conferences among Pike County officials, the county sheriff, in a midnight raid, arrested an AV fieldworker named Joe Mulloy and two organizers for the Southern Conference Education Fund on charges of violating a Kentucky sedition law. (The man charged with the prosecution was a former president of the Independent Coal Operators Association who was then a candidate for state office.)

In indicting the three, the Pike County grand jury concluded that "a well organized and well financed effort is being made to promote and spread the communistic theory of the violent and forceful overthrow of the government of Pike County" and that "the employees of the Appalachian Volunteers and other federally financed antipoverty programs have collaborated and cooperated with known communist organizers to help them organize and promote the violent overthrow of the constitutional government of Pike County." The grand jury, said Harry M. Caudill, the Whitesburg attorney who is probably the most eloquent spokesman for the mountains, "was certain that the revolution was about to begin in Pike County, and that the neighboring counties, in domino fashion, would then fall to the enemy."

Although the sedition law was quickly declared unconstitutional by a federal court, the Pike County affair reinforced suspicions not only about the Appalachian Volunteers, but about everything that smacked of community action. In many eastern Kentucky counties VISTA workers are no longer welcome. In West Virginia, Governor Hulett Smith, while praising the VISTA program in mental health, charged the AVs with "misconduct" and demanded an OEO investigation. In Kentucky, Governor Breathitt (who could not succeed himself as governor but was nonetheless involved in the political campaign) demanded and received assurances from OEO Director Sargent Shriver that some current OEO grants to the Appalachian Volunteers would not be renewed, and that the cancellation of other federal support for AV activities would receive "most serious consideration." In Hazard, Kentucky, a few months later, an exasperated staff member of the Community Action agency declared that "we're still trying to beat this Red rap. People in the Work Experience and Training Program have been told that if they had anything to do with us they'd be off the rolls."

What is most in jeopardy now is not merely the budget of the Appalachian Volunteers (who are trying to find private funds to

replace their uncertain federal support), but the principle of independent community action itself. The efforts of the past three years
have (in some areas at least) generated a degree of independence
that will be difficult to arrest: Even before the poverty program
began, the Appalachian Group to Save the Land and People, composed entirely of mountaineers, had begun to campaign for stricter
strip-mine laws and for the imposition of a severance tax on the
minerals that now flow untaxed from the region. In the creeks and
hollows, residents have stopped bulldozers, sometimes with their
bodies, sometimes with shotguns and dynamite. When Youth
Corps funds ran out during the 1967 Congressional debate on the
poverty program, the staff members in many Appalachian communities came to work anyway, and when Shriver announced the
curtailment of AV support, the residents of a number of mountain
communities signed letters and telegrams of protest. This fall, for
the first time in history, teachers in an eastern Kentucky county
went on strike for higher pay. Nevertheless, if prime responsibility
for the Appalachian portion of the war on poverty is delegated to
the established regimes, the basic political arrangements will remain unchanged: Every dollar in federal funds will make the
politicians that much stronger.

* * *

It is difficult to cheer the results of Appalachian development or
the war on poverty: The harmonious interplay of poverty, politics,
and the welfare mind combine to frustrate even the most valiant
effort. But it is even more difficult to criticize the intent of these
programs or the officials who are charged with running them. They
have been forced to live with a limited and reluctant mandate that
prohibits them from anything more than making poverty bearable
and, if posible, invisible. The vested Appalachian interests in the
status quo—coal companies, railroads, banks, local bar associations,
insurance agencies, politicians—are so vast that they represent a
fair cross section of American society itself. Their stockholders
and beneficiaries live all over the nation; they help sustain our
affluence. If Appalachia hasn't changed, it may be in part because
too many are dependent on it as it now is. "The reason little has
happened," said Perley F. Ayer, the chairman of the Council of the
Southern Mountains, "is that America doesn't have its heart in it."

13 / THE ILLEGALITY OF POVERTY

Edward V. Sparer

We are participants in a constitutional and human crisis. An increasing segment of the American people will no longer accept what has been, and remains, acceptable to the rest of the population and to those who exercise the power of government. There are young people who refuse to fight and kill in other lands, despite the legal demands of an elected government. There are blacks, browns, and reds who refuse to tolerate inequality, despite the manner in which certain forms of inequality are protected by the legal process of government. There are American poor, in and out of "welfare," who refuse to tolerate starvation conditions on the ground that neither Constitution nor statute nor court decision appears to impose upon our government an obligation to protect all of its citizens against starvation. There are also large numbers of Americans, apparently drawn from various classes, who would cast such folk outside the pale of constitutional protection and withdraw all their rights.

It is argued that the Constitution is designed to assure democratic results: the majority governs through the elective process; the minority is guaranteed the right to dissent. Those are the ground rules by which all members of American society must abide. These rules are subject today to increasing challenge. Upon what moral premise must the starving man or woman accept the majority's vote on whether he or she shall live or not? What moral premise requires that the youth accept the majority's vote on whether he must kill other men? What moral premise requires that the black man accept the results of the white majority vote on whether obstacles to his equality shall be removed?

The persuasive argument on such issues has not been moral, but pragmatic: If you do not accept these ground rules, the result

From *Social Policy*, March/April, 1971.

will be chaos. To which some who suffer under such ground rules, and their sympathizers, reply: We do not prefer the *status quo* to chaos; only the relatively comfortable see the issue of change in such terms. The ground rules must do more than guarantee the right to persuade the majority; they must guarantee the right to live, whatever the majority thinks. The right to live is a *sine qua non* of the social contract.

The welfare recipient lawyer started his struggle in 1965 not merely as a technician whose function was to help the welfare system conform to what the elected representatives of the majority had decreed it should be. His mission was to utilize the legal process to help change the very nature of welfare and, thereby, to change the ground rules of American society. No mere legal technician, he was a grand strategist. No mere advocate of other people's yearnings, he yearned for the change with his clients. And for a brief moment in the 1960s when it appeared that a majority, or at least their elected representatives, were ready to accept some basic change, his mission appeared possible. In 1971, it does not. No more a significant participant in grand change, he appears reduced to what the revolutionist has often accused the lawyer of being—a technical aide who smooths the functioning of an inadequate system and thereby helps perpetuate it. Thus we find among some welfare and other antipoverty lawyers the growing conviction that their profession is but a trade which does more to support the lawyer than it does his impoverished and often hungry client; that their work may be more negative than positive in its social consequence. Drift and anomie set in.

It is painful to abandon the grand strategist's role. It is painful to be defeated in ambitious schemes. It is painful to realize that the struggle for a humane society is long-term, not short-term. It is painful to share the yearning of the dispossessed, presumably speak on their behalf, and observe that one earns a comfortable living in the process. (Why not abandon role-playing and become one of the dispossessed?) But the real problem is not the lawyer's self-satisfaction. The human and constitutional crisis of America has to do with the situation of the poor, not of the lawyers. The issue for the lawyer is whether he can do useful things to increase the rights of welfare recipients through the legal process. He can.

WELFARE LITIGATION AS PART OF
A POLITICAL CAMPAIGN

Rather than suffer demobilization from defeats or become giddy from success, the welfare lawyer's job, among others, is to understand the highly political nature of welfare litigation and to act upon that understanding. This is not simply a matter of evaluating what legal arguments will be acceptable to a particular court at a given time. It is also a matter of seeing litigation as one element among several that may be required to induce a particular change in welfare policy. Some cases—the durational residence cases are an example—are "right" for the time without doing more than engaging in well-prepared litigation. Others, however, can succeed only where various non-litigational efforts have also been made in order to make the time "right."

For a narrow illustration of the point, consider *Goldberg v. Kelly* and the "prior hearing" success. The theory underlying *Goldberg* was first developed in 1965. Although the issue dealt with procedural due process and was therefore more amenable to courtroom success than some other issues, numerous obstacles stood in the way. Welfare, at the time, was a very novel area to judges, who would approach the area with great caution. Welfare department opposition in many places was extreme. The federal agency, HEW, not only found prior hearings unnecessary for "fairness": it refused to provide federal matching funds for state payments for the period between an ineligibility determination and a hearing determination (except, where the recipient was successful, on a retroactive basis). Consequently state agencies argued, with some force, that it was unreasonable to require them to make categorical program payments to which HEW would not contribute; the financial burden would be enormous. Yet a legal attack on HEW for not matching such payments might weaken rather than strengthen the position in the early days on welfare litigation.

Goldberg v. Kelly was the culmination of a number of efforts in what was, in essence, a coordinated political campaign to change the odds. A carefully prepared comment in a very respected law journal laid a scholarly basis for court action. HEW conferences, in which invited "experts" were asked to criticize state fair-hearing procedures, were turned into assaults on HEW's failure either to require or offer federal matching to state prior hearings. The first effort in a federal courtroom was deliberately made in Mississippi. Since HEW at the time did not pay attention to "antipoverty" lawyers but was sensitive to civil rights lawyers, the prior hearing issue was converted into a Southern civil rights issue. Some machinery in HEW was able to respond, federal matching was offered, the case was settled, and Mississippi became the first state to hold prior hearings.

As the "Poor People's Campaign" of the summer of 1968 developed, prior hearings became a campaign demand, in response to the welfare rights movement. The politics of 1968 was such that the Johnson Administration sought concessions that it might offer to the Poor People's Campaign. One of these became the welfare prior hearing. HEW issued a regulation, postponed in its effective date, requiring such hearings. New litigation was surely influenced by the fact that the federal agency responsible for welfare now regarded prior hearings as so significant to "fairness" that it saw fit to require them. But as national administrators changed, the HEW regulation was further postponed—with an eye on what the Supreme Court would do. In the meantime, however, the regulation affected what the Supreme Court in fact did.

Would *Goldberg* have turned out the way it did without the development of a general sensitivity to the issue as a result of efforts on many different fronts? Perhaps, but probably not. It is striking, when one considers other even more promising issues which lost in the courts, that far less effort was expended on anything other than the litigation process. The rule should be: The more difficult and "political" an issue is, the more a multifaceted campaign should be carried out, especially at a time, as now, when the court system is unreceptive to litigation involving social change.

But on precisely what issues can lawyers be of assistance to recipients today? What are the connections between those issues and political strategy generally; and what is the grand strategy for advancing welfare legal rights?

THE LAWYER'S JOB IS TO PROVIDE TECHNICAL AID, AND NOT TO DETERMINE GRAND STRATEGY IN PLACE OF THE RECIPIENTS

Deflating perhaps, but a grand role that strikes more at the heart of the "welfare system." The task is to help bring into full being that which did not exist and is struggling now to develop: a constituency for the welfare lawyers, who will decide for themselves (1) the question we raised earlier, whether legal maneuvers are simply covers for our present inhumane system or whether they are of real value to the poor, and (2) the question we now raise, what legal maneuvers should be, insofar as they reflect an overall strategy. There are two levels on which such a constituency-building task is carried out by lawyers. The first is with regard to individual clients. It requires an effort to avoid the usual professional role of telling the poor and relatively powerless client what is to be done. Because they know the technical aspect of the subject better than the client, welfare lawyers are prone to tell rather than advise, confine their advice to one option rather than the many that usually exist, shape and control the client's decision although it is made to appear the client is deciding, and generally manipulate and dehumanize in much the same way as the system they are presumably helping the client fight.

The second effort is the central one: to put themselves at the service of the organized recipients—the welfare rights movement—so as to help it become a more forceful part of American politics. Individual recipients are not positioned to decide "grand strategy" and the overall use to which lawyers are to be put. The organized movement is. Individual recipients cannot affect national welfare politics. Organized recipients can, if their organizations are strong enough and if they have sufficient support.

Unfortunately, in only a few communities have welfare lawyers aided welfare organization, and in these there has been little sophistication in fulfilling the task. On a national level, there has been only minimal assistance to the National Welfare Rights Organization. There was in 1970, and there will be for at least a few years, a pronounced lack of enthusiasm for such work on the part of the federal government. Since almost all welfare lawyers are government-funded, the financial base for their work probably will shrink in the years immediately ahead.

Helping to build a constituency of welfare recipients who decide legal strategy for themselves is an extraordinarily difficult task. It does not mean organizing by the lawyers, but it does require the closest work with organizers. It does not mean abandoning "test case" litigation, but it does mean assessing the value of such litigation with the organized recipients. It may mean spending more time writing welfare rights manuals and training recipients and organizers in the content of manuals and in the manipulation of grievance procedures. It may mean spending more time helping the organized groups develop alliances with the working poor, or helping the organized AFDC mothers find allies among the unorganized recipients of old-age assistance. It may mean that the national legal centers will put at least part of their staff directly at the service of the national movement. It means finding new financial bases for such work. It may mean that welfare lawyers from around the country will have to volunteer a few weeks a year to serve NWRO, and maybe even pay for their own upkeep while so doing. It may mean that some of the newly sprouting "public interest" law firms, or departments of existing private firms, should also volunteer their time.

What is urged here is that the use of lawyers' time on welfare matters, and the strategy they are to follow, be worked out with the organized recipients—with the ultimate decisions made by the recipients. In other words, the first step in a grand strategy for lawyers in advancing welfare rights is to serve, and thereby help build, an independent rights movement.

BASIC CHANGE IN THE WELFARE SYSTEM REQUIRES NEW ANALYSIS AND SCHOLARSHIP

Although there will be those who doubt the possibility of changing anything through "analysis and scholarship," as long as we are talking about America as it is we must analyze what we want by way of a welfare system, what other goals are inconsistent with our own goals, and what facts we must find and put before recipient organizations as well as the general public.

At least two issues require the most serious analysis. The first concerns the "work test" and "work incentive" issue. Anglo-American welfare programs throughout their history have been pegged to the "work test" as a means of guaranteeing that able-bodied men or women will not turn to welfare as a substitute for work. At times the "work test" has been used to exclude whole categories of able-bodied people; for example, our categorical system, with the exception of the unemployed parent category, is designed to exclude the able-bodied man and his family. When included in the welfare system, the able-bodied person's willingness to accept an available job—no matter how menial in nature or inadequate in salary—has been a condition for the welfare grant. The great fear has been that the poor will lose interest in menial jobs and that without the "work test" there no longer will be a supply of desperate workers.

Work tests have been brutal in their exclusions and bureaucratic and harsh in their administration. When they are humanely administered, there has been some reason to believe that the "incentive" to work at certain jobs is reduced. Would black mothers agree to stoop labor in Georgia's fields if adequate welfare grants were available and not conditioned on their accepting such work?

To all of this, the "welfare liberal" and the "negative income tax" proponent have worked out what they believe to be a good answer. Instead of imposing a "work test" for needy, able-bodied people, why not create a "work incentive"? Let us end the system, the argument goes, wherein every working poor person is "taxed 100 per cent" for every dollar he earns. That is, when a poor person takes a job, let us exempt part of his earnings for the purpose of determining welfare eligibility. For instance, if the applicants' family is eligible without work for $2,000 and the applicant earns $2,000, let him keep 50 per cent and deduct only the other 50 per cent from his grant. Thus there will be an "incentive" to work; by working, the person in this example will receive $3,000 annually (instead of $2,000 on welfare or $2,000 solely from his job without an "incentive" system).

THE "WORK INCENTIVE" TRAP

The "work incentive" proposal seems widely attractive. Economists Milton Friedman and James Tobin endorse it. Congress accepted a limited version in 1967 for AFDC recipients (allowing 30 per cent of income to be retained), and President Nixon has proposed that the "work incentive" be broadened to 50 per cent and be applied to all families with children whose income falls below his proposed federal floor. Welfare recipients, by and large, like the idea; some are even enthusiastic. (Why should their job income be "taxed 100 per cent"?) The nonwelfare working poor like it; their total income would be raised. All America seems united on a good idea; who ever said that the different classes have different interests?

It is, I suspect, a trap. There are at least four closely related problems: (1) it is extremely expensive to finance a good "work incentive" and an adequate base grant for those who cannot work; (2) as illustrated by President Nixon's proposal, it is the base grant which will be sacrificed in favor of the incentive, thus leaving those who cannot work with an inadequate grant; (3) it pumps most new money to be put into a welfare system into federal subsidy for every sweatshop, every menial job, every poorly paid job in the country; and (4) it thereby conditions survival of the needy poor on their willingness to accept menial jobs, just as effectively as the most harshly administered work test—or perhaps even more effectively.

Thus, when the 1969 White House Conference on Hunger and Malnutrition was considering the NWRO proposal that it support the $5,500 welfare line for all persons in need, Robert Harris was quick to advise the participants what was wrong with the proposal. On the assumption that $5,500 was necessary for decent survival, Harris calculated that to guarantee such income would require $20 billion more in income maintenance programs, a manageable figure (once we abandon war-making). But, he argued, without either a work test or work incentive, it would cost far more because many persons would not work at lower-paid jobs when they could get $5,500 without such jobs. A 50 per cent work incentive on a $5,500 base would cost some $70 billion more, an unmanageable figure, and subsidize persons making up to $11,000 a year. This is purely ridiculous. Harris argued, naturally, that the solution would be to lower the base grant—even though $5,500 is not high enough to support a family decently.

We must identify our primary concern. Is it to guarantee that people who cannot or should not work will have enough aid so as to live with the minimum decency, or to assure that people who can work will do so regardless of what work they are forced to accept? Suppose a welfare system offered an adequate grant to all those in need (with income below it) and a right to refuse work which paid less than the welfare grant. If private business and government were forced to reorganize the economy to ensure that it provided purposeful and well-paying work, would not this be desirable? Are we not producing the opposite result when we subsidize (through the "work incentive") the most pointless and exploitive jobs in the economy while denying decent welfare grants to those who cannot work?

THE RIGHT TO LIVE

The second and quite different issue concerning which we need more analysis and scholarship is the extent to which the Constitution imposes upon government an obligation to support individuals who cannot survive without such support. Is there a constitutional "right to live"—that is, is there a basis upon which we can fairly interpret the Constitution as implying such a right under modern conditions?

Earlier, we briefly mentioned the equal protection strategy which was moving in that direction and, for the time being, has failed. There probably will not be any major judicial or legislative changes on this matter in the next few years. But the issue is not and must not be dead forever. Legal argument will revive not simply when times change, but also when enough scholarly work has been done to provide the groundwork for forward movement.

For example: Have not even "judicial activists" too readily assumed that the equal protection clause does not impose a governmental obligation to sustain the lives of those who would otherwise perish? Should not the views of such men as Jacobus Ten Brock be more vigorously pursued? Is it not time to answer fully the simplistic equation between equal protection, "special scrutiny," and the due process abuses of fifty years ago? Even assuming traditional concepts, does not an affirmative duty under the equal protecton clause arise when, as a result of government action designed to enrich one group of citizens, other citizens are stripped of the means of survival? Has not this pattern characterized much of government policy in recent decades? Agricultural policy and tenant farmers? Inflation policy and unemployment? Cannot a substantial case be made that there is a direct, causal relationship between affirmative government policy on behalf of the middle class and rich and the substandard condition of the poor? These examples, in my opinion, merely touch the surface of the scholarly work that is needed.

We are not in a period of dramatic advance. By doing what we can: by engaging in scholarship and analysis of where we are going, by holding and expanding the gains we have made, by aiding recipient organization, we can hasten a better time. Too many persons, including a large percentage of welfare lawyers, do not understand that large forward movements are possible only as the expectations of people increase as a result of numerous small struggles, reforms, and increased understanding.

C. THE WORKER

14 / THE BLUE COLLAR WORKER'S LOWDOWN BLUES

Time Staff

The competing power groups that make up the American system have never operated in complete harmony. They have moved ahead according to the clout—electoral, financial and sometimes moral—that they could muster. During the 1960s, the blacks, the poor and the young spoke up and pushed forward. The blue collar workers, who sweated in the mines and factories, built the roads and drove the halftracks, seemed to accept stoically the role of providers and members of the Silent Majority. No longer. Today they are making themselves heard as they have not done since the turbulent 1930s. Their voices are loud, angry and aggressive.

Blue collar power has become a mighty and unpredictable political force that was bound to swing many House and Senate races this week and will heavily influence the decisions of the 92nd Congress. Throughout the campaign, both parties assiduously courted the blue collar vote, and many candidates even donned the new symbol of rock-ribbed Americanism, the hard hat. Vice President Spiro Agnew appealed to the workers' fears of crime, drugs and bombings, and to their suspicion of intellectuals. After President Nixon had A.F.L.-C.I.O. President George Meany in for a cozy chat "to discuss foreign policy," Republicans made good use of pictures of the meeting around workingmen's neighborhoods. (Feeling that he had been used, Meany later roasted the Republicans in radio speeches.) On the other side, the Democrats and their old friends in the union leadership played up the pocketbook issues of unemployment and inflation.

The blue collar workers have been wooed not only by the political parties but also by the New Left. For Election Day this week, the Students for a Democratic Society planned a march on General Motors' Detroit headquarters in clenched-fist support of the auto workers, who are now in the eighth week of a bitter strike against G.M. Reviving the faded dream of a Socialist alliance with labor, the S.D.S. hoped to draw 10,000 students and strikers to the demonstration. Considering the way that workers generally feel about the long-hairs and left-wingers, however, the students seemed to be more in danger of violence than the company.

While they are being hotly courted on all sides, blue collar workers are also being severely criticized by traditional friends and opponents alike. Political liberals, who once considered working-men their most reliable allies, now often see them—rather simplistically—as supporters of racism and repression. Black leaders condemn many unions for systematically excluding Negroes. Many other Americans think of labor as fat, lazy and arrogant, a condition exemplified in their minds by the $10-an-hour auto mechanic, the $15-an-hour plumber and the $18,000-a-year carpenter.

Business leaders complain that the workingman's extravagant wage demands are the real cause of inflation. Unless labor costs can be held down and productivity pushed up, they argue, the basic nature of the economy will be changed; economic growth, profits, exports and the global power of the dollar will dwindle. General Electric Chairman Fred Borch blames the nation's economic ills on "an unbalanced concentration of power in the hands of organized labor." One top industrialist compares the wage raises in the building trades, which have been running at 12 per cent this year, to "a kid in class with a case of measles. You've got to isolate it before they all catch it." Inspired in part by the construction workers' successful militancy, unions in general have wrung out wage-and-benefit increases averaging 10 per cent in major contract settlements so far this year.

THE CAUSES OF ANGER

From this odd combination of public criticism and political courtship, blue collar workers are gaining a renewed sense of identity, of collective power and class that used to be called solidarity. It often takes a negative form, because workers are the Americans most affected by rapid social disruption and technological change—and least prepared for it. The workingman is angered and bewildered by what he sees happening in the nation. As psychologists and social researchers have confirmed, he believes in God and country —if not necessarily in equality for all and the right of dissent. He is convinced of the virtues of hard work, the necessity of saving and a steady, ordered way of life. He is proud of paying his own way and standing on his own feet. He is respectful toward authority but not subservient, and he still has faith in the future, even though that faith has diminished somewhat of late.

Now he finds his values challenged on every side. He sees young people—sometimes his own children—turning on with drugs or even turning to revolution (or what he considers revolution). His neighborhoods, formerly bastions of familiar order, are often being transformed by the upheaval in the cities. Says Eugene Schafer, a hardhat ironworker and Democratic candidate for the state assembly from Brooklyn: "I think that I'm a forgotten American because my community is falling apart. The streets are caving in, the sanitation's lousy, the sewer system stinks, industry's gone out of the community, welfare's on the rise."

CRUEL ILLUSIONS

As wrenching change has overtaken the blue collar worker's neighborhood and home, technology has changed his life on the job— for the worse. The celebrated productivity gains of the 1950s were largely accomplished by the expansion of automation and by breaking down jobs into smaller and smaller functions, enabling the assembly lines to move faster. A great many workers have lost any sense of control over what they are doing and often have to move so fast and steadily on assembly lines or at piecework that there is hardly time even to go to the toilet. The image of Charlie Chaplin, in *Modern Times*, leaving a plant and turning and twisting an invisible wrench all the way home is less funny than ever. "Do you know what I do?" asks a striker outside G.M.'s assembly plant at Tarrytown, N.Y. "I fix seven bolts. Seven bolts! Day in and day out, the same seven bolts. What do I think about? Raquel Welch."

Often lacking the education to seek better jobs or the money to flee to suburbia, blue collar workers live with nagging fears of muggings, of illness or layoffs at work, and of automation. According to a recent survey by the University of Michigan, one-half of all industrial workers worry continually about their job security, and one-quarter are concerned about their safety; 14,000 were killed in on-the-job accidents last year, more than the number of U.S. servicemen men who died in Viet Nam in 1969. Fully 28 per cent have no medical coverage, 38 per cent no life insurance and 39 per cent no pension beyond Social Security.

The affluent society and a rising standard of living are cruel illusions to most blue collar workers. They are incensed by the charge that they have caused inflation; in fact, they are its chief victims. The average weekly wage of factory hands and clerks rose from $95 five years ago to $121 in September. But in real purchasing power, adjusted for inflation, it has actually declined (see accompanying figures). Over the last decade, according to the Labor Department, the financial needs of a family with growing children have risen by 61 per cent. In the same years, the average earnings

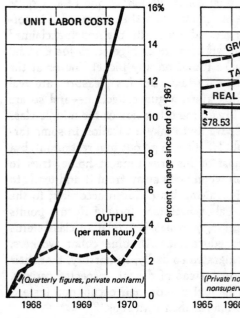

of skilled workers have increased only 41 per cent, compared with 64 per cent for blacks as a group and 61 per cent for executives. "The blue collar worker has seen the smart guy and the poor guy get theirs and has been wondering what was happening to him," says Economist Robert Nathan. "Now he is beginning to catch on." He has learned that those who push and speak up get attention and results.

Blue collar anger has burst out this year in the worst epidemic of strikes since just after World War II, and in the form of hardhat riots in New York City, St. Louis and elsewhere. This year postal employees have gone on strike for the first time in history, city workers have stomped off the job in Cincinnati, and tugboat crewmen and gravediggers have struck in New York. Municipal employees in San Francisco and Atlanta, rubber workers in Akron, and teamsters across the country—all have walked out. In this year's first nine months, the U.S. lost 41.5 million mandays through strikes, up 32 per cent from the equivalent period last year.

* * *

NOT MAKING IT

The real-life world of the blue collar worker is one of not quite making it, and a keen sense of diminished status. Some of it is portrayed, in crude and exaggerated form, in the much-acclaimed movie *Joe*. Certainly not all workers are as bigoted as Joe Curran, though his counterpart can be found on any picket line or at the wheel of many a New York City taxi. But his pleasures are real enough—whisky, the bowling alley, a gun collection—and so are his yearnings for a taste of life on the other side of the middle-class line. The blue collar worker wants to take a vacation in some far-off place, but usually cannot. He likes to go out to a restaurant, but seldom does. He spend most of his free time at home, tries to avoid thinking about the job when he is away from it and tends to have a close-knit family life, raising his children according to the strict, old rules. Assistant Labor Secretary Jerome Rosow points out that "the American workingman has lost relative class status with the growth of higher education. All blue collar workers, skilled or not, have been denigrated so badly, so harshly, that their jobs have become a last resort instead of decent, respected careers. Fathers hesitate—and even apologize—for their occupation instead of holding it up as an aspiration for their own sons."

Often the sons have no choice but to follow their fathers into the hated plant. William West, a crane operator in a coil plant at Braddock, Pa., for example, brings home $100 a week, and he sees no way that he can finance a college education for his eight-year-old son. West asks: "What kind of a future does my kid have when you can't even get a job with a high school education?" In some blue collar neighborhoods, the high school dropout rate reaches 30 per cent—the continuation of a cycle that locks the sons into the same working class as their fathers.

RUMBLES FROM THE YOUNG

The average age of workers in auto plants has been declining, and often on the less desirable night shifts it is close to 20. The young workers are of the same generation as the students who have turned the universities into battlegrounds. Like college students, they are feisty, ebullient and unwilling to put up with things as they are. As union members, they are an unsettling force, pushing labor leaders to heighten their demands for fear of being voted out of their own jobs. In many instances, young unionists have ousted the old leadership. This year rank-and-file members have rejected a record one out of twelve contracts negotiated by their embarrassed and harassed leaders. In San Francisco last month, the ironworkers won a 30 per cent increase in a one-year contract, a raise of $2.01 an hour. Even so, says their leader Jewel Drake, 56, "the younger leadership is not satisfied. I don't understand what they really want, what it would take to satisfy them."

Money alone will not do it. The young workers are revolting against the job itself, or at least the way it is organized. They reject the principal enunciated in 1922 by Henry Ford I: "The average worker wants a job in which he does not have to put much physical effort. Above all, he wants a job in which he does not have to think." The job that has no meaning must often be performed in factories that seem bereft of human feeling. Auto plants are often old, dirty and so noisy that conversation is impossible. "That's why so many young people just go from shop to shop," says Eugene Brook, director of labor education at Detroit's Wayne State University. "They can't believe that it's this bad. A young guy will start working at Dodge, and after a week he'll be so shocked at how dull the job is and how unpleasant the working conditions are that he'll figure it has to be better somewhere else. So he goes to G.M. for three days, and then to Ford—and then he sees it's all the same. The young guy asks: 'Is this all there is to America?' They're not buying the myth any more."

The worker is also blamed by management for product defects, and there is much truth to the bosses' charge that craftsmanship is a thing of the past on the assembly line. Sabotage is not uncommon; upholstery is slashed or a tool welded inside a fender compartment to cause eternal rattles. But there is also some justice in the workers' countercharge that they are not given time to do their jobs properly. Says Raymond Calore, 51, president of U.A.W. Local 664 in Tarrytown, N.Y.: "Sure, we read how the workingman today has no pride in his work, and it's true. But what you don't read is how the company has broken down the work into smaller and smaller units, so that no man can feel pride in what he's doing. If they'd just let us build a car occasionally. Just one." Manhattan Psychologist Harold Greenwald sees union grievances—frequently a long list of niggling complaints—as representing "a cry for recognition that the complainer is a man and not a machine."

REVOLT OF THE COUNTER CULTURE

The worker is also trapped between the technology of the past and of the future. In return for hard and automaton-like work on the assembly lines, the technology of the past promised to provide leisure and plenty for all—and has not fully delivered. Future technology still holds out that promise, at a cost of making many blue collar workers obsolete by replacing them with machines. Thus the worker has paid one high price for yesterday's technology and will have to pay another for tomorrow's; meanwhile, he has received a short measure of the promised benefits. Under those circumstances, he can hardly be blamed for wanting out of the trap.

The New Left and a handful of scholars, led by Theodore Roszak, author of *The Making of a Counter Culture*, believe that technology in America has been enshrined as an end, rather than as a means to a better life. They challenge the proposition that society must be organized around the requirements of mass production and technology—and so do the militant young workers. Machines, they say, should work, and people should live; their own personalities are simply more important. If a machine will soon take over their jobs, then there is no reason to dedicate their lives to a dead end. The auto companies and other manufacturers have already designed machines to handle many assembly-line tasks— welding, stamping, hauling and lifting. But for now it is still cheaper to rent people than to buy machines.

The inherent contradiction is that the American worker's dream remains what it always has been: in modern terms, a house in the suburbs and two cars in the breezeway. Yet he is no longer willing to pay the traditional price of increased productivity—or, perhaps more accurately, unable to endure any more speedups. His contradictory yearnings were expressed by one striking G.M. worker in Tarrytown: "What I hope is, by the time my kids grow up, this plant will be automated. They'll sit here in business suits, looking at a panel of instruments, and they will be called technicians or technologists and get twice as much as I do for half the work."

Younger workers want at least part of the dream now, and they have the power to demand it. Unions have often been paid off at the expense of the consumer. The large unions in industries like trucking or construction have far more strength than the small, independent employers, who simply bow to wage demands, accept restrictive labor practices and pass on the increased costs to their customers. But many other industries—notably autos, steel and chemicals—run grave risks of losing markets when they kick prices up. Foreign automakers already build 15 per cent of the cars that Americans buy. G.M.'s new Vega subcompact, which was designed to compete against the Volkswagen, had to be priced $211 higher than the Beetle. Other companies, similarly pressed, are shifting operation overseas for cheaper labor. The production of most typewriters, sewing machines and radios has been moved abroad.

TICKING TIME BOMB

The unions are thus in a series of binds. Pressed by their members, they can demand higher wages and get them, but often only at the expense of forcing employers to shift more of the work to other countries or to machines. Even if the unions could force employers to pay higher wages out of profits, that would lead to a cutback in capital investment, postponing technological innovation and labor's share of its benefits.

Labor's white-haired leadership just does not understand what the younger members are saying. The average age of the A.F.L.-C.I.O. executive council is 63, which makes the council one of the oldest governing bodies in the world, in roughly the same league as the Vatican Curia and the Chinese Politburo. Seemingly innocent of new ideas, labor's gerontocracy has lost the loyalty of the young and the idealistic, which it had held in the time when labor led the battle for reform. Today, instead of seeking to change and improve the system, the union leadership has become a part of it. Textile-union leaders, for example, accompany mill owners to Congress to plead for higher tariffs.

The isolation of labor leaders from many of their own members is a ticking time bomb. "The '70s will be far more turbulent than the '60s," predicts Columbia Economist Eli Ginzberg, chairman of the National Manpower Committee. A major source of turbulence will be the civil service employees' rising drive for organization. There will be more disruptive strikes by teachers, police, garbage collectors, hospital workers and other public employees. Unless the unions form a coalition with minority groups like the blacks, who have their own insistent demands on squeezed municipal and federal budgets, those two forces are likely to conflict even more sharply.

The Nixon Administration wants to win more of the blue collar workers' support by doing more for them, yet the Government is limited in what it can do. It cannot give them subsidies or generous tax relief because the sheer numbers of people involved would make the cost out of sight. At the President's order, Administration leaders are closely studying a much-discussed memo written by Assistant Secretary Rosow, who has a cornucopia of ideas. All of them fall far short of labor youth's demands but meet specific needs of their elders. The Administration, for instance, is considering legislation for the Government to regulate corporate pension plans more closely and require that all of them be vested, becoming the workers' property after ten years on the job. Partly because workers often quit their jobs before they qualify for pensions—and also because many plans are badly funded and ill-managed—half of the 30 million employees covered by them now will never draw a penny in benefits.

Other ideas must wait for the day that the budget squeeze is eased. Then the blue collar worker's new-found power will assure him at least a place in line for federal aid. One high priority: child-care centers (in half of the blue collar families, wives also hold jobs). More federal aid to community colleges would help working-class children rise beyond high school. Revenue sharing with the states could ease regressive local property taxes that often fall most heavily on blue collar families. In addition, the Government might update disability insurance laws. What Washington cannot do is give the workingman a renewed sense of pride in his job.

Much of the blue collar worker's lost sense of self could be restored by evidence that his employer cares about him, if only in little ways. Do the managers eat in the same cafeterias as the men, share the same parking lots? Are management's decisions clearly—not condescendingly—explained? Does the company offer small, appreciated extras, like Ford Motor's provision of a tow truck with jumper cables to help any worker who cannot start his car on winter nights? Companies are trying to find more and more incentives for executives, and Rosow argues that they could extend some of those ideas, like profit-sharing plans, to the men down in the plants. Health and safety conditions, he adds, "require dramatic improvements"—and higher federal standards.

Companies that neglect to consider the blue collar workers' worries and dissatisfactions pay a hidden price in low production, goofing off, absenteeism, high job turnover and union grievances. By contrast, management's reward for concerning itself more deeply and more knowledgeably about the blue collar worker's cares has been an increase in productivity. That, in turn, is the key to raising labor's living standards and meeting the demands for more leisure. Since World War II, U.S. productivity has risen an average of about 3.3 per cent annually, but for the whole period from the end of 1967 to early this year it increased less than 2 per cent. Lately, output per man-hour has rebounded, but only as a result of layoffs and the shutting down of older machines. (U.S. plants are operating at only 76 per cent of capacity, the lowest rate in almost a decade.)

Managers have discovered that at least in certain jobs, they can push production up by applying what labor economists call "participative management" and "job enrichment." The ideas are so new that only a handful of companies have tried them. One of the largest is Polaroid, where workers participate in planning changes in their job routines and help decide what new machinery to buy. They can also take company-sponsored courses ranging from English to engineering, either after hours or on company time, and they are encouraged to apply for higher positions. Polaroid officers say that the program has certainly enriched morale.

* * *

FITTING THE JOB TO THE MAN

The apostles of enriched labor insist that the idea can be profitably applied even to auto plants or steel mills. The cost would be high, since the assembly line would have to be redesigned to give each worker at least some responsibility for assembling an entire component rather than tightening a single bolt. In Volkswagen's Wolfsburg plant, for instance, groups of workers put together large components. That allows for more human contact and freedom on the line, relieves the boredom and permits a worker to take several minutes off from time to time. Comparisons with Detroit's plants are not wholly valid because Volkswagens are much simpler than almost all American cars, but Wolfsburg produces autos at three or four times the rate of U.S. plants. In Detroit, the U.A.W. has suggested that teams of workers assemble whole cars, but the notion was dropped by the union when the auto companies concluded that it was not feasible on present assembly lines. But in 1970 it is not too soon to suggest that the nature of the job should be changed to fit the man rather than the other way around. The time may come when it will be cheaper for the companies to enrich the workers' jobs than to pay ever higher wage increases as the price of continuing discontent.

Western industry long ago disproved Karl Marx's prediction that the workingman would become ever poorer in a capitalistic state. But it has yet to prove wrong his less well remembered forecast that workers would become progressively more alienated from their jobs. The young people now entering the factories present an opportunity for employers to end that alienation. Blue collar youngsters are as eager as the college students to become involved and to genuinely earn the pay and leisure that they seek. Essentially it is the task of management to give them that chance.

As it is, the alienation of the blue collar worker compounds all the other ills of the U.S., making it more difficult to integrate the blacks, or to bring the realities of the American system into closer conformity with the ideals of the young. The blue collar worker is exerting his new power to resist some social changes because the developments of the last decade have not been kind to him, and he has for too long been ignored. He is now insisting that the nation listen to him. He must accommodate himself to social change, but somehow he also must be accommodated if American society is to continue to progress.

15 / UNEMPLOYMENT: ANY QUICK REMEDY IN SIGHT?

U.S. News & World Report Staff

With nagging persistence, the high rate of unemployment hangs on as one of the toughest domestic problems for the U.S.

At a time of increasing buoyancy in business, the rate of joblessness has remained at 5.9 per cent for three months.

That rate is nearly as high as the peak of 6.1 per cent reached in December, 1970, when the economy was starting to recover from recession—and a drive by the Nixon Administration to cut unemployment was already under way.

Reprinted from *U.S. News & World Report*, June 19, 1972.

Around the country, the question is: With business improving and Government working hard to combat unemployment, is a quick solution now in sight? A study just completed by the Economic Unit of "U.S. News & World Report" suggests that the answer is "No"—and indicates why.

The prospects.   Two major conclusions reached in the study:

1. Although the Nixon Administration hopes for a jobless rate of 5 per cent by the end of this year, signs are that this goal will be very hard to reach.

2. Over the long run, reduction to 4 per cent—a rate that most economists regard as "full" employment—might bring an "unacceptable" amount of inflation. Thus, the likely prospect is an unemployment rate ranging between 5 and 6 per cent for an indefinite period.

The study puts the problem in perspective. It explains why some areas are hit harder than others, tells who is hurt most, analyzes the difficulties confronting government and business.

The issue, of course, is not new. Since World War II, the jobless rate has dipped below 4 per cent in just three periods: the

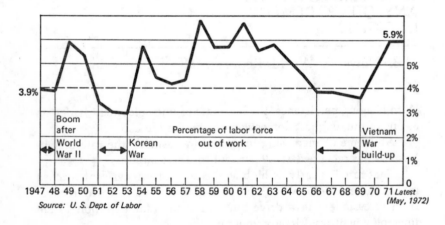

THE JOBLESS RATE: BELOW 4 PERCENT ONLY IN WAR BOOMS

Source: U. S. Dept. of Labor

THUS: In the past quarter century, only during wartime—or in periods of postwar boom—has the unemployment rate in U. S. dipped below 4 percent of the labor force. Government officials, more and more, are becoming convinced that a 4 percent unemployment rate is an impractical goal—unless the country is willing to tolerate high levels of inflation.

postwar boom of 1946–48; the Korean War years of 1951–53, and the Vietnam-war build-up in 1966–69.

Basic changes. This time, though, a new set of circumstances complicates the task of cutting down the jobless rate.

For one thing, the study shows, a basic change is under way in the composition of the labor force—chiefly the addition of greater numbers of women and teen-age workers. Unemployment among these groups is almost always higher than among men.

For example, nearly 17 per cent of teen-age boys and 15 per cent of teen-age girls looking for work are unable to find jobs—compared with 2.9 per cent of married men. The rate of joblessness among adult women in the labor force is 5.9 per cent.

In the present period of business recovery, 6 out of every 10 new job hunters are teen-agers and adult women. The reason is that when business is expanding, these categories flock to the job market because they feel they have a better chance of finding work.

Even before the current recovery, more women were entering

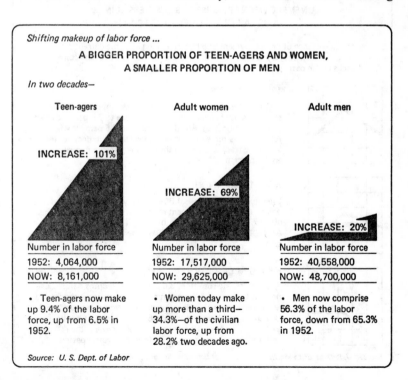

Shifting makeup of labor force ...

A BIGGER PROPORTION OF TEEN-AGERS AND WOMEN, A SMALLER PROPORTION OF MEN

In two decades—

Teen-agers	Adult women	Adult men
INCREASE: 101%	INCREASE: 69%	INCREASE: 20%
Number in labor force	Number in labor force	Number in labor force
1952: 4,064,000	1952: 17,517,000	1952: 40,558,000
NOW: 8,161,000	NOW: 29,625,000	NOW: 48,700,000
• Teen-agers now make up 9.4% of the labor force, up from 6.5% in 1952.	• Women today make up more than a third—34.3%—of the civilian labor force, up from 28.2% two decades ago.	• Men now comprise 56.3% of the labor force, down from 65.3% in 1952.

Source: U. S. Dept. of Labor

job markets, seeking to supplement family income—in many cases to cope with inflation—or to fulfill personal ambitions.

Flood of job seekers. What's more, says George Perry, a Brookings Institution economist:

"Women and teen-agers are more likely to work part time than adult males. In general, they offer less skills to employers. Also, their productivity is lower. Therefore, their availability for work, as measured by their unemployment, does not meet the manpower needs of many employers."

The current rush of women and teenagers seeking work is part of a broader flood of job seekers. The "baby boom" after World War II is still swelling the labor force. Also, the winding down of the war in Vietnam has affected an estimated 2.2 million men separated from the armed forces or from payrolls in defense plants.

UNEMPLOYMENT PERSISTS AS BUSINESS CLIMBS —A BREAK IN RECOVERY PATTERNS

The persistence of unemployment at a high rate, long after the current recovery got under way, is a sharp break with the pattern of most business comebacks in the past. A look at the last three recessions—

1957-58 RECESSION

A year before the low point of the recession, unemployment stood at a 3.9 percent rate. The rate rose to 7.4 percent when business hit bottom, edged up further to 7.5 percent when the recovery was three months old—then started to decline steadily. When recovery was 18 months old, the jobless rate was down to 5.7 percent.

1960-61 RECESSION

Unemployment rate was 4.8 percent a year before the low point. It rose to 6.9 percent at the recession's bottom, inched up to 7.1 percent three months later. Then a steady decline. At the 18-month mark, the jobless rate had fallen to 5.7 percent.

1969-70 RECESSION

The jobless rate rose from 3.5 percent 12 months before business hit bottom to 5.8 percent at the low point. A month later, as the recovery was under way, unemployment was up to 6.1 percent. And there, around the 6 percent level, it has hovered ever since. In May, 18 months into the recovery, the rate was still 5.9 percent—a striking shift from the typical pattern.

Source: U. S. Dept. of Labor; National Bureau of Economic Research, Inc.

Since the end of the recession in November, 1970, 2.5 million job seekers have found new employment or have been rehired—but in the same period, 2.5 million new job seekers have entered the labor market. So a surge in hiring has not reduced total unemployment.

Another key factor in the unemployment picture is the pattern of recovery. In 1971, the rise in private output—2.9 per cent—was the smallest in any of the five postrecession years since the end of World War II. Because of the slow upturn, employers were cautious in hiring, to hold down labor costs.

In the first quarter of 1972, output rose at an annual rate of 5.9 per cent over the fourth quarter of last year, and man-hours of work grew 3.6 per cent. But employers were as likely to raise production by having people work longer hours, or otherwise increasing efficiency, as by taking on new workers.

"Essential hiring." T. Vincent Learson, chairman of the board, International Business Machines Corporation, put it this way:

"For two years now we have been hiring only absolutely essential people, some bright college graduates, professionals and other essential talents. We have used reassignments and retraining of our people to balance our work load without reducing our ability to serve customers.

"Adapting to new situations and demands will continue to be a way of life for us. Semiconductor technology is developing so rapidly that we will require fewer man-hours to assemble, test and service our equipment. The outlook is that this trend will continue."

Adding to the unemployment problem are such elements as these:

■ The impact of foreign competition in certain industries—and the prospect of fierce competition still to come.

Some examples: All of the 35-mm still cameras bought in the U.S. are imported; 96 per cent of the magnetic tape recorders are made overseas; 75 per cent of calculating machines sold in this country are manufactured abroad.

■ Mismatches between the skills in demand—largely in professional and technical areas—and the people looking for jobs.

To illustrate: Professional and technical workers had an unemployment rate of only 2.4 per cent in May, while the rate for laborers was 10.9 per cent. At any given time, the poor, who lack job skills, have almost twice as much unemployment as the national average.

■ Reluctance of many workers—particularly in blue-collar occupations—to leave familiar surroundings, even when jobs are available elsewhere. Example: A study by the Conference Board, a non-profit research group, showed that even though the demand for skilled workers in Rochester, N.Y., was high, craftsmen as close as 60 miles away were not moving there, despite increasing unemployment in their home towns.

■ Lack of significant growth of job opportunities in whole sections of the economy—mining, construction, manufacturing and farming, for examples. Most new jobs have been in service industries. A comparison of two cities—Jacksonville and Seattle—points up that problem.

■ In 1971, Jacksonville had an unemployment rate of only 2.4 per cent, against the national average of 5.9 per cent. Only 24,000 of its 195,000 workers were in manufacturing. More than 86,000 were employed in trade or government services—areas less affected by ups and downs of the economy.

■ Seattle, where the jobless rate reached 13.2 per cent in 1971, is a manufacturing city, geared to defense and aerospace products. Cutbacks in defense contracts and suspension of the supersonic-transport-plane project (SST) were major causes of the increase in numbers of people out of work. When the Vietnam-war effort was intense and the SST was being funded in 1969, Seattle's unemployment rate was 4 per cent.

The official line. What are the prospects for lowering the unemployment rate? The official Administration view is that Government stimulation—resulting in the biggest budget deficits ever, except for the World War II years—will spur business enough to reduce the jobless rate to 5 per cent by year's end, and even lower next year.

In the view of Herbert Stein, Chairman of the President's Council of Economic Advisers, the unprecedented growth of the

Among major areas . . .		Percentage of labor force unemployed in March, 1972	
WHERE JOBLESS RATE IS HIGHEST		**. . . AND WHERE IT IS LOWEST**	
Muskegon, Mich.	13.0%	Charlotte, N.C.	1.9%
New Britain, Conn.	12.7%	Austin, Tex.	2.0%
Lowell, Mass.	12.5%	Richmond, Va.	2.2%
Seattle	12.5%	Durham, N.C.	2.3%
Waterbury, Conn.	12.2%	Greensboro, Winston-Salem, High Point, N.C.	2.3%
Bridgeport, Conn.	11.8%	Denver	2.4%
Tacoma	11.7%	Jacksonville, Fla.	2.4%
Fall River, Mass.	10.0%	Washington, D.C.	2.5%
Atlantic City	9.8%	Harrisburg, Pa.	2.6%
Huntington-Ashland, W. Va.	9.7%	Dallas	2.6%
Springfield-Chicopee-Holyoke, Mass.	9.6%	Tampa-St. Petersburg, Fla.	2.7%
Utica-Rome, N. Y.	9.5%	Little Rock	2.7%
Detroit	8.8%	Greenville, S.C.	2.7%
Jersey City	8.5%	Jackson, Miss.	2.9%
Buffalo	8.4%	Atlanta	3.0%
Spokane	8.3%	Norfolk-Portsmouth, Va.	3.1%
Grand Rapids	8.2%	Columbus, Ohio	3.2%
New Haven	8.1%	Knoxville	3.3%
Fresno	8.0%	Memphis	3.6%
Providence, R. I.	7.8%	Chattanooga	3.7%
Hartford, Conn.	7.6%	Des Moines	3.7%
San Diego	6.6%	Phoenix	3.8%
Newark, N. J.	6.5%	Omaha	3.8%
Gary-East Chicago	6.4%	Savannah	3.9%

Source: U. S. Dept. of Labor

labor force can't go on indefinitely because "there has to be a point when people stop joining" the force in such numbers.

From the Conference Board comes this prediction: "At some point, the pool of persons 'waiting in the wings' for job opportunities to appear will be largely exhausted and rising employment will begin to make more substantial inroads on the uncomfortably high unemployment rates with which we have been living for a year and a half."

Andrew F. Brimmer, a member of the Federal Reserve Board, is not so optimistic. He projects an increase in total employment of 2 million for 1972 and a decline in unemployment of only 250,000, leaving the jobless rate "somewhat above 5 per cent."

"Jobs beneath skills."   Over the longer run, Tilford Gaines, senior vice president and economist of Manufacturers Hanover Trust in New York, sees it this way:

"The United States has reached a condition of affluence in which it probably is able to produce more with a fully employed labor force than the consumption needs and wants of the public would require.

"If this is the case, two problems emerge. First, many new entrants to the labor force will find it necessary to work at jobs beneath their skills. Second, a growing number of unskilled or low-skilled people will find it impossible to obtain productive employment."

There is a rising conviction among economists, in fact, that the "full employment" jobless rate of 4 per cent as a national goal over the next few years may not be feasible without significant inflation. As Dr. Perry of Brookings views the problem:

"Today we have high unemployment with a less effective labor supply, due to the large influx of women and teenagers. When unemployment moves to a level of 4 or 4.5 per cent, over-all labor markets are tight. Labor is scarce in many fields where teen-agers and women are not heavily employed. And it is this tightness that touches off inflation."

Wary of Inflation.   A top U.S. Government economist remarked:

"We have the tools to get unemployment as low as 4 per cent, but we don't want to make the same mistake that was made earlier —sparking off a 6 per cent rate of inflation."

In the search for solutions to the unemployment problem, much attention is being given to an expanded program of public-service employment—similar to the Works Progress Administration (WPA) of the depression in the 1930s.

Last year, Congress approved a billion-dollar program to provide jobs in public service for 150,000 or more of the unemployed. Expansion of such steps appears likely.

Senator Alan Cranston (Dem.), of California, has introduced

JOBS IN MAJOR INDUSTRIES:
THE GAINERS AND LOSERS

	1969	Now	Percentage Change
State-local government	9,444,000	10,628,000	UP 13%
Finance, insurance, real estate	3,564,000	3,918,000	UP 10%
Services	11,229,000	12,286,000	UP 9%
Retail and wholesale trade	14,639,000	15,617,000	UP 7%
Transportation, utilities	4,429,000	4,536,000	UP 2%
Federal Government	2,758,000	2,668,000	DOWN 3%
Mining	619,000	603,000	DOWN 3%
Construction	3,435,000	3,260,000	DOWN 5%
Manufacturing	20,167,000	18,959,000	DOWN 6%
Farming	3,606,000	3,353,000	DOWN 7%

A CLOSER LOOK AT JOBS IN MANUFACTURING—

	1969	Now	Percentage Change
Rubber, plastics	596,000	626,000	UP 5%
Petroleum, coal	182,000	189,000	UP 4%
Furniture, fixtures	484,000	490,000	UP 1%
Printing, publishing	1,094,000	1,095,000	—
Food products	1,791,000	1,755,000	DOWN 2%
Apparel	1,409,000	1,366,000	DOWN 3%
Fabricated-metal products	1,440,000	1,378,000	DOWN 4%
Chemicals	1,060,000	1,004,000	DOWN 5%
Electrical equipment	2,020,000	1,838,000	DOWN 9%
Primary metals	1,361,000	1,223,000	DOWN 10%
Nonelectrical machinery	2,033,000	1,825,000	DOWN 10%
Transportation equipment	2,061,000	1,778,000	DOWN 14%
Ordnance	316,000	187,000	DOWN 41%

Source: U. S. Dept. of Labor

legislation for a permanent public-employment program to provide a million jobs. Senator Walter Mondale (Dem.), of Minnesota, and Representative Henry Reuss (Dem.), of Wisconsin, have introduced separate bills to authorize federal funds providing 500,000 public-service jobs.

Senator Gaylord Nelson (Dem.), of Wisconsin, is drafting a manpower reform bill that would double public-service-job programs in the next two years, and shift operating control of current labor-training programs from federal to State and local governments.

10-billion-dollar program. Mr. Stein, the President's chief economic aide, notes that the Nixon Administration is spending this year "about 10 billion dollars for manpower programs and unemployment compensation."

For all the steps under way, and in prospect, to cut into unemployment, though, the Economic Unit study makes it clear that no quick and easy solution is in sight.

Most economists agree that the problem is getting tougher, and that fresh approaches are needed.

D. CRIMINALS

16 / THE SHAME
OF THE
PRISONS

.

Time Staff

> *It is with the unfortunate, above all,*
> *that humane conduct is necessary.*
> —Dostoevsky

President Nixon calls them "universities of crime." Chief Justice Burger has become a crusader for their reform. Legislators have taken to investigating them—and citizens have finally begun to listen. After decades of ignoring their prisons, Americans are slowly awakening to the failure that long neglect has wrought.

It is not just the riots, the angry cries of 426,000 invisible inmates from the Tombs to Walla Walla, that have made prisons a national issue. Public concern is rooted in the paradox that Americans have never been so fearful of rising crime, yet never so ready to challenge the institutions that try to cope with it. More sensitive to human rights than ever, more liberated in their own lives and outlooks, a growing number of citizens view prisons as a new symbol of unreason, another sign that too much in America has gone wrong.

It is a time when people have discovered with a sense of shock that the blacks who fill prisons (52 per cent in Illinois) see themselves as "political victims" of a racist society. It is a time when many middle-class whites are forced to confront prisons for the first time, there to visit their own children, locked up for possession of pot or draft resistance. A time when many judges have finally begun to make personal—and traumatic—inspections. After a single night at the Nevada State Prison, for example, 23 judges from all over the U.S. emerged "appalled at the homosexuality," shaken by the inmates' "soul-shattering bitterness" and upset by "men raving, screaming and pounding on the walls." Kansas Judge E. Newton Vickers summed up: "I felt like an animal in a cage. Ten years in there must be like 100 or maybe 200." Vickers urged Nevada to "send two bulldozers out there and tear the damn thing to the ground."

THE BIG HOUSE

It will not be easy to raze, much less reform, the misnamed U.S. "corrections" system, which has responsibility for more than 1.2 million offenders each day and handles perhaps twice as many each year. Since 1967, four presidential commissions, dozens of legislative reports and more than 500 books and articles have pleaded for prison reform. But the system remains as immutable as prison concrete, largely because life behind the walls is still a mystery to the public. Most Americans think of prisons only in terms of the old "big house" movies starring James Cagney and more recently Burt Lancaster.

In fact, the corrections system is not a system at all. It is a hodgepodge of uncoordinated institutions run independently by almost every governmental unit in the U.S. Pacesetting federal institutions (20,000 prisoners) range from maximum-security bastilles like Atlanta Penitentiary to a no-walls unit for tame young offenders in Seagoville, Texas. The states offer anything from Alabama's archaic road gangs to California's Men's Colony West, one of the nation's two prisons for oldsters. There are forestry camps for promising men and assorted detention centers for 14,000 women. Some juvenile institutions are the best of the lot because reformers get the most political support at that level. But many areas are still so lacking in juvenile facilities that 100,000 children a year wind up in adult pens.

THE JAIL MESS

Two-thirds of all U.S. offenders technically serving time are actually outside the walls on parole or probation, but most offenders have at some point encountered the worst correctional evil: county jails and similar local lockups. Such institutions number 4,037—a fact not even known until last week, when the federal Law Enforcement Assistance Administration published the first national jail census. Jails usually hold misdemeanants serving sentences of a year or less. More important, they detain defendants awaiting trial: 52 per cent of all people in jails have not yet been convicted of any crime. Of those, four out of five are eligible for bail but cannot raise the cash. Because courts are overloaded, unconvicted defendants may linger in crowded cells for months or even years.

To be sure, jails vary widely from two-cell rural hovels to modern urban skyscrapers. But the vast majority treat minor offenders—and the merely accused—more harshly than prisons do felons, who commit graver crimes. The jail mess is typified by New Orleans' Parish Prison, a putrid pen built in 1929 to hold 400 prisoners. It now contains 850—75 per cent of them unsentenced. Money and guards are so short that violent inmates prey on the weak; many four-bunk cells hold seven inmates, mattresses smell of filth and toilets are clogged. Prisoners slap at cockroaches "so big you can almost ride them."

Jail conditions frequently breed hardened criminals who then go on to the prisons themselves, the second anomaly in a pattern that stands as a monument to irrationality. The typical U.S. felon is sentenced by a judge who may have never seen a prison and has no idea whether x years will suffice. Leaving the courtroom, where his rights were scrupulously respected, the felon has a good chance of being banished to one of 187 escape-proof fortresses, 61 of them built before 1900. Now stripped of most rights, he often arrives in chains and becomes a number. His head sheared, he is led to a bare cage dominated by a toilet. In many states his cellmate may represent any kind of human misbehavior—a docile forger, a vicious killer, an aggressive homosexual.

In this perverse climate, he is expected to become socially responsible but is given no chance to do so. He is told when to wake up, eat and sleep; his letters are censored, his visitors sharply limited. His days are spent either in crushing idleness or at jobs that do not exist in the "free world," such as making license plates for a few cents' pay an hour. In some states, he cannot vote (even after his release), own property or keep his wife from divorcing him. He rarely gets adequate medical care or sees a woman.

Everything is a privilege, including food, that can be taken away by his keepers.

If he is accused of violating one of scores of petty rules, he is haled before the "adjustment council" without right to counsel. If he denies guilt, he can be punished for implying that his accuser guard lied; if he admits it, he may lose "good time" (eligibility for parole) and perhaps land in solitary. The lesson is clear: truth does not pay.

If he happens to be a rich criminal, a Mafia type, life in some prisons can be easy. Ill-paid "hacks" (guards) may sell him anything from smuggled heroin to a girlish cellmate. More often he is a complete loser; for him, prison is synonymous with poorhouse. Already angry at life's winners, he becomes even more insensitive to others in a doomed universe whose motto is "Do your own time": trust no one, freeze your mind, be indifferent. Unequipped for normal society, he may well be headed back to prison as soon as he leaves. In fact, he may come to prefer it: Why struggle in a world that hates ex-convicts?

Everyone knows what prisons are supposed to do: cure criminals. Way back in 1870, the nation's leading prison officials met in Cincinnati and carved 22 principles that became the bible of their craft. "Reformation," they declared, "not vindictive suffering, should be the purpose of the penal treatment of prisoners." Today, every warden in the U.S. endorses the ideal of rehabilitation. Every penologist extols "individualized treatment" to cure each inmate's hangups and return society's misfits to crime-free lives. But the rhetoric is so far from reality that perhaps 40 per cent of all released inmates (75 per cent in some areas) are reimprisoned within five years, often for worse crimes. Says Rod Beaty, 33, who began with a $65 forged check, became an armed robber, and is now a four-time loser in San Quentin: "Here you lose all sense of values. A human life is worth 35¢, the price of a pack of cigarettes. After five years on the inside, how can you expect me to care about somebody when I get outside?"

SLAVERY IN ARKANSAS

Without question, the U.S. boasts some prisons that look like college campuses—humane places that lack walls and shun official brutality. Guards chat amiably with inmates; men are classified in graded groups, promoted for good conduct and sped toward parole.

And yet, rehabilitation is rare. By and large, mere aging is the main cause of going straight. For inmates between the ages of 16 and 30—the vast majority—neither the type of prison nor the length of sentence makes any significant difference. The repeater rate, in fact, is rising. Something is clearly wrong with a system that spends $1 billion a year to produce a failure record that would sink any business in a month. Consider a random sample of prisons from the worst to the best:

Arkansas. Whether in 110° F. summer heat or winter cold, 16,000 acres of rich southeastern Arkansas land will always be tilled. This is the Cummins Prison Farm, where 200 convicts stoop in the vast cotton fields twelve hours a day, 5½ days a week—for zero pay. Such are the wages of sin in what may be the nation's most Calvinistic state.

A virtual slave plantation in the 20th century, Cummins takes all kinds of errants and turns them into white-clad "rankers" who work or perish. Toiling from dawn to dusk, they move in a long line across the fields, supervised by a horseman in khaki and five unmounted "shotguns" (guards) who "push" the serfs along. At each corner of the field stands another guard, armed with a high-powered rifle. All the guards are convicts, the toughest at Cummins. Hated by rankers, the trusties are picked for meanness in order to keep them alive off duty. They are killers, armed robbers, rapists—ready to gun down the first ranker who strays across an imaginary line in the fields.

After three skeletons were dug up on the farm in 1968, national publicity moved the state to do a little fixing. Gun-toting trusties lost some power, 60 more free-world staffers arrived, $450,000 was allotted to replace some men and mules with farm machinery. Robert Sarver, head of the Arkansas penal system, is pushing hard for improvement against stiff odds. But Cummins still lacks any schooling, counseling or job training. For a college-trained social worker, the state pays only $593 a month; Cummins can barely attract civilian guards ($330). Says Sarver: "We can't guarantee a man's safety."

Last year U.S. District Judge J. Smith Henley ruled that imprisonment in Arkansas amounts to unconstitutional "banishment from civilized society to a dark and evil world." He ordered the state to reform Cummins by the fall of 1971 or face an order to close the place. But the evil world persists. With no pay, Cummins prisoners survive by selling their blood or bodies. To blot out the place, they sniff glue and gobble smuggled pills. Some mornings, 200 men are too stoned to work. Since gambling is pervasive, loan sharks top the prison pecking order. They charge 50¢ per dollar a week and swiftly punish defaulters. In a single month last summer, Cummins recorded 19 stabbings, assaults and attempted rapes. The worst of it is the privacy-robbing barracks, where 100-bunk rooms house all types, from harmless chicken thieves to homicidal sadists, and the young spend all night repelling "creepers" (rapists). "You're all there in the open," shudders a recently released car thief named Frank. "Someone's stinking feet in your face, radios going, guys gambling. You never really get to sleep. What's worse is the fear. There's no protection for your life. I kept thinking 'if' I get out—not 'when.' "

Indiana.   With its 40-ft. walls, the gray castle in Michigan City looks its part: a maximum-security pen for 1,800 felons, including teen-age lifers. Inside, the walls flake, the wiring sputters and the place is falling apart. Indiana spends only 1.5 per cent of its state budget on all forms of correction.

Like many legislatures, Indiana's insists that prisons make a profit. Last year Indiana State Prison turned out 3.5 million license plates, among other things, and netted the taxpayers $600,000— no problem when inmates get 20¢ an hour. Inmates also provided the prison's few amenities. Many cells are jammed with books, pictures, record players and tropical fish in elaborate tanks. There are two baseball diamonds, three miniature golf courses, tennis, basketball and handball courts—all equipment paid for by the inmates' recreational fund.

The prison needs far more than play. It teems with bitter men, one-third of them black. Some of the toughest are young militants transferred from Indiana State Reformatory at Pendleton, where 225 blacks staged a sitdown last year to protest the prolonged solitary confinement of their leaders. Instead of using tear gas or other nonlethal weapons, Pendleton guards fired shotguns point-blank into the unarmed crowd, killing two blacks and seriously wounding 45. One official gasped: "They slaughtered them like pigs."

At Indiana State, Pendleton survivors and other young blacks grate against 245 guards, most of them middle-aged whites and some close to 70. This is a U.S. pattern: only 26 per cent of all prison guards are younger than 34; only 8 per cent are black. To compound Indiana State's age and racial tensions, only a third of the inmates actually work. Boredom is chronic. The prison has only 27 rehabilitation workers; job training is absurd. Since the state provides few tools, vocational classes make do with donated equipment: archaic sewing machines, obsolete typewriters, TV sets dating to Milton Berle.

Why not send some promising Indiana inmates to work or school outside? "Their victims would disagree," says warden Russell Lash, a former FBI agent. Lash, only 29, is a good man hampered by his budget and the voters' fears. His first duty, he says, is "custody."

California. Though it leads all states in systematic penology, California has the nation's highest crime rate. Critics also claim that the system is characterized by a kind of penal paternalism that becomes psychological torment. In a much touted reform, California judges give indeterminate sentences; corrections officials then determine each offender's fate according to his presumably well-tested behavior. Thus 66 per cent of all convicted offenders get probation, 6 per cent work in 20-man forestry crews, and only 13.5 per cent of felons go to prison. Despite rising crime, California's prison population (26,500) has actually dropped by 2,000 in the past two years.

All this saves millions in unneeded prison construction. But it fills prisons with a higher ratio of hard-core inmates who disrupt the rest. And because of indeterminate sentences, California "corrects" offenders longer than any other state by a seemingly endless process (median prison stay: 36 months) that stirs anger against the not always skilled correctors. Says one San Quentin official: "It's like going to school, and never knowing when you'll graduate."

Something is not quite right even at the state's cushiest "correctional facilities" (bureaucratese for prisons), some of which could pass for prep schools. At no-walls Tehachapi, near Bakersfield, inmates can keep pianos in their unbarred rooms, get weekend passes and join their wives at "motels" on the lush green premises. Yet Tehachapi is full of repeaters, prison-dependent men who soon violate their paroles and return.

These days, California's black prisoners are rebelling at places like Soledad, a seeming garden spot in the Salinas Valley that looks like a university campus. Soledad's 960 acres throb with activity: tennis, basketball, weight lifting, a dairy, a hog farm. Inmates earn up to $24 a month turning out toilet paper and handsome furniture for the judges and prosecutors who got them the jobs. But for 180 rebels confined in Soledad's "X" and "O" wings, there is no play or work. Because they scorn prison rules, they are locked up tighter than lions in a zoo.

Many are blacks who see themselves as political victims, others whites who hate the blacks. Racial tension is so bad that some prisoners wear thick magazines strapped to their backs to ward off knife blades. In January 1969, the prisoners were allowed to exercise together in a small yard. Before long, a guard shot and killed three blacks. According to the guard's testimony before a Monterey County grand jury, the blacks were beating a white inmate. The guard said that he fired a warning shot, then killed the attackers. Though black witnesses insisted that there was no warning shot, the grand jury ruled justifiable homicide. At Soledad not long after that ruling, a white guard was thrown off a balcony to his death.

The accused killers are three unrelated blacks who call themselves the Soledad Brothers. They include George Jackson, one of the angriest black men. In one of his many despairing letters to Angela Davis, the black Communist, Jackson wrote: "They've created in me one irate, resentful nigger—and it's building."

COSTLY CAGES

The idea that imprisonment "corrects" criminals is a U.S. invention. Before the 18th century, prisons mainly detained debtors and the accused. Punishment itself was swift and to the point. Europeans castrated rapists and cut off thieves' hands; the Puritans put crooks in stocks and whipped blasphemers—then forgave them.

In 1790, Philadelphia's Quakers started a humane alternative to corporal punishment: they locked errants in solitary cells until death or penitence (source of penitentiary). Soon the U.S. was dotted with huge, costly, isolated cages that deepened public fear of those inside and reinforced a U.S. spirit of vengeance against prison inmates.

Caging has crippled the entire system. Burdened with vast forts that refuse to crumble (25 prisons are more than 100 years old), wardens cope with as many as 4,000 inmates, compared with the 100 that many penologists recommend. Archaic buildings make it difficult to separate tractable from intractable men, a key step toward rehabilitation. The big numbers pit a minority against a majority, the guards against the prisoners. Obsessed with "control," guards try to keep inmates divided, often by using the strong to cow the weak. The result is an inmate culture, enforced by fist or knife, that spurs passivity and destroys character.

Even though two-thirds of all offenders are on parole or probation, they get the least attention: 80 per cent of the U.S. correctional budget goes to jails and prisons; most of the nation's 121,000 correctional employees simply guard inmates and worry about security. Only 20 per cent of the country's correctors work at rehabilitation and only 2 per cent of all inmates are exposed to any innovative treatment.

Federal prisons lead most of the U.S. in job training; yet few released federal inmates find jobs related to their prison work. With notable exceptions, like California, most states provide no usable training, partly because unions and business have lobbied for laws blocking competition by prison industries. At least one-third of all inmates simply keep the prison clean or do nothing. Most of them need psychiatric help. Despite this, there are only 50 full-time psychiatrists for all American prisons, 15 of them in federal institutions, which hold only 4 per cent of all prisoners.

The failure of American prisons, humane or inhumane, to change criminal behavior is hardly their fault alone. The entire American criminal justice system shares the blame. It is perfectly human, if somewhat bizarre, for a criminal to see himself as a victim. The U.S. reinforces that defense: most crimes are committed for economic reasons by the poor, the blacks and other have-nots of a society that stresses material gain. In fact, only 20 per cent of reported U.S. crimes are solved; half the crimes are never even reported. Since justice is neither swift nor certain, the caught criminal often sees his problem as mere bad luck in a country where "everyone else" gets away with it.

He has a point. Americans widely ignore laws they dislike,

whether against gambling or marijuana. The nicest people steal: roughly 75 per cent of insurance claims are partly fraudulent. Uncaught employees pocket $1 billion a year from their employers. To poor offenders who go to jail without bail the system is unfair, and the legal process strengthens that opinion. If a man cannot afford a good lawyer, he is pressured to plead guilty without a trial, as do 90 per cent of all criminal defendants. He then discovers that for the same crime, different judges hand out wildly disparate sentences, from which 31 states and the federal courts allow no appeal.

So the prison gets a man who sees little reason to respect state-upheld values. Even if he actually leaves prison as a reformed character, he faces hazards for which no prison can be blamed. In a Harris poll, 72 per cent of Americans endorsed rehabilitation as the prison goal. But when it came to hiring an ex-armed robber who had shot someone, for example, 43 per cent would hesitate to employ him as janitor, much less as a salesman (54 per cent) or a clerk handling money (71 per cent). This is obviously understandable; it also teaches ex-cons that crime pays because nothing else does.

Even parole supervision is often cursory and capricious. Many parole agents handle more than 100 cases; one 15-minute interview per month per man is typical. The agents can also rule a parolee's entire life, even forbid him to see or marry his girl, all on pain of reimprisonment—a usually unappealable decision made by parole agents, who thus have a rarely examined effect on the repeater rate. To test their judgment, Criminologists James Robison and Paul Takagi once submitted ten hypothetical parole-violator cases to 316 agents in California. Only five voted to reimprison all ten men; half wanted to return some men but disagreed on which ones.

* * *

25¢ ON THE DOLLAR

Criminologist James Robison, who does research for the California legislature, is among those who question the accuracy of many penal statistics. He even disputes the much-vaunted results of the California Youth Authority's Community Treatment Project, a famous experiment in which convicted juvenile delinquents were not confined but given intensive tutoring and psychotherapy. After five years, only 28 per cent had their paroles revoked, compared with 52 per cent of another group that was locked up after conviction. As a result, the state expanded the project and cut back on new reformatories, saving millions. Robison, though, has proved, at least to his satisfaction, that the experimenters stacked the deck by ignoring many of the kids' parole violations. He argues that most penal-reform funds are wasted on salaries for bureaucrats, who mainly worry about pleasing their bosses. "For every dollar spent on the criminal justice system," he insists, "we get back about a quarter's worth of crime control."

Given the facts of penal bureaucracy and sheer ignorance, critics like Robison sometimes wonder whether the only rational solution is simply to unlock all jails and prisons, which clearly breed crime and hold only 5 per cent of the nation's criminal population while costing far more to run than all the crimes committed by their inmates. Pessimism is well founded, but the encouraging sign is that few if any Americans defend the system as it is. From the President to the lowliest felon, the nation wants a humane system that truly curbs crime. This is the year of the prisons, the year when Congress may double federal spending (to $300 million) to spur local reform, the year when something may finally get done and Americans may well heed Dostoevsky's goading words.

17 / ADDICTS AND ZEALOTS

Marion K. Sanders

Nineteen-seventy may well be remembered as the year of the great drug panic, the year when addiction was a permanent theme in the press and on TV and when government officials and office seekers made instant headlines by pledging a "massive attack" on the

From *Harper's Magazine*, June 1970. Copyright © 1970 by Minneapolis Star and Tribune Co., Inc. Reprinted by permission of author.

problem. People old enough to recall previous waves of hysteria about drugs and similar promises of action view these pronouncements with cynicism verging on despair. They concede, however, that something new has been added. The image of the addict has changed. Suddenly, he is seen not merely as a criminal derelict. He may, it turns out, be a young child who not only knows how to tie a tourniquet around his arm and stick a needle in his vein but also sells drugs to his schoolmates.

Last December young Walter Vandermeer died of a heroin overdose two weeks after his twelfth birthday. Since then New York newspapers have published a daily body count of OD fatalities, a phrase which no longer needs explanation. Although the vast majority of the victims—young and old—are slum dwellers, affluent America is also represented on these grisly lists.

With mounting evidence that this plague can no longer be quarantined in the ghettos, there is less talk about "getting the addict off the streets" and more about what can be done to salvage him. One result is that the treatment of addicts has become a growth industry with proponents of various theories fiercely vying for public funds to support their enterprises. This competition, it should be said, is not motivated by greed. Treating addicts is heart-and-back-breaking and generally unprofitable work. It is a task for zealots.

Over the past several months I have taken a first-hand look at what some of them are doing in New York, heroin capital of the U.S.A. where half of the nation's addicts are believed to live. Appropriately, this city has been the chief proving ground and battle ground for rival theories about the cause and cure of addiction.

Paralleling the vogue for "sensitivity training" and other forms of group psychotherapy is the current enthusiasm for programs which apply similar strategy to addiction. Known as "therapeutic communities," these are modeled after Synanon, which was launched in Santa Monica, California, twelve years ago. Its founder, Chuck Dederich, an ex-alcoholic, propounded the theory that the addict can change his faulty behavior patterns only by voluntarily joining a sternly disciplined but loving pseudo-family. There he must be guided by ex-addicts who have unique insight into his weaknesses and evasions and provide living proof that his habit can be overcome. This is accomplished through a "self-help" regime which includes plenty of physical work plus the now-familiar techniques of group dynamics which have given such words as "encounter" and "confrontation" a special meaning.

Among those attracted to Dederich's ideas were two psychiatrists, Dr. Daniel Casriel of New York and Dr. Efren Ramirez of Puerto Rico. With the blessing of city officials, Dr. Casriel obtained a grant from the National Institute of Mental Health to set up on Staten Island a privately operated Synanon-type institution to be known as Daytop Village.

Almost immediately, the project ran into a predictable difficulty —a dearth of skilled and reliable ex-addicts needed to run it. After many months, the right man was found, David Deitch, a talented Synanon graduate. Under his leadership Daytop flourished. A play performed by Daytop residents became an off-Broadway hit in 1968 and offered persuasive evidence to hundreds of theatergoers that "The Concept" (its title) actually worked.

In 1966, Mayor John Lindsay invited Dr. Ramirez to come to New York to coordinate and expand the city's battle against narcotics. Preceded by glowing reports of his success in treating addicts in his native Puerto Rico with a mix of the Synanon formula and his own brand of existential psychiatry, Dr. Ramirez found the going rough in New York. The black community which most needed help turned its back on any program headed by a Puerto Rican. The medical establishment was affronted by the claim that nonprofessional therapists could succeed where it had failed. In fact, few ex-addicts went into action, for scarcely any could meet the educational requirements of civil service. The acquisition of buildings and equipment was mired in municipal red tape. Dr. Ramirez departed after a stormy year, turning the job over to his deputy, Larry Alan Bear, who now heads the city's Addiction Services Agency.

A resourceful administrator with keen political antennae, Bear, a lawyer by profession, has forged rapidly ahead on the path Ramirez charted. The city now operates a chain of therapeutic communities known as Phoenix Houses, as well as a growing network of storefront outposts aimed at reaching young people, and has embarked on a program of prevention through schools and community organizations. With the help of a private foundation, emergency purchases can be made quickly. A new civil-service category, "addiction specialist," has been established with minimum formal educational requirements. Part of the cost of operating the Phoenix Houses is met by having residents who are on welfare contribute their welfare checks.

Bear has had to expend much of his considerable energy defending his efforts against the sniping of private-program operators who miss no opportunity to aggrandize their own projects by denigrating all others. The most strident has been the psychiatrist Dr. Judianne Densen-Gerber who opened up her own treatment center, Odyssey House, in 1967.

Like the majority of philanthropies nominally under private auspices, most "private" addiction treatment programs in New York are heavily dependent on government support. Odyssey's "Mother House," with seventy residents currently in treatment, has received $770,000 from the state since its inception. Last summer Dr. Judy, as she is known to her charges, moved some 35 adolescent heroin users into an abandoned convent previously occupied by nine nuns, and applied to the state for an additional $250,000 to operate a separate facility for adolescents there. She was turned down on the grounds that no further funds were available for private agencies in the current fiscal year and that Odyssey House was not licensed to care for children. Subsequently she was hauled into court for violating city building regulations. In a press interview she blamed her troubles on the "malevolence" of politicians.

A non-stop talker with an ample bosom and an ego to match, Dr. Judy appeared last winter at a televised legislative hearing with a puny twelve-year-old boy, Ralph de Jesus, seated on her lap. The audience was moved to tears as he told his story which included mainlining (injecting into the vein), mugging, and pushing to support his habit. The next day I visited the shelter where Ralph was spending his fourth day of abstinence and found him sitting forlornly on his bunk. "It was kinda scary," he said of his television debut. Shortly afterwards he left the shelter. A *New York Times* reporter tracked him down in his South Bronx home and asked him whether everything he had said at the hearing was true. "Some of it," Ralph replied.

While Dr. Judy has performed a service in sounding the alarm about a tragically neglected problem, her methods are open to criticism. By preempting the limelight she has diverted public attention from much more extensive efforts, particularly the city's sixteen Phoenix Houses where nearly 1,000 addicts, ranging from young adolescents to middle-aged men and women, are currently in treatment.

Each house is run by a small paid staff of ex-addicts with the help of residents nearing the end of their treatment. Residents do all the work of the place, starting out as each new house is opened by making a dilapidated building habitable through a strenuous roach-and-rat extermination campaign, plastering, partitioning, painting, rewiring, and replumbing. Cooking, cleaning, and all maintenance work are also done by residents, who start out on the lowliest tasks such as KP and scrubbing toilets. They are promoted to clerical and administrative jobs as they demonstrate progress by carrying out assignments responsibly, and by personality changes which are tested at encounter sessions, held three times a week.

There are three cardinal rules: no chemicals; no violence; no threats of violence. Infractions are dealt with by demotion to a lowlier work squad or by what are known as "learning experiences." The minor offender may incur a "haircut"—that is, a public reprimand or temporary ostracism by the group. At Phoenix House and similar centers, you also see young men and women going about their tasks with large cardboard signs dangling from their necks hand-lettered with such phrases as, "I am a baby," "I must stop testing the program," "I am a liar." There are boys with shaved heads and girls with their hair stuffed into stocking caps. ("We don't shave the girls' hair, it means too much to them emotionally," I was told. "They tried it on one girl at Daytop and she went into the bathroom and cut her wrists.")

Phoenix Houses, like most therapeutic communities, are coeducational except for the sleeping quarters on the upper floors. There is an easy camaraderie among residents, and one hears over and over again identical phrases about the merits of the program and about "responsible concern" for one's fellows which includes reporting their misdeeds or "wrong attitudes" at encounters. Visitors are welcome at "wake-up sessions" held at eight in the morning, where coffee is served to an accompaniment of songs and impromptu speeches or readings from the day's newspapers. All residents must attend, since learning to get out of bed at a fixed hour is a basic step in moving out of the benumbed, erratic life of addiction.

Outsiders are not generally encouraged to attend encounters

both because an alien presence might inhibit their spontaneity and because the tone and content of the dialogue are likely to be jolting to anyone who has not undergone "sensitivity training" or its equivalent.

Such is, in truth, my own experience when I find myself seated on a hard wooden chair in a circle along with a dozen young people —black, white, and Puerto Rican. All wear long-sleeved blouses or sweaters, the uniform of the mainliner whose needle-striped and abscess-scarred arms are the permanent badge of his affliction. Leader of the group is Charlotte, a pretty blond college dropout who is ready for "reentry" after eighteen months of treatment. There are several other fairly advanced residents. The rest are candidates for admission to Phoenix House. This is an "induction encounter" designed to test their readiness.

The air is thick with cigarette smoke as a verbal barrage is directed at a handsome sloe-eyed Negro youth who persists in mumbling almost inaudibly despite exhortations to "speak up" and "contribute some input." Charlotte finally goads him into reciting a halting memoir with much prodding from the rest of the group.

"My name is Raymond. . . . I'm twenty-two. My father died when I was six."

"What do you remember about him? Did you like him?"

"He was big and husky. . . . He worked in a chemical plant. Once when my mother wouldn't buy me a cap pistol he got it for me. . . . My mother remarried."

"How did you feel about your stepfather?"

"He was mean to me. He yelled at me when I didn't straighten up my room . . . stuff like that . . . I don't like nobody to yell at me."

"What did you do? Just sit there and listen like you do here?"

"Well, I stumble when I talk so I don't talk good. One of my brothers got killed. He got hit in the temple with a stick. . . . My oldest brother has been in and out of jail most of the time. My mother didn't want that to happen to me. . . . She died in the hospital when I was fifteen or sixteen. I was smoking reefers then, staying out nights. . . . The dean caught me and threw me out of school. I was running in the street for a year . . . started shooting dope. I went to live with one of my sisters. . . . I stole from her. I took a portable TV, a record player, and her watch. I always meant to get her another watch but I never did. . . . When my niece got married there were a lot of wedding presents in the house. I stole them. My sister threw me out. I moved in with my other sister. She axed me in. I took her camera. And her watch. An eighty-dollar watch. Not the TV . . . it was too big to carry. I got picked up by the housing detectives. My sister come to court with me. . . . I got probation. Then I'm picked up on possession."

"You keep blowing a good thing."

"That's right."

"Well, you got an advantage here. Who you got to look bad before? We're all just a bunch of dope fiends. Inside we're all babies. We say to ourselves, it hurts. Who has to hurt? I can get high. How do you see yourself today?"

"I see myself as a liar, a thief, and a dope fiend."

For Raymond, this degree of candor is rated as progress. With what seems savage intensity the group now turns on Dolores, a plump, swarthy girl who has been in and out of several treatment centers—a common pattern. Her last sojourn was at Boerum Place, a recently opened city facility for children, where she was sent because she is only fifteen. She walked out after less than a week. Dolores is given to turning her head away and giggling at some private joke.

"Why you split from Boerum Place?"

"All those little kids. I didn't like it. I want to be back in Phoenix with my friends."

"You're inconsistent. You're selfish."

"What you want me to do?"

"Talk about your hang-ups."

"I don't have no hang-ups."

"You're a lying bitch. One guy split from this program because of you. There's a lifetime ban on somebody like you—a split-ee. You're like a cancer. You sound fucking poisonous."

"I think she's dealing."

"Maybe she's a spy from another program."

"She's a spoiled brat with a cute little female body."

"You liked it on Hart's Island [another treatment center] where there were two hundred boys and thirty girls?"

Dolores responds with a nostalgic giggle.

"You know what a whore is?"

"I know. But I'm not a whore. Sure, I turned tricks when my boyfriend didn't have money for dope. He got me tricks. But I'm not a whore."

"Then why you go around balling everybody? You couldn't fuck at Boerum so you went out to shoot dope and get down with Tom. . . ."

Though their prospects of success seem dim, Raymond and Dolores will probably be admitted whenever space is available. In fact many applicants are no more promising. Few addicts spontaneously seek salvation in a place where they know they will be under close surveillance by their fellows even though the front door is unlocked. Most come because of pressure from parents, on order from the court, or because their welfare checks will be cut off unless they go into treatment. Others simply find the rigors of street life temporarily unbearable.

Since they have taken on an assignment that is inherently so risky, the therapeutic-community advocates object strenuously to being judged by the "numbers game." They prefer not to mention that more than half of those who enter drop out quite early. When they cite a "success rate" of 90 per cent or better—as do Odyssey, Phoenix, and Daytop for example—the base they are using is the handful of residents who have run the full course and who can be checked a year or more after they leave.

A high proportion of their graduates remain in addiction work as staff members. The most extreme example of this trend is Synanon, which, on the theory that no ex-addict can cope with the realities of the square world, encourages its members to remain permanently hooked on Synanon, spending the rest of their days in one of several outside business enterprises operated by alumni on Synanon property and enjoying lifetime membership in a utopian society.

Some do leave, to be sure. Along with the graduates of other programs, many ex-addicts have proved themselves highly effective therapists and forceful lecturers who have a unique credibility for young audiences. They also tend to attribute almost divine powers to group dynamics, which is, in fact, by no means the sole or even the most promising therapy for drug addiction.

There is, indeed, considerable evidence that the most effective treatment that could be used on a large scale is not psychiatric but medical—a technique known as methadone maintenance. It grew out of experimental work begun in the late 1950s by Dr. Vincent Dole of the Rockefeller Institute, a distinguished metabolic researcher. Seeking an entirely new approach to the drug-abuse problem, he teamed up with Dr. Marie Nyswander (now Mrs. Dole), who had spent twenty frustrating years treating addicts with the methods of classic psychiatry. After trying a variety of possible antidotes to heroin they chose methadone, a synthetic opiate developed in Germany during World War II when morphine was scarce. Small doses of methadrone block the craving for heroin. The Dole-Nyswander experiments showed that if the dosage is gradually stepped up, the euphoric effects of heroin are also blocked. Though it is a narcotic, methadone, taken by mouth, causes virtually no undesirable reactions.

When he reaches the "maintenance level," the patient comes to the hospital daily to drink his dose of methadone dissolved in Tang under the watchful eye of a registered nurse. (At a later stage he comes once a week to pick up his supply.) He leaves with her a urine specimen to be checked for drug usage by means of a test developed by Dr. Dole which has become the standard method of policing all therapy programs.

A number of New York hospitals now offer methadone-maintenance therapy under the general direction of the Morris Bernstein Institute of Beth Israel Hospital, the program's main base. To be admitted, patients must be eighteen or older, with at least a two-year history of addiction and a record of arrests and failure in other types of treatment.

Statistically monitored by the Columbia University School of Public Health and Administrative Medicine since its inception, methadone maintenance has rolled up an impressive score, with a better than 80 per cent success rate. As of September 1969, 2,205 individuals had been admitted to the program. Of these, 18 per cent dropped out. The rest remained in treatment and after three years only 2 per cent had been rearrested; 96 per cent were in school or gainfully employed (as compared to only 29 per cent on admission) and none had become readdicted.

Figures like these do not impress doctrinaire believers in the therapeutic communities, who consider methadone a "cop-out," simply substituting one addiction for another. Dole, Nyswander, and their followers do not deny that their patients are dependent on methadone. Addiction, they say, is a disease for which the addict needs medication, just as a diabetic requires insulin and the cardiac patient digitalis. So long as he takes it only by mouth and in the proper dosage, the patient can lead a normal life. On the basis of experiments with animals Dr. Dole has propounded the theory that narcotics addiction causes metabolic changes in the body which necessitate lifetime treatment. This view (disputed by other researchers) stirs heated emotions in the anti-methadone forces who point to the considerable number of ex-addicts who have managed to remain "clean" for a good many years by other means. They also hint darkly at a vast illicit traffic in methadone, known on the street as "dollies" (Dolophine is the trade name of methadone in tablet form). Addicts are known to use dollies to cut back a habit that has grown too expensive. Though there is at present no evidence of an extensive illegal trade in methadone, it obviously should not be dispensed like aspirin and it is hazardous —as is almost any drug—if injected. Furthermore, the end of his drug craving is only the beginning of rehabilitation for the addict who needs—and is given, under well-organized programs—continuous help in finding a job and otherwise adjusting to the square world. Methadone is being misused in some bogus programs hastily set up to convince taxpayers that the drug problem is being dealt with.

The guerrilla war between New York's addiction experts took a novel turn last March. One morning at four o'clock, the *New York Post* city desk received a call from a man identifying himself as Dr. Thomas Butler of Roosevelt Hospital. He reported two deaths due to methadone: one man, he said, had hanged himself in jail after receiving a methadone injection in a hospital; the other had been found dead in his home after renewing his methadone supply. The caller was at pains to say that "methadone acts as a depressant whose use has not been carefully researched. It can often do more harm than good." He was so quoted in the story that was published after a check with the police confirmed the fact that the deaths had indeed occurred.

The next day, the *Post's* able medical reporter, Barbara Yuncker, decided that the matter needed further investigation. Her sleuthing revealed that Roosevelt Hospital had never heard of Dr.

Thomas Butler and that no such name is listed in the state medical directory. Furthermore, the medical examiner's office, which did not perform autopsies until many hours after the story was phoned to the *Post*, flatly said that neither death could be attributed to methadone. The small dose given intravenously to one man in the hope of easing his withdrawal agonies would have been more likely to cause a high than a depression. The other man—who was being phased out of a maintenance program at Harlem Hospital because of alcoholism—succumbed to massive bleeding from a ruptured spleen apparently suffered when he fell in an alcoholic convulsion. The perpetrator of this hoax has not been found.

* * *

As with other commodities, the traffic in narcotics is a matter of supply and demand. In Harlem, there is a buyers' market in heroin. Prices are at an all-time low and the quality is said to be better (*i.e.*, less adulterated) than ever before—a fact which may account for the mounting death rate from overdoses. The rise in youthful addiction may well be the result of a sales campaign deliberately aimed at the teen-age and juvenile market; innovative packaging— the $1 and $2 bag—has been designed for this trade. (The $5 bag is the adult size.) Because of overstocked inventories, heroin—long sold strictly for cash—may be bought on credit. When an addict says, "The man's about to ice me," he means that he is so heavily in debt to his dealer that he fears for his life. And in all probability if he does not pay up he will be stabbed or pushed off a roof.

In a six square-block section of central Harlem, a militant tenants' organization, after conducting a door-to-door census last year, has concluded that 80 per cent of the population is addicted and that on every block there are at least twelve "shooting galleries" where addicts congregate for their daily fix.

The leader of the tenants' group is Mrs. Beraneece Sims, a softspoken gray-haired black woman whose gentle manner cloaks a seething rage and an iron will. A few months ago she set up her own addiction program, calling it "The Community Thing." Sitting in her shabby office—a store on Lenox Avenue acquired simply by "occupying" it—one gets a perspective on the narcotics problem quite different from the view downtown.

Mrs. Sims sees the "hard-core addict" not as a single stereotype but as two distinct breeds. The older ones, whom she calls the "Bible Belt type" have usually had some stabilizing family ties which gave them the rudiments of a value system. Although they are professional thieves, forgers, shoplifters, passers of bad checks, they seldom resort to violence and they do not operate in their own community. "They would rather be sick in the street than do that," she says. Because they hustle downtown, they are not perceived in Harlem as dangerously antisocial characters. Their loot, which finds eager customers at bargain prices, is regarded as a kind of tithe on white society and there is even a certain admiration for the skill with which they practice their specialities. Some, for instance, have perfected the art of walking out of department stores in broad daylight carrying off two portable TV sets. Others are "cattle rustlers" who steal meat to order for housewives, charging them half the market price. (The real experts swap labels in the store so that the purchaser winds up paying half the price of a porterhouse for the chuck steak she gets.)

These older addicts, along with all other ghetto residents, view with horror the new, younger breed—the mugger or the purse snatcher who has not even the skills of the professional thief but is simply a ruthless predator preying on his own people. "These adolescents came along when our community fabric had fallen apart," Mrs. Sims says. "What can you expect when you don't have to walk half a block for a fix, when dealing in drugs is the easiest money in Harlem?"

The Community Thing has acquired squatter's rights to a row of venerable buildings which were scheduled for demolition, and is using them for its own therapy program. On one door is a sign, "Come into my house, child." Here are lodged some twenty addicted youngsters ranging in age from seven to fourteen.

"We don't believe in encounters, confrontation—all that," she says. "Not for our children anyway. They have been damaged too much. They need to find out who they are, to develop some pride and purpose, they need *habilitation* not rehabilitation. We take them off drugs, cold turkey. Then we try to find out what their *thing* is and get them busy at it."

For some, the thing is "growing something." This spring a steep slope in a nearby park glowed with tulips and daffodils planted on land terraced and cultivated by some of the children who are being taught by a volunteer landscape gardener.

Any addict who makes a "soul decision" to change may join The Community Thing, even though the decision may be merely to cut back his habit. All are encouraged to go to work or to school and to get involved in community-action programs. Some become scouts for the drug program, roaming the streets, housing projects, tenements, and playgrounds in search of "copping" youngsters.

"We also use addicts who are not going to change themselves but who want to help us anyhow," Mrs. Sims explains calmly. "We need them most for our Special Child Detail Squad. They are the ones who help us find the pawned children."

"Pawned children?"

"When an addicted mother owes her dealer more than she can ever pay, she might become a pusher. Or she might go to work in a factory where they package heroin. If she is really desperate she may pawn her child to the dealer. She hopes she'll be able to redeem it someday, but she never does. If it's an infant the dealer may sell it to a childless couple. The eight-, nine-, and ten-year-olds become pushers and sometimes the boys work as homosexual prostitutes, the little girls as prostitutes for 'specialty sex acts.' Only an addict can find these children for us. An ex-addict is respected but he's not trusted like the one who's still using."

Except for a mini-grant of a few thousand dollars from the state, The Community Thing has been supported entirely by contributions, mostly from Harlem people. "Our addicted brothers and sisters understand, as we all do, that we've got to save our children or we're finished as a race, *finished*," Mrs. Sims says. "Some of the older addicts give us 15 per cent of their take every week. That's mighty generous you know—they have that much less left for a fix. The numbers people help us too."

The ideal way to solve the drug problem would be to cut off the supply. But as Americans sadly learned during Prohibition, a multimillion-dollar business operated by organized criminals, who corrupt public officials ranging from the cop on the beat to the highest levels of government, presents a formidable law-enforcement problem. It is not solved by the sporadic seizure of smuggled drug shipments or periodic arrests of dealers and pushers.

"A big collar makes a big noise," said a Harlem clergyman. "But these fellows are just straw bosses. We want to know who's the big plantation boss sitting back with his mint julep, raking in the millions."

On rare occasions one of these overlords is seized, and a temporary panic in the street follows. "I remember a time like that back in 1965," an ex-addict told me. "The story was that the cops had collared a big gumbah of Frank Costello's and made a deal with him. They agreed to let him go home safe to Italy if he would get the heroin out of Harlem. Forty-eight hours later, 116th Street was full of addicts puking in the gutter, lighting bonfires, throwing their money around. You literally couldn't get a fix. Of course, this only lasted a week or so."

The federal Narcotics Bureau has recently been transferred from the Treasury to the Justice Department, which, with the help of local crime commissions, has sent an unusual number of Mafia bosses to jail in New York and New Jersey. However, the drug traffic is no longer a Mafia monopoly: freelancers from Latin America have moved in and dominate the cocaine-smuggling industry whose trail begins in the coca bushes of Peru and Bolivia and moves into the United States via Miami.

Most heroin originates in the poppy fields of Turkey, where part of the crop, grown chiefly for conversion into medicinal morphine, is sold at much higher prices to the bootleg market. It is refined into heroin in Marseilles. There the American importer may pay $5,000 to $15,000 for a kilo, which, when cut, will bring in $250,000 at retail after passing through a chain of jobbers and dealers each of whom skims off a profit. The earthquakes which recently struck the Turkish poppy fields may somewhat shrink the supply. Pressure could also be exerted on France, Turkey, and other exporters to cut off the traffic at the overseas source.

Meanwhile vigilante groups in some drug-infested communities are waging their own wars against dealers and pushers. Others clamor for higher mandatory jail sentences for drug offenders, despite abundant evidence that this has never been an effective weapon against crime. A few politicians urge us to adopt the British system, under which all criminal sanctions are abolished and doctors prescribe freely to all addicts the drugs they need. This proposal was widely touted in the 1950s by liberal critics of the punitive philosophy of Harry J. Anslinger, longtime chief of the Bureau of Narcotics.

Even at that time it was apparent that what might work in Britain, with a minute addicted population, was irrelevant to the monstrous American problem. Most of Britain's addicts then were well-to-do people who were introduced to morphine during a painful illness. Within the past few years the drug problem in England has escalated as a new breed of addicts have proved adroit at hoodwinking several doctors into supplying them and then selling the surplus. Many British experts concede that their system is in disarray. For the tragic fact is that, though a few addicts may be able to function despite their habit (one per cent of American doctors are said to be addicted), heroin turns most people into befuddled, stuporous, totally disorganized and unproductive members of society.

E. MEN AND WOMEN

18 / THE
NEW
WOMAN

Time Staff

The "New Woman" has been proclaimed with a certain regularity for a century and more. Ibsen brought Nora Helmer out of her doll's house in 1879, and succeeding generations have invented her anew: in Shaw's drawing-room heroines, Laurentian sensualists, Brett Ashleys, flappers, women who smoked and drank and swore and brushed their teeth with last night's Scotch, got divorced or did not bother to get married at all, wore pants, and perhaps in the mellow suburban '50s, lived to grow old as Auntie Mame.

As often as not, the New Woman was a masculine fantasy—Greta Garbo as a Soviet virago, titillatingly mannish yet secretly craving French perfume and Melvyn Douglas. Such, at least, was popular mythology—women, even in their supposed emancipation, have often been, as it were, prisoners of the male imagination. Always there was the secret, insistent vibration of sex: rebellion ends when Rhett Butler kicks down the door.

Sex emphatically remains, but something complex and important has occurred in the relationship between American men and women. Another New Woman has emerged, but she is, perhaps for the first time on a massive scale, very much the creation of her own, and not a masculine imagination—an act of intellectual parthenogenesis. The New Feminism cannot be measured entirely by the membership lists of the National Organization for Women and other liberation groups. It is a much broader state of mind that has raised serious questions about the way people live—about their families, home, child rearing, jobs, governments and the nature of the sexes themselves.

Or so it seems now. Some of those who have weathered the torrential fads of the last decade wonder if the New Woman's movement may not be merely another sociological entertainment that will subside presently, like student riots, leaving Mother, if not Gloria Steinem, home to stir the pudding on the stove while Norman Mailer rushes off to cover the next moon shot.

Certainly the movement itself has invited the ironist's eye. Foreigners have traditionally regarded American women with a sort of wary bemusement; they seemed a race of cool, assertive, pampered and sometimes savagely domineering women. In 1898, the Scots traveler James F. Muirhead observed, with what was surely a chauvinist's exaggeration: "Man meekly submits to be the hewer of wood, the drawer of water, and the beast of burden for the superior sex." Yet now the New Feminists assert—an irony that does not invalidate the argument—that it is they who are dominated.

It seems certain, at least, that sex is too important to be left entirely to ideologues. Some men have spoken of it as the last frontier of free expression. Yet in a way, the opposite is true. The appeal of sex, at least to some, is not freedom but order, represented by the clear definition of roles. Marriage is a remnant of a fixed social order that, in the past, was thought to be a reflection of a fixed natural order. In sex, of course, men and women feel that they must prove themselves, but they do not so often feel under the bewildering obligation to define themselves. It is one area in which definition is usually unambiguously understood—one simply is a man or a woman. Perhaps for this reason, many people, male and female, are troubled by the notions of sexual equality and interchangeable social roles.

In its belief that old traditions can be changed and that men and women can learn anything—even how to be men and women —the feminist movement is characteristically American. As Critic Elizabeth Hardwick has noted, the movement rests "upon a sense of striving, of working, and it has the profoundly native ethical themes of self-reliance, personal responsibility, and equality. Preparation, study, free choice, courage, resolution: these are its images and emblems." The women's movement, she points out, is antipathetic to "the youth culture, which appeared more as a refusal, a pause in the labor of the vineyard, sometimes a sort of quietism."

Miss Hardwick notes that when Hawthorne wrote his great parable about men and women in America, *The Scarlet Letter,* in which Hester Prynne decides to make a lonely stand against Puritanism and hypocrisy, Mrs. Hawthorne read it and said that she liked it, but "it gave her a headache." In a sense, that is where we are still.

The women's issue could involve an epic change in the way we see ourselves, not only sexually but historically, sociologically, psychologically and in the deeper, almost inaccessible closets of daily habit. Its appearance has startled men and women into self-perception. It has outraged some, freed others, left some sarcastically indifferent. Men and women have shared equally in all three reactions.

It seems prudent to admit that the subject remains mysterious. If men to some extent have lost their mystique as gods and kings and hunters, women somehow have not yet lost—not quite—the aura of earth mother or Kali. To say that over 99 per cent of women are not lawyers—and why not?—reckons without the residual mystique of women defined not so much by what they do as what they are. Perhaps all of that will change and should change. Meanwhile, we have attempted to describe what women are doing and thinking, what they are and might become.

WHERE SHE IS AND WHERE SHE'S GOING

> *There is a tide in the affairs of women,*
> *Which, taken at the flood, leads*
> *—God knows where.*
> —Byron, *Don Juan*

By all rights, the American woman today should be the happiest in history. She is healthier than U.S. women have ever been, better educated, more affluent, better dressed, more comfortable, wooed by advertisers, pampered by gadgets. But there is a worm in the apple. She is restless in her familiar familial role, no longer quite content with the homemaker-wife-mother part in which her society has cast her. Round the land, in rap session and kaffee-klatsch, in the radical-chic salons of Manhattan and the ladies auxiliaries of Red Oak, Iowa, women are trying to define the New Feminism. The vast majority of American women stop far short of activist roles in the feminist movement, but they are affected by it. Many of them are in search of a new role that is more independent, less restricted to the traditional triangle of *Kinder, Küche, Kirche* (children, kitchen, church).

The most lordly male chauvinist and all but the staunchest advocate of Women's Liberation agree that woman's place is different from man's. But for the increasingly uncomfortable American woman, it is easier to say what that place is not than what it is. Most reject the Barbie-doll stereotypical model of woman as staple-naveled Playmate or smiling airline stewardess. Marilyn Goldstein of the Miami *Herald* caught the feeling well when she wrote about the National Airlines' celebrated "Fly me" advertising campaign: "If God meant men to 'Fly Cheryl,' he would have given her four engines and a baggage compartment."

The new Feminism includes equality with men in the job market and in clubs, though it is not restricted to that. Already, women have invaded countless dens once reserved exclusively for the lion: there are women at McSorley's Old Ale House in New York, women in soapbox derbies and stock car races, women cadets in the Pennsylvania state police. Women have come to protest what seems to them to be the male chauvinism of rock music. An all-female group in Chicago belts out:

> *Rock is Mick Jagger singing*
> *'Under my thumb, it's all right'*
> *No, Mick Jagger, it's not all right*
> *And it's never gonna be*
> *All right again.*

The New Feminism has increasingly influenced young women to stay single, and it has transformed—and sometimes wrecked—marriages by ending once automatic assumptions about woman's place. In the first issue of *Ms.*, New Feminist Gloria Steinem's magazine for the liberated woman, Jane O'Reilly writes of experiencing "a blinding click," a moment of truth that shows men's preemption of a superior role. An O'Reilly example: "In New York last fall my neighbors—named Jones—had a couple named Smith over for dinner. Mr. Smith kept telling his wife to get up and help Mrs. Jones. Click! Click! Two women radicalized at once." The term Ms. itself, devised as a female honorific that, like Mr., does not reveal marital status, is winning wider acceptance: for example, the Republican National Committee and the federal Equal Employment Opportunity Commission now use it.

American men and women are looking at each other in new ways—and not always liking what they see. Reactions are ambivalent. Men feel threatened; yet sometimes, by marginal amounts, they appear more favorable than women do toward strengthening women's status in society. A Louis Harris poll taken for Virginia Slims cigarettes ("You've come a long way, baby") indicates that men favor women's rights organizations 44 per cent to 39 per cent, whereas women narrowly oppose them (42 per cent to 40 per cent). But unquestionably, consciousness has been raised all around, particularly among the more liberal and better educated. *Psychology Today* got almost 20,000 replies to a questionnaire that sampled men, women not associated with a women's group and women who were. Of the men, 51 per cent agreed that "U.S. society exploits women as much as blacks." Nongroup women agreed by 63 per cent, group women by 78 per cent.

Second-Class. The New Feminism has touched off a debate that darkens the air with flying rolling pins and crockery. Even *Psychology's* relatively liberated readers are not exempt. Male letter writer: "As far as Women's Lib is concerned, I think they are all a bunch of lesbians, and I am a male chauvinist and proud of it." Female: "It's better to let them think they're king of the castle, lean and depend on them, and continue to control and manipulate them as we always have."

Activist Kate Millett's scorching *Sexual Politics (Time,* Aug. 31, 1970) drew a frenetic reply in Norman Mailer's celebrated article, "The Prisoner of Sex," which excoriated many of Millett's arguments but concluded in grudging capitulation: "Women must have their rights to a life which would allow them to look for a mate. And there would be no free search until they were liberated." Arthur Burns, chairman of the Federal Reserve Board, complained last month: "Now we have women marching in the streets!

If only things would quiet down!" Washington Post Co. President Kay Graham left a recent party at the house of an old friend, Columnist Joseph Alsop, because her host insisted upon keeping to the custom of segregating the ladies after dinner. Other social habits are in doubt. A card circulating in one Manhattan singles bar reads: If you're gonna say no, say it now before I spend all of my goddam money on you.

Many currents of social change have converged to make the New Feminism an idea whose time has come. Mechanization and automation have made brawn less important in the marketplace. Better education has broadened women's view beyond home and hearth, heightening their awareness of possibilities—and their sense of frustration when those possibilities are not realized. As Toynbee had noted earlier, middle-class woman acquired education and a chance at a career at the very time she lost her domestic servants and the unpaid household help of relatives living in the old, large family; she had to become either a "household drudge" or "carry the intolerably heavy load of two simultaneous full-time jobs."

A declining birth rate and the fact that women are living increasingly longer—and also longer than men—has meant that a smaller part of women's lives is devoted to bearing and rearing children. The Pill has relieved women of anxiety about unwanted pregnancies.

All of this helped ensure a profound impact for Betty Friedan's *The Feminine Mystique*, published in 1963. In it, she argued that women lose their identities by submerging themselves in a world of house, spouse and children. The book came just at the height of the civil-rights movement in the South; the pressures to give blacks a full place in society inevitably produced a new preoccupation with other second-class citizens. The Viet Nam War also led to far-reaching questions about traditional American assumptions and institutions, to a new awareness of injustice.

First in Wyoming. The 1960s were not the first time in American history that civil rights and feminism were linked. Early American woman was conventionally seen, and conventionally saw herself, as the frontiersman's helpmeet in building the new nation—wife and mother of pioneers. It was the Abolitionist movement before the Civil War that helped get American feminism under way. In working against slavery, women emerged as a political force. The 1848 Women's Rights Convention at Seneca Falls, N.Y., was the first of several to demand the vote, equal opportunity in jobs and education and an end to legal discrimination based on sex.

The 14th Amendment in 1868 enfranchised blacks, but not women. In 1913 some 5,000 women, many of them bloomer-clad, marched down Washington's Pennsylvania Avenue carrying placards addressed to Woodrow Wilson: Mr. President! How long must women wait for liberty? About 200 women were roughed up by unsympathetic bystanders, and 169 were arrested for obstructing traffic in front of the White House. Anger over the shabby treatment of the demonstrators, plus the momentum of state women's suffrage movements—Wyoming in 1890 was the first to enfranchise women—finally got women the vote throughout the U.S. with ratification of the 19th Amendment in 1920.

"The golden psychological moment for women, the moment at which their hopes were highest, was in the 1920s and 1930s, when they won the vote and began to go to college in considerable numbers, with the expectation of entering the professions," says Clare Boothe Luce, politician, diplomat and author. "Women then believed that the battle had been won. They made a brave start, going out and getting jobs." World War II made Rosie the Riveter a figure of folklore, and many women never before in the work force found that they liked the independence gained by working. The postwar reaction was the "togetherness" syndrome of the Eisenhower era, a doomed attempt to confer on suburban motherhood something of the esteem that pioneer women once enjoyed. From the affluent housewife's suicidal despair in J. D. Salinger's "Uncle Wiggly in Connecticut," it was not far to *The Feminine Mystique.*

Oddly, women characters have never had a particularly important place in American literature; as a rule they have had smaller roles than in English, Russian or French fiction. In *Love and Death in the American Novel*, Critic Leslie Fiedler argues that U.S. writers are fascinated by the almost mythological figures of the Fair Maiden and the Dark Lady, but "such complex full-blooded passionate females as those who inhabit French fiction from *La Princess de Clèves* through the novels of Flaubert and beyond are almost unknown in the works of our novelists." There are memorable figures, of course: Hawthorne's Hester Prynne, John O'Hara's

Grace Caldwell Tate and Gloria Wandrous, Fitzgerald's Daisy Buchanan, Dreiser's Sister Carrie, Steinbeck's Ma Joad, Margaret Mitchell's Scarlett O'Hara, Nabokov's Lolita, Roth's Sophie Portnoy.

Still, Fiedler finds American writers displaying at least covert hostility to women. Probably none has matched in misogynist invective Philip Wylie's diatribe in *Generation of Vipers* (1942): "I give you mom. I give you the destroying mother . . . I give you the woman in pants, and the new religion: she-popery. I give you Pandora. I give you Proserpine, the Queen of Hell. The five-and-ten-cent-store Lilith, the mother of Cain, the black widow who is poisonous and eats her mate, and I designate at the bottom of your program the grand finale of all soap operas: the mother of America's Cinderella." It is a mark of the wondrous sea change of public attitudes that in a scant three decades Wylie's castrating bitch has become, in much popular mythology if not in fact, part of the wretched of the earth.

Twenty Years Older.   Just where is American woman today? In a statistical overview, she is nearly 106 million strong, at the median age 30 and with a bit more than a twelfth-grade education. She is likely to be married (61.5 per cent). She makes up more than a third of the national work force, but according to a Department of Labor survey, she generally has a lower-skilled, lower-paying job than a man does. In many jobs she does not get equal pay for equal work. (Her median earnings have actually declined relative to men.) In a recession she is, like blacks, the first to be fired. Because of the instability of marriage and a growing divorce rate, women head more and more households; 20 million people live in households depending solely on women for support.

As Patrick Moynihan pointed out in his controversial report on black family life, black women tend to be the center of households more often than white women. Black women, interestingly, are more likely to go to college than black men are. According to Christopher Jencks and David Riesman in *The Academic Revolution*, "Among other things this reflects the fact that at least until recently they have had a better chance than their brothers of getting a professional job once they earned a degree."

Early in 1964, Lyndon Johnson sent out a presidential directive pushing for more women in Government. Only in 1967 did the federal civil services start making full-scale reports on the numbers of women at the upper civil service levels of the U.S. Government. In the top grades, at salary levels beginning at $28,000 a year, 1.6 per cent of the jobs were held by women in 1966 *v.* 1.5 per cent four years later. Midway in his present term, President Nixon promised to appoint more women, and to that end he created a brand-new position on the White House staff for a full-time recruiter of women. She is Barbara Franklin, 32, a Harvard Business School graduate who was an assistant vice president of New York's First National City Bank. She claims to have more than doubled the number of women in top Government jobs within a year.

But women in Washington seldom scale the highest reaches of power like the National Security Council. There has never been a woman Supreme Court Justice, though both Pat Nixon and Martha Mitchell lobbied for one before Nixon wound up nominating William Rehnquist and Lewis Powell. Only two women have ever sat in the Cabinet: Frances Perkins under F.D.R. and Oveta Culp Hobby under Eisenhower. Ten years ago, there were two women in the U.S. Senate and 18 women Representatives; now there are only Senator Margaret Chase Smith and eleven women in the House. The first woman in Congress, Jeannette Rankin, elected from a Montana constituency in 1916 and still starchy at 91, ventured recently that if she had it to do all over again she would, with just one change: "I'd be nastier."

At the state and local levels, women have yet to make much impression on government. New York is the only state that has a special women's advisory unit reporting to the Governor, but its head, a black ex-newspaper-woman named Evelyn Cunningham, readily confesses: "We're a token agency." There are 63 separate agencies in the New York State government, she notes, and only 13 of them have women in jobs above the rank of secretary. Round the U.S. there are a few women mayors—among them Anna Latteri in Clifton, N.J., Patience Latting in Oklahoma City, Barbara Ackerman in Cambridge, Mass.

The last female state Governor was Lurleen Wallace in Alabama, a stand-in for her husband George, forbidden by the state constitution to succeed himself. (The first: Nellie Tayloe Ross was elected Governor of Wyoming in 1924.) The legislatures of the 50 states have a total membership of more than 7,000—including only 340 women. Few of these women have much influence, though there are stirring exceptions: New York Assembly Member Constance Cook, for example, represents a small upstate county, but led a successful fight for liberalizing the state's abortion law in 1970.

In a man's world, women still have only a ritualized place: they are received regularly and warmly only in women-centered trades like fashion or in acting. As Clare Luce puts it, "Power, money and sex are the three great American values today, and women have almost no access to power except through their husbands. They can get money mostly through sex—either legitimate sex, in the form of marriage, or non-married sex." Sexual freedom is not enough; "what leads to money and power is education and the ability to make money apart from sex."

It is not an easy goal to achieve. Many women fear it; they want to have their cigarettes lit and their car doors opened for them. Far more seriously, they are afraid that, as working mothers, they simply would not be able to give their children the necessary personal care and attention. And Richardson Roiphe, a novelist with five children, worries about the de-emphasis of the family. She has written "These days I feel a cultural pressure not to be absorbed in my child. Am I a Mrs. Portnoy sitting on the head of her little Alex? I am made to feel my curiosity about the growth of my babies is somehow counter-revolutionary. The new tolerance should ultimately respect the lady who wants to make pies, as well as the one who majors in higher mathematics."

Utopian. In a sense, if the feminist revolution simply wanted to exchange one ruling class for another, if it aimed at outright female domination (a situation that has occurred in science fiction and other fantasies), the goal would be easier to visualize. The demand for equality, not domination, is immensely complicated. True equality between autonomous partners is hard to achieve even if both partners are of the same sex. The careful balancing of roles and obligations and privileges without the traditional patterns to fall back on, sometimes seems like an almost utopian vision.

While nearly everyone favors some of the basic goals of the New Feminism—equal pay for equal work, equal job opportunity, equal treatment by the law—satisfying even those minimum demands could require more wrenching change than many casual sympathizers with the women's cause have seriously considered. Should women be drafted? Ought protective legislation about women's hours and working conditions be repealed?

Still, American women cannot be forced back into the Doll's House. More and more, American women will be free to broaden their lives beyond domesticity by a fuller use of their abilities; there will be fewer diapers and more Dante. Anatomy is destiny, the Freudians say. It is an observation that can hardly be dismissed as mere male chauvinist propaganda, but it is simply no longer sufficient. The destiny of women and, indeed, of men, is broader, more difficult than that—and also more promising.

19 / HOW MEN WILL BENEFIT FROM THE WOMEN'S POWER REVOLUTION

Marya Mannes

A great many men must be not only bewildered by, but sick of, the increasing sound and fury of the Women's Liberation movement. They may also feel threatened.

To these men I would like to extend sympathy and hope. You must know you are not only indispensable but desirable! (Some of my best friends are men.) And if I thought this revolution (and it is one, in spite of those too young or too confused to know what the word really means) concerned the weakening, emasculation, or domination of the male, I would have no part of it.

For if this movement of women towards social, economic, and

From *PTA Magazine*, January 1971. Reprinted by permission of Harold Ober Associates Incorporated. Copyright © 1970 by Marya Mannes.

political parity with men is ever to succeed it will do so only if men, too, are freed of certain burdens and limitations. Those women who consider men the enemy would fare much better if they enlisted men as allies—by understanding them. Once men recognize that their new partners in a life that extends beyond the home and into the world are no less women, they may realize the first fruits of a new masculine freedom.

One, very simply, is relief from the prolonged weight of female dependence, emotional and economic. I realize that there is a protective instinct in you men that needs to be satisfied. To take care of a helpless or at least passive woman is not only a natural male desire but the source of a satisfying equation: stronger-to-weaker. It is also one of the easiest ways to bolster an ego not otherwise secure.

So you are often the sole support of a woman and family. And you feel, as your wife does, that it is a perfectly fair and equitable return for her to be mother, lover, housekeeper, and cook also. You are supposed not only to keep her forever but love her always.

The irony is that you might love her more if you kept her less. And I do not mean only physically but as a human being. For the first very often militates against the second.

You spend your years at jobs that very often do not satisfy you and living a life that becomes more and more of a pattern. Office hours all week, car or train two or three hours a day, evenings with your wife at your lowest ebb, weekends with your family that end too soon (or not soon enough), TV and small talk fill the gaps, and endless worry about meeting bills. Your bills, her bills.

"But I love my family!" you may say, or "I love my job." But, surely, sometimes you dream of another life, with another (perhaps less domesticated) woman and time to do all those things you never manage to do?

If you do break away, you are still stuck for life with supporting your wife. Especially if she is of that age when the prospects of marriage in a society of youth are increasingly dim.

Because you have made all the major decisions in her life, she has become almost incapable of making her own. She has lived for twenty years through you and her family and, if you leave her, she has nothing left but alimony and memories. Her capacity to support herself is negligible.

And if you stay, put your children through a costly education that not all of them really want or use and pay for a home which, once flown, they seldom inhabit, what have you got? At the very best a dear companion who cooks and tidies for you and will join you in some retirement community until death.

More often, perhaps, your life has become a habit, with a wife to whom—precisely because she has had no other resources, no other life, no other competences—you have little to say except in the small coinage of daily existence.

She is, if you will, the best possible argument for female—and male—liberation. She is also one of the women who still resist it most. For it is easier for her to depend on a man than on herself. But even if her marriage fails, the dependent woman will say, "But I have my children!" Has she?

After loving care (cook, servant, chauffeur, tireless user of detergents and waxes) what happens to them? The exclusive company of their peers and almost any messy pad but their tidy homes.

Not all, of course. There is always the daughter brought up to marry in church as early as possible, the son brought up to make it in business. Either way, here is the woman who has lived through everyone but herself and ends up by never knowing what "herself" is.

Now, at last, a rising tide of women are doubting this destiny. And a rising number of men will begin to understand that women's insistence on themselves as identities and not as accessories is a mirror-image of their own needs.

There is no reason any more why a man should be the sole provider all his life. There is no reason why he should not achieve a life-style in which the labors of work and home and raising children are given equal priorities and time.

It is my firm belief, in fact, that a major cause of the alienation of the young from their elders is the absence of their fathers from their lives. Here is the real and dangerous domination of women. In the home—not in the world.

Ironically again, the men take this separation from their families as necessary and preferred because their business lives are more interesting than their wives and homes. They prefer the company of men, with whom they have more in common than with the woman they have chosen to live with (one-fifth of the time).

Let me hasten to say that there are a great many men and women who find nothing wrong with it. These are free to pursue accepted patterns and find satisfaction in them, and the wiser female militants should not tamper with the happiness of home-bound females by suggesting that they are unhappy.

A major point of the liberation movement is freedom of choice: freedom of man and woman as individuals to pursue the life that they most want to live. And if a woman enjoys a purely domestic role, she has every right to it.

But for a great many it is not enough. We do not want to spend our days without men, without the formulation and execution of ideas, without the use of what special talents or skills we have, whether for science or art, for engineering or business, for journalism or technology, for philosophy or broadcasting, for government or law. And whether men like it or not, the universities of this nation are turning out more and more women who are prepared to use their skills and demand that they be used without fear, favor, or discrimination. Many of us—perhaps most of us—want to live with men and bear their children—no more, hopefully, than two. And even, perhaps, none.

Society forgets that not all women are naturally maternal. And all of us must know by now that the large family is no more a blessing than the childless couple is a crime. In fact, the woman who is a copious breeder is doing infinitely more harm than good to this suffocating planet and its crowded broods.

The rest of us really want more men in our lives, not fewer. We want their comradeship at work as well as their company at home. We refuse a life that forces us to live ten hours of every weekday confined to the company of children and women.

We have close women friends, but we choose them more for their intelligence and spirit and talents than for what is repulsively called "girl-talk." We find on the whole that women who work are infinitely more interesting than women who don't.

And I think you men will find that out, too, in time. As a matter of fact, the happiest marriages I know have been between men and women who collaborate in work as well as in the home . . . whether in research, writing, science, or the arts.

At this point, I would like to relieve the male mind of one major apprehension: competition and aggression. You've heard those words time and time again: Why do women want to *compete* with men? Or, "I don't like *competitive* women—they're *aggressive*," or, "*aggressive* women are unfeminine."

Gentlemen, why is it that if you describe a man as competitive and aggressive it's a compliment and in a woman it's a curse? Are ambition and drive and energy exclusive male attributes? And if they are also possessed by many women, why are they feared?

We are not trying to *compete* with you; we want to collaborate with you. We don't want to be better than you—even if we could be. We don't even want to be *like* you. We merely want to be equal companions. In honesty, however, I must admit that aggressive militance is no more attractive in a woman than it is in a scruffy youth who yells obscenities while he hurls rocks. You may get attention but you don't get love.

The real aggressors you men should be aware of, in fact, are the killer-sharks in the guise of submissive females. Guerrilla tactics pale before their techniques of ambush and conquest of the male—not necessarily for himself but for his money, power, or his position.

Having had work experiences with both sexes in situations of at least some importance, I have found separation of man and woman to blur and fade entirely. I said separation, not difference. For in the difference lies our greatest contribution to the work both must do together.

This work is the making of decisions. Decisions that affect every segment of society and its organization, from the Cabinet to the Town Hall from state to village, from city to block.

Because of our long experience as nurturers and housekeepers, our constant intimacy with the daily details of life and environment, we can bring to these decisions elements that humanity sorely needs.

Surely, no intelligent and rational man will deny that his long, absolute, and exclusive reign over the destiny of men and nations has brought neither peace nor order nor joy nor happiness for the vast majority of people.

In other words, gentlemen, not only do you need help, but we want—and intend—to work for it and give it. We are 51 per cent of the population. Even if only a quarter of us care to, or can, prepare ourselves adequately for participation, we can offer a mighty force for good that cannot be ignored or rejected.

To accept the offer will mean—unquestionably— many alterations of thinking, of patterns, of accommodation, in men and women. It will mean a wholly new look at work schedules in terms of time, job alteration, provision for the children of working women and for the dreams of men who are better fitted to be artists than providers, farmers than tellers, wanderers than desk-sitters.

Love between a man and a woman should not depend on domination but on fusion. And the fact that above the body a man loves is a mind that equals his own should not be a source of conflict but of pride. Whatever happens, the male ego should remain intact. Not as the conqueror of woman, so long its most abiding source, but as the sovereign of himself.

PART THREE
THE ILLS OF A NATION

THE ILLS OF A NATION

Part III has been divided into three major headings—ecology, protest, and responses to change. Although the topics relate to quite different phenomena and, usually, quite different behavior, we have placed them together because they consist of problems that can best be seen on a community or national level and are not easily analyzed on an individual level. Although it would conceivably be possible to study the personality of the pollutor, or the characteristics of those taking part in protests, the emphasis is generally not so much on the individual as it would be in the study of the criminal, the worker, or the adolescent.

Traditionally the word ecology was used to refer to the interrelationships of organisms and their environments. More recently the word has been used primarily to deal with man's relationship with his environment, in social as well as purely biological ways. This category is thus relatively new among the list of major social problems. This is not to say that people have not been concerned with their environment. To some the conservation of natural resources has been a problem for generations. But only in the last few years has the magnitude of the problem come to the attention of the public, for it has only been in the last few years that many of us have begun to realize that without major controls we are likely to be overcome by the problems of the environment. The population problem (which will be discussed in the next section) is closely related to the problems of ecology. From that discussion we will see that in the world today we not only have a large number of people, but we have them in increasingly concentrated areas. Under the heading of ecology we must study the effects of urban crowding on our environment. Material is needed for housing and other industries, but attention is not always given to the long-range effects of using up these materials. Transportation is essential to get the city-dweller from his place of work to his residence, but little attention has been given to the effects of many cars on the air in the city. Food must be transported, stored, and distributed in large quantities and, therefore, preservatives have been added to some foods with little consideration of their effects on the health of the consumer or the nutritive value of the food. Then there is the problem of getting rid of all the waste created by an affluent society. Sewage and garbage, become more than economic problems, they have become major health problems and over the last few years have emerged as a genuine social problem. Of course, the items listed do not exhaust the problems that could be studied under the heading of ecology.

The study of social protest provides an excellent opportunity to observe the complexities of social problems. When we study protests, just what is the social problem? Is it the "issue" that generated the project—racial prejudice, war, and so on? Is it the protesters, who frequently disrupt the ongoing operation of society —closing down colleges, blocking freeways, boycotting various products? Or is the real problem in the reaction of society to the protests—mass arrests, shootings, counterprotests (see the Hard Hat article)? There are some who would say that there is no problem at all, but rather that the protests are a healthy means of communicating dissatisfaction within a democratic society. However, others would argue that the protesters and the methods they employ create a major problem. This argument suggests that there are other, more "proper" means of bringing about change in a democratic society, such as voting behavior of one type or another. There is a third view that suggests that social protest is neither healthy nor improper, but rather that the protesting reflects larger problems within the society. This view would argue that it is not necessarily healthy to disrupt the Democratic Convention, but instead of questioning whether or not it is proper, we ought to be asking why it is that so many persons feel that they have to express their discontent in such a drastic way.

The last broad topic in this part of the book, deals with reactions to changes taking place in society. Some feel that it is necessary to keep a close tab on some members of society. Others feel that this act of keeping tab, or spying, is far more dangerous than any problem it is aimed at solving. As you read these articles, try to understand the interrelationship between different dimensions of society and social problems.

A. ECOLOGY

20 / THE GARBAGE EXPLOSION

Charles A. Schweighauser

The accumulation of solid waste in the United States is reaching alarming dimensions. Each person throws away more than half again as much waste as he discarded fifty years ago. A larger and more affluent population, buying an increasing quantity of goods designed to be discarded after temporary use, produces a gigantic disposal problem. Each one of us in a year throws away 188 pounds of paper, 250 metal cans, 135 bottles and jars, 338 caps and crowns, and $2.50 worth of miscellaneous packaging. And every year we amass 2 per cent more refuse which, coupled with a 2 per cent annual population growth, indicates a 4 per cent annual growth in the solid waste disposal problem.

In 1920, the daily per capita disposal was somewhat less than 3 pounds; in 1965 it was 4.5 pounds, not including industrial solid wastes, which account for an equal amount. In 1920 the citizens of this country were throwing away 100 billion pounds per year; today the amount is more than 720 billion pounds per year—not including 6 trillion pounds of mineral and agricultural solid wastes. By 1985, household wastes alone will amount to an estimated 1.25 trillion pounds per year.

The trend is illustrated by the history of glass containers. The first "no deposit, no return" beer bottle was made in 1938; in 1958 more than 1 billion bottles were made, and in 1965, nearly 5 billion bottles were distributed. The throwaway soft-drink production was more than 1 billion. By 1970, the estimated combined

From *The Nation*, September 22, 1969. Reprinted by permission of *The Nation*.

beer and soft-drink use will exceed 12 billion nonreturnable bottles. That's 33 million bottles a day.

Nearly all major urban areas have run out of suitably inexpensive land for solid waste disposal, and are forced to dispose of solid waste by either long-distance removal or incineration. Incineration is more expensive than land disposal because of smoke pollution laws, and incinerator residue must be disposed of somewhere on the land.

The traditional method of disposing of solid waste was to put it either on the land, under the land, or down the side of a bank, where it decayed and was covered by vegetation. Very little thought was given to the pollution that resulted from using the land as a dump. Water, air and visual pollution weren't noticeable because their effects weren't very large. With an increasing population producing proportionately more waste, the physical insult to the land and to human sensibilities can no longer be tolerated. Urban areas must look for new methods and procedures to handle solid waste, as traditional techniques become unsatisfactory.

Few successful attempts have been made to re-use the paper, glass, plastics, rubber, rags and garbage that make up most of our domestic solid waste. About 35 per cent of total paper production, and about 10 per cent of plastics are recycled; glass not at all. The re-use of some metals is higher, as most major nonferrous metals can be economically salvaged. Copper re-use accounted for about 40 per cent of the supply in the United States in 1963, discarded lead was recovered at a rate that was more than double that produced from domestic mines, and scrap aluminum accounted for about 25 per cent of the total supply in the same year. Recovered scrap iron and steel currently account for about 50 per cent of total production. The recovery of rubber for chemicals, rubber and fibers is beginning to increase, and now stands at about 15 per cent.

The nearly 180 million tons of annual municipal refuse are estimated to contain ferrous and nonferrous metals valued at more than $1 billion. Each ton of residue from incineration contains 500 pounds of iron and 50 pounds of aluminum, copper, lead, tin and zinc. Fly ash from incinerators weighs about 20 pounds for every ton of refuse incinerated, and contains enough silver and gold to be comparable to a normal mine assay in the West.

Our solid waste disposal problems would be much worse if some materials were not recycled. A great deal more recycling could be done, but rising labor costs, uncertain markets, synthetics, and the mixing of refuse all make re-use costly and difficult.

Our industry is organized to use continuous input of new, rather than recovered, materials, and is sustained by constantly increasing consumer affluence and demands, built-in obsolescence, self-service merchandising, and competitive enterprise. We collect sometimes widely scattered resources, process and distribute them. But the responsibility of the private enterprise manufacturers stops at the shipping door. Neither distributors nor the retailers ever took responsibility for the disposal of the material they distribute (returnable bottles were an exception). Goods are used and then discarded; there are no consumers in the literal sense of the word. Responsibility thus passes from producer to user to a local government disposal agency.

So far it has been economically more feasible to build a new product out of new resources, because our industrial systems are so constituted, than to recover and re-use old products and their parts. Re-use systems could work in one of two ways: the material to be recycled could be collected by the producer, or the public agency or private individual keeps responsibility for returning the product to the producer/manufacturer (reverse distribution). The former system has worked, but in a rather disorganized and unsystematic manner; missing are economic incentives to encourage an efficient re-use system. Compounding the problem is our resistance to investment of money in an item that we will never use again. Solid waste disposal, therefore, has a low priority status with the general public and its agencies.

Recycling of garbage presents some interesting and difficult situations. Before urbanization, domestic garbage was recycled through pigs, chickens and other farm animals. Piggeries still use domestic garbage, but on a lesser scale. Garbage must be separated from nonorganic solid waste, usually in the home, which causes problems. Most states require domestic garbage to be cooked before it is fed to swine in order to stop the trichinosis cycle, a requirement that is necessary for public health but that is also expensive and time consuming for the piggery operator.

Another recycling method for garbage is composting, a process that involves biochemical degradation of the organic material. This material must be separated from ferrous metal, usually by magnet, and from all other metals, glass, paper, rubber and plastics by hand. The remainder is shredded, put through a short aerobic period to increase bacterial action and to hasten decomposition, and then allowed to cure for several months. The final product is a soil conditioner.

The product is of good quality, but the cost of producing it is greater than that of other types of soil conditioners. The cost of compost material from other sources is higher in Europe than in the United States, and thus composting of solid waste is much more widely practiced there. Contribution to the cost factor is labor (including pickers), rather expensive equipment, time for the product to mature, and the relatively low percentage of organic material in the total refuse. About 30 per cent of the original material must still be disposed of by other means. Vermin are also hard to control in a compost operation.

A number of schemes have been proposed, and a few are being developed, using other kinds of technology. For example, containers that dissolve in water or by the action of soil acids and sunlight are being investigated. Organic solid waste, mixed with sewage sludge, may give a highgrade composting material, provided that the pathogens can be removed. This process may also be valuable in curtailing excessive use of nitrogen, and thereby slowing down the tendency toward entropy in lakes and waterways.

Home solid waste grinders, analogous to contemporary garbage grinders, have been proposed. These larger and more rugged units might handle objects of paper, glass, plastics and light metal up to a cubic foot or more in size. After grinding, the material would be disposed of through sewer systems.

The Japanese have built large compactors to reduce solid waste to high-density blocks, which are then encased in an asphalt sealer and used for building foundations and other construction purposes. The city of Cleveland is also experimenting with a similar technique, using a mixture of solid waste, fly ash, dried sewage sludge, river and lake dredgings, and incinerator residue made into small, compact bricks for use as fill material to reclaim submerged lands adjacent to Lake Erie.

Paper products make up the largest percentage of most domestic solid waste. Since paper is nearly all cellulose, and since ruminants (cattle) can digest cellulose and turn it into protein, a number of public and private groups are experimenting with the use of paper products, supplemented with vitamins and minerals, as cattle feed. Today's newspaper may be tomorrow's steak. Power production from incinerated solid waste has also been proposed. Milan, Italy, will soon be running all of its streetcars and subways by electricity generated by incinerated solid waste. Similar attempts in this country have been less successful, however, because of the inconsistent quality of the refuse to be incinerated and the production of electricity by other, hitherto less expensive means.

Other ideas have been put forward, such as adding hydrogen to wastepaper to make a high-grade fuel. Sanitary land-fill techniques along the sides of highways, power lines, sewer interceptors and other public rights of way have also been suggested. Such innovations have met with little enthusiasm, however, due to economic factors, entrenched procedures and lack of organized promotion campaigns.

The annual sum spent on solid waste collection and disposal in this country is large in comparison with other services. The annual cost of refuse collection and disposal, according to a recent federal document, is estimated at more than $4.5 billion, an amount that is exceeded only by schools and roads among public services. An estimated additional $750 million will have to be spent each year over the next five years to bring the collection and disposal systems of the nation to an acceptable health and aesthetic level.

The figures show only how much we have extracted from our natural environment, used briefly, and discarded permanently. They tell nothing about the supply of metals, pulp and other resources still left in the natural environment, that we will use once and discard. Will we run out of resources before we choke on our own midden?

We can no longer treat solid waste as something to be shoved so far away that we'll never see it. There just isn't anywhere left to put it. We must learn to treat solid waste as a fact of life, and learn how to live with it, as we have learned to live with, or at least tolerate, sewers, automobiles, manufacturing plants and all other aspects of our modern age.

It should also be realized that our traditional attitude toward solid waste disposal is untenable in view of further environmental deterioration. This attitude can be characterized by the phrase "symptom-chasing." The disposal problem will not be solved by improving procedural techniques: it can only be postponed for a few years at best. The ultimate goal of refuse disposal—or any pollution control—is 100 per cent recycling of materials and energy. Advanced refuse recycling systems for urban areas are in the distant future; for the countryside they are even further away.

The problem can be viewed from another perspective. To control the effluent of our affluent society one must understand and rectify the causes in human behavior, and not just the symptoms. If a man has a brain tumor we would hardly expect his total treatment to be an aspirin. We must somehow convince the refuse makers—both the producers and the consumer-users (that means all of us)—that our overpackaged, overstuffed, throw-away lifestyle will bring long-term ecological and economic disaster. We probably will not much longer have the luxury of making decisions that will affect the ecosystem, as nearly all decisions ultimately do, based solely on economic and political expediency.

It is comparatively simple to write about solid waste practices and to recommend certain changes and improvements. It would be infinitely more difficult—but much more to the point—to study ways of drastically reducing solid waste effluent. And we must recognize that our solid waste situation, as well as our larger environment, can be improved only by self-imposed restraints.

21 / NADER:
NO VICTIMIZATION WITHOUT
REPRESENTATION

Leonard Schecter

There are tiny, curled gray hairs at the back of his neck. And his face, animated, dominated by those immense dark eyes, has

From *Intellectual Digest*, Vol. III, No. 1, September 1972. Copyright © 1972 by Communication/Research/Machines, Inc. Reprinted by permission.

taken on some of the firming lines that signal the surreptitious departure of youth. His hands are too large to have slipped through the buttoned white shirt cuffs, too much of which are revealed below the sleeves of his navy blue suit. His shoes, black, heavy, plain-toed, serviceable, are on the edge of needing a shine and his socks droop unfashionably—and somehow predictably. Just as predictable is the clutter and metal-shelved Spartanism of his third-floor walk-up office on 19th St. NW in Washington. Well, it's not really his office. It's the office of Ted Jacobs, one of his bustling disciples, and Ralph Nader, who doesn't have an office, uses it from time to time. He sits on a metal chair on the wrong side of the desk, pink phone messages accumulating at an astonishing rate from the moment he says he will not take any calls for a while. He is bigger somehow than he appears in photographs, more bear than hawk, conveying an odd mixture of impatience and dedication to being understood. . . .

Q: Given, let us say, ultimate success in your endeavours by 1976, our 200th anniversary, what will our nation be like?

Nader: Women will no longer be wearing cosmetics. We'll have ended the high priority we put on that kind of activity.

(Nader has been watching Susan Lombardo, who is taking pictures for ID. She is young and fresh faced. He was rather pleased with his remark, and one guesses that it will be incorporated in the Nader litany, taking its place with "energy crisis" and "time crisis" and "base lines for a whole conglomerate of problems.")

Nuclear power is a problem. Why? Because we need more power for air conditioning. We need air conditioning because our cities are polluted and the wind can't blow through them. More growth means more emphasis on material goods, which means more pollution, more demand for air conditioning, more demand for power. That has to change. There must be more emphasis on services than on goods. Health services, cultural, educational, democratic government services. There has to be a new ethic that can replace economic growth and still lead to full employment and better distribution of wealth and income.

Q: That all?

Nader: No. Government. There has to be a change there. We have to move toward a more sophisticated form of self-government. Citizens have delegated more and more power to governments. Now we need a new politics, a *wave* of citizen action. You can't rely on giant government agencies to do the job for the people. What citizen, for example, can challenge the Port of New York Authority? Government has become immune to its citizens.

So there has to be a challenge function. And there is one. At least there's a trend toward it. That's what civil rights means. That's the real New Federalism. That's what revenue sharing is about. In 1776 the cry was no taxation without representation. We can still make the same cry. No victimization without representation. The fact of victimization gives the citizen rights. Victims of pollution have the right, ipso facto, to sue. The same is true of any government bureau. You have a whole panoply of rights. But there are no rights if you don't avail yourself of them. You have to use these rights. But what if you can't afford to go into court? So then, every person should have the right to have a lawyer, just as in criminal cases if you can't afford a lawyer you are provided with one. The trouble is that while we all have rights, only corporations have lawyers. Up to now.

Q: Anything else?

Nader: Yes. Contamination. Those who contaminate the environment should be treated the same way we would treat somebody who sold contaminated food. *We* are the environment. Contaminate the environment and you contaminate the individual. That's a crime.

And speaking of crime, there is, I believe, a corporate crime wave. Pollution is a crime. Deceptive sales practices are a crime. Price-fixing is a crime. Bribing politicians is a crime. Serious occupational hazards are a crime. Cheating consumers by putting certain additives in their food is a crime. Stuffing hot dogs with fats is a crime. There comes a point when waste is a crime. There is waste in defense. There are subsidies to industries and businesses that don't need it or deserve it. Government agencies violate their own regulations. There is a refusal to enforce pesticide laws. General Motors says there is nothing wrong with the motor mounts on seven million cars and then recalls them. Then they say that a broken motor mount can be dealt with as easily as a flat tire. And what's the penalty? I call this crime in the suites. We need to have more even-handed application of the law. If corporate executives were tried, convicted and sent to jail—well, at the very least it would improve our jails.

Q: All right. An interesting vision. Pragmatically, though, what are our chances of getting there by 1976, or 1984 or 2000?

Nader: I don't know. There are too many factors you can't predict. I do think, though, that people will develop a sense of injustice.

Q: Is it possible though, whatever our sense of justice and no matter how highly it is aroused, that the implementation of your vision will lead to an even more elephantine government bureaucracy, and to less and less freedom for the individuals?

Nader: There are two kinds of freedom, freedom from and freedom to. The freedom to is the freedom toward greater control by the citizen. That's what the civil rights movement is. The freedom to depends on leadership, grass-roots leadership. The people who defeated the detergent lobby in Miami defeated Procter & Gamble. Who were they? Elderly retired people. We didn't know leadership could come from them. The trouble is that there are no farm clubs for leadership in this country. And that's what we're trying to do. Get retired people. Get student activity groups. Students are assessing themselves $3 a year and hiring people to represent them.

All occupations require expertise. But who works on citizenship? Now citizens are beginning to say "How?" They're saying "What can we do?" They're saying "How do you develop a strategy of political action?"

Well, take pollution.

One. Find out who's affected by the pollution.

Two. Find out who can help, who has the skills, the time.

Three. Analyze the corporation involved and their problem. How much will it cost to correct? Can they afford it?

Four. What about the union? Can you enlist their help?

Five. What about whistle blowers inside the company?

Six. Think about opening up a new front. Maybe the company isn't paying its fair share of taxes. Make it a *cause célèbre*. Keep it building. It becomes a science.

The civil rights movement developed a lot of these techniques, but what we need now are full-time citizens. There is some $17 billion donated each year to traditional charities. Now we need a new charity; we need a charity to support these full-time professional citizens. We had a pilot program in Connecticut that raised $50,000 in nickels and dimes from three-quarters of a million people. The leverage is enormous when truth and right are on your side.

Q: What else?

Nader: We have hearing-aid frauds. With one office and one lawyer we could clear them up in four years. We have to redeploy our professional manpower, appeal to the desire to escape boredom. The people who play bridge, watch television, go to football games, could be doing important work. They have professional skills. There is a great deal of manpower out there. Retired people, people with too much leisure, students, young people.

Q: Do you think this was an idea whose time had come or, modesty aside please, it all happened because of R. Nader?

Nader: I think I was an important factor. The really important thing is the knowledge that you *can* take on General Motors. You see, we've always had defense lawyers. We now have to develop offense lawyers.

Q: You are the latest in a line of respected American muckrakers. . . .

Nader: Yes. But most of them, maybe all of them, were writers. They wrote and let other people take action.

Q: Correct. You are more of an activist than other muckrakers. But my question was going to be whether it has struck you that our muckrakers don't come from the newspaper business as one would expect?

Nader: Muckrakers have no place to go on newspapers. They leave. They write books. As publishing action groups develop, there will be room for them. Until then, they are like fish out of water.

Q: Are you planning to look into the American newspaper business?

Nader: We're looking into freedom of information.

Q: Where do you stand politically?

Nader: You mean whether I'm a Republican or a Democrat?

Q: No. But in the reality of politics you must have found a comfortable place.

Nader: I'm an activist. And I believe in the rejection of ideology. Ideology is a crutch. It stops people from thinking. I don't know what the best system is. The best system is what grows out of citizens' activity. The most fundamental reforms are those that grow out of people's needs and desires. Laws that are not supported by people don't work. Suppose we passed a law against phosphate detergent. If people didn't agree with it, they would bootleg the detergent as they bootlegged whiskey during prohibition. But if people understand that phosphate detergent is bad, it will be an effective law.

Q: Possibly the most serious criticism leveled against you is that you behave like the FBI. If somebody doesn't agree with you, you investigate him. An example would be the AAA in the air bag controversy. Because they didn't agree with you about the air bags, you put a task force on them.

Nader: If that were true, we'd be investigating everybody in the country. The fact is that we started looking into the American Automobile Association long before the air bag became an issue. I have been criticizing the AAA since the year one. It's a good example of what happens if members don't take part in an organization.

Q: The next most serious, if that's the word, is that you have become scattergun, making a great many charges but accomplishing very little.

Nader: Anytime anybody says that, I ask if he has read our reports. There is always an embarrassing silence. No, the reports haven't been read. They are available but unread. The fact is they are detailed and intense. The very opposite of scattergun.

Q: Again, in the same area, the charge is that you have learned to manipulate public opinion but that outside of real changes in the automobile industry, you have not accomplished much at all.

Nader: Influencing public opinion is not an option. The first step *is* to influence public opinion. In any case, we've been in operation a half decade as opposed to how long these things really take to change. We're developing an ability to litigate. We've had great impact in many areas. Automobiles. Nutrition. Environment. It's all had a great penumbra effect. Take the milk thing.

(As a "consumer of milk," Nader brought suit in the U.S. District Court, alleging that in return for campaign donations of $322,500, the Nixon Administration had illegally increased the Federal price support level for milk. The U.S. District Court dismissed the suit. It is pending before the Court of Appeals.)

The best part of it is the part you can't see. It's the part that now a lot of officials will say, "We can't do that. We'll get caught." That's the penumbra effect. The real witnesses of how effective this is won't say. Still, I must admit we've only scratched the surface. For the year ending last June we had a budget of just a million dollars. That's 20 minutes of gross revenue to General Motors. In May of 1963 there was one person with me. Now we have 39 or 40. It's a lot by comparison, but obviously far from an enormous organization.

Q: The intemperate language in your reports is often stronger than the research.

Nader: To the contrary. The reports are deliberately understated. If we talk about gross injustice, criminal activity such as price-fixing, it's only because these are accurate terms. We don't use words like "fascist pigs."

(As time goes by, Nader gets increasingly edgy. He seems to be sliding off his little metal folding chair into space. There are more questions, but they will hold, I say, until we are on the way to the airport. That's in something less than an hour. Two hours later, Nader strides very purposefully toward a cab, leaning forward as though battling a wind. After he tells the driver that he should be able to make the airport in 12 minutes, we talk again.)

Q: Aren't you really aiming at public ownership and operation?

Nader: No. TVA is owned by the people and it behaves like a giant corporation. Even a cooperative that starts out democratically can end up like Lumbermens Mutual. The bureaucracy has a vested interest of its own. Once you have the Post Office there is no way out. Private industry can be kept in line through the courts. But will the Justice Department sue the TVA? So the question is, where is the potential greater? I don't think it's in public ownership.

Q: Outside of bringing General Motors to its knees, what do you consider your greatest accomplishment?

Nader: The public-interest lawyer role. Lawyers without clients. It's now accepted that there are such lawyers and that they do act in the public interest. There are probably about 150 of them and I think the numbers will grow geometrically rather than arithmetically.

Q: I get the feeling that there will come a time when you can consider politics as a viable career. Is that true?

Nader: It's very, very doubtful. Most people can't work outside of an institution. I can. And what we're trying to do is develop more noninstitutional sources of power. So I can't see myself going into an institution. I'm more comfortable pushing against them than supporting them.

Q: Still, it would be fun to see you leaning on the Senate from the inside.

Nader: As long as change depends on personality, it will be temporary. The idea is to make laws that can't be rewritten. You can't rewrite *Brown* v. *Board of Education*. At least not easily. Eventually the changes will be internalized. But if you have nobody outside pushing, nobody inside will be interested in changing. Let's assume John Lindsay wanted to do a good job as mayor. What could he do? He's in a jungle. But suppose he had a 300-man law firm working for him. And real newspapers. It would be a different ball game. Do you expect bureaucracy to monitor bureaucracy? It's a tribute to our institutions that they're not any worse than they are.

Q: Where do you think you'll be in 1976?

Nader: Same place, doing the same thing.

The cab pulls up at National Airlines and Nader leaps out. He is still leaning against the wind. He has only minutes to catch his plane. I am happy to pay the cab fare. It's the least I can do.

22 / THE "HEALTHIEST NATION" MYTH

Abraham Ribicoff

About two years ago the wife of a forty-three-year-old house painter in Alabama was hospitalized for cancer of the cervix and colon while pregnant with the couple's fifth child. Over an eighteen-month period she had several major operations, round-the-clock nurses, and heavy dosages of expensive drugs, but she died. Her husband was left with a $30,000 medical bill, of which only $9,000 was covered by insurance.

Ruinous medical bills like this are only one example of what is wrong with American health care. (If the painter had lived in Sweden, which has national health insurance, his wife's hospital bill would have been $1.40 a day, doctors' visits would have cost $1.35 each, and drugs, if not free, would have been provided at minimal cost.) Another is that this woman was among 100,000 Americans who die of cancer each year who might be saved by earlier or better care.

There are serious and growing defects in American medicine. They range from shameful efforts at prevention—in which the patient is partly at fault—to a lack of manpower, equipment, and facilities, in which the patient clearly is a victim. From the patient's standpoint this translates to a fear that he will not find a doctor in an emergency, that he will receive inferior care, and that his rights as a consumer will be ignored by physicians and other health professionals. (A Harris poll showed that 64 per cent of the public—nearly seven of every ten people—believed that "most doctors don't want you to bother them.")

These fears are well founded; many Americans, even when they can pay, cannot find a doctor. This shortage is due basically to the "professional birth control" the American Medical Association practiced in the 1930s and, more recently, to the development

From *Saturday Review*, August 22, 1970. Copyright © 1970 by Abraham Ribicoff. Reprinted by permission.

of specialists and the tendency of doctors to pursue careers in teaching, research, industry, and public health instead of patient care. Those who can't find a doctor generally descend on already overburdened hospital emergency rooms, with the result that only one-third of the people waiting there for care are true emergency cases.

Those physicians we do have are distributed unevenly throughout the country and not necessarily according to need. A 1965 survey of 1,500 cities and towns in the upper Midwest showed that 1,000 had no doctor at all and 200 had only one. Highly populated areas have their problems as well. In Rochester, New York, the Monroe County Medical Society receives thirty to fifty calls every day from people looking for a doctor, according to Medical Society officials who testified during my 1968 Senate hearings on health care.

Yet, this year alone, medical schools turned down 15,000 well-qualified students who wanted places in freshman classes. There was only enough space for 10,000. That is an involuntary rejection rate of three of every five applicants, a loss this country cannot afford. And medical schools face such severe financial problems that forty-three of 107 in the U.S. received "financial distress" grants from the government. At the same time, cutbacks in federal funds have limited construction money to one of every four potential new medical schools this year.

The best the government's efforts for fiscal 1969 and 1970 will do is produce—by 1975 at the earliest—another 1,600 physicians, an increase of slightly more than one-half of 1 per cent in the current physician population. In the meantime, as health coverage expands, the demand for more doctors will automatically increase. Unless the country is willing to provide significant incentives to correct the poor geographic distribution of physicians, the situation can only worsen for certain groups in the population. The picture would be even darker were it not for foreign medical graduates, who comprise 14 per cent of the nation's active physicians and 28 per cent of its interns and residents.

Specialized hospital expertise also is distributed unevenly. A 1967 report of the President's Commission on Heart Disease, Cancer, and Stroke surveyed the 777 U.S. hospitals equipped to perform open-heart surgery. Such operations are complicated and demanding, with constantly changing procedures that require frequent use and a well-trained staff. Nonetheless, a full one-third of the hospitals surveyed by the commission had no open-heart surgery cases that year, more than 60 per cent had fewer than one a week, and 30 per cent had fewer than one a month.

Nor are hospital medical practice standards in general what they should be. The scandal of publicly owned hospitals has been well documented by young interns and residents, forcing the Joint Commission on the Accreditation of Hospitals to strip some large-city hospitals of their already minimal levels of accreditation and to threaten others with similar action. Also, physicians in voluntary, nonprofit hospitals admit privately that they cut too many corners and take too many chances with the lives and safety of patients.

There are stories of heart attack patients placed in halls near nurses' stations when cardiac units are full, of hospitals failing to separate infectious gynecological patients from obstetrics areas containing newborn infants, and special emergency units that function without any blood bank and that provide X-ray service only between 8 a.m. and 4 p.m. and not on weekends at all. It is impossible to ignore the warning from the chief of medicine at one of New York City's public hospitals: "You come to this hospital, and we're telling you somebody's going to take care of you. The fact is, you're going to lie in a pool of feces, develop an ulcer, septicemia [blood poisoning], and perhaps ultimately die because of inadequate nursing care."

The poor have known for years that medical care was expensive, hard to get, and uneven in quality. So has much of rural and small-town America. Now the urban middle class, which must receive its care from the same poorly organized system, is learning all this, too. Although high costs have hit harder than any other problem so far, the American middle class is beginning to understand that poor organization also can result in death or disability.

Obstetricians and pediatricians at one major teaching hospital insist that many infant deaths and cases of brain damage and blood disease could be prevented if communities devised better systems of identifying women who were "high-risk" pregnancies. What troubles these physicians is that such cases often are identifiable, the risk to the mother and child predictable, the treatment known, and the resources available.

Meanwhile, some individuals still contend that the medical

crisis in this country is exaggerated and overblown, that the doctor shortage is not severe, and that many communities without doctors may be even healthier than those with doctors. But none of those individuals who argue this position is willing to live in a community without doctors. They point out that our finest medical care is second to none and that people from other countries come here for open-heart surgery as well as for complex brain and eye operations. But the shocking truth is that in too many instances it doesn't even extend beyond their own doorstep to the approximately twenty million Americans who receive inadequate care or no care at all.

Defenders of American medical care also argue that the Swedish system, good though it may seem, is not as cheap as it appears: The Swedish citizen pays 20 per cent of his taxes—the highest in the world—for health. Even so, Sweden still devotes 1 per cent *less* of its Gross National Product and $45 *less* per person for health than does the United States.

If cost were any indication of quality, then America would be the healthiest nation in recorded history. We spend more money on health and medical care than any other people in the world: $63-billion a year, 6.7 per cent of our Gross National Product, $294 per person. No other country can match any of these figures.

But a dozen nations, each of which spends less per country and per person, can match us and do a better job of preventing infant deaths. Twelve nations also have a lower maternal mortality rate. In seventeen countries, men live longer than in the United States. Women have a better chance of surviving in ten other countries. And the percentage of men who will die between the ages of forty and fifty is less in seventeen other nations. Obviously, we are not the healthiest nation in the world. We are not even close. Personal habits, life-styles, education, income, genetics, and physical and social environment have combined, along with medical care deficiencies, to produce the data that destroy this myth.

Medical care may play only a secondary role in these world rankings (although the countries that come out on top, such as Sweden, also have good and inexpensive medical care). Public health officials often contend they could do more for the nation's health by getting rid of the slums and ending pollution than by making sure everybody has a thorough physical exam once a year.

Rank	Country	Infant mortality per 1,000 births
	INFANT MORTALITY FIFTEEN COUNTRIES	
1	Sweden	12.9
2	Netherlands	13.4
3	Finland	14.2
4	Norway	14.6
5	Japan	15.0
6	Denmark	15.8
7	Switzerland	17.5
8	New Zealand	18.0
9	Australia	18.3
10	Britain	18.8
11	France	20.6
12	East Germany	21.2
13	Canada	22.0
14	United States	22.1
15	West Germany	22.8

Source: U. N., U. S. Dept. of Health, Education and Welfare

Early death, they say, seems related more to income and life-style than to medical care. And although infant mortality occurs mostly among poor blacks, who often do not see a doctor, a recent California study found that whites with regular medical care do not have that state's lowest infant death rate. Japanese-Americans do. In fact, they outrank whites on every index of good health.

But none of these considerations should obscure or minimize the point that when most Americans speak of health they mean medical care, because that is what the $63-billion is supposed to buy. Nor can we minimize the fact that health costs continue to rise out of proportion to other prices, and that few signs of relief are visible on the manpower horizon. Just five years ago the national health bill was a fraction of today's $63-billion figure—$37-billion. Rough estimates predict that it will reach $100-billion in the next five years and may even double and reach $200-billion in the early 1980s.

If current trends continue, the major share of that increase—

47 per cent in the past—will be due to rising prices caused by inflation, technology, long-overdue wage increases for hospital employees from nurses to kitchen workers, and just plain higher charges. Thirty-five per cent will come from more services provided per person, and 18 per cent from population increases. Hospital charges, which doubled between 1956 and 1966, already have gone up another 50 per cent in the last three years. Doctors' fees during the 1960s rose twice as fast as the general cost of living, with the biggest boost coming since the advent of Medicare.

A reliable prediction—one that a health economist would stand by—is not available. Too many political uncertainties cloud the picture. But no special wisdom is needed to understand that unless efficiencies and controls are adopted, the cost of health care will skyrocket out of sight. Reliable predictions of medical manpower needs also depend upon basic decisions the country makes regarding the organization, financing, and delivery of medical care. But all the evidence suggests that manpower shortages will continue.

This, then, is where we stand today: high costs, not enough doctors, nurses, or other health professionals, too many people receiving poor care or no care at all, inadequate health insurance, and most medical care organized and operated in a manner that rewards inefficiencies and perpetuates inequities. All that keeps the medical care system afloat, as Dr. John Knowles suggested at my 1968 hearings, is the fact that millions literally have no knowledge of their medical needs.

Thus, when one large metropolitan hospital recently gave medical examinations in a ghetto junior high school, 20 per cent of the students were found to have hearing and sight problems. Because nobody had ever examined them before, many had spent half their public school lives in schools for the retarded.

The same type of problem shows up again when eye examinations are given suburban children. The National Center for Health Statistics estimated that in 1967 nearly half the people in this country had at least one chronic disease or impairment.

Why should these conditions exist? Why should medical care be on the verge of collapse for so many Americans?

One compelling reason was contained in a letter last fall from the Department of Health, Education and Welfare. I had asked how each of the twenty-four departments and agencies that spend the government's $20.6-billion health budget contributed to the formulation and implementation of the national health policy. With refreshing candor, HEW answered: "Up to and including the present there has never been a formulation of national health policy as such. In addition, no specific mechanism has been set up to carry out this function."

That in itself is an intolerable situation. If there is no policy, there can be no goals. If there are no goals, there can be no strategies. This is what we have today, and the result is that medical care, instead of being a public responsibility, is a private business. It is operated more for the convenience of its practitioners than according to the needs of the sick.

Washington's $20.6-billion health budget is one-third the money the United States spends on health. Clearly, the government has both the potential and the responsibility to spend its money as a lever for improvements in manpower, organization, and efficiency in addition to whatever action is taken on national health insurance.

If Washington does not assure all Americans access to adequate medical care at a cost they can afford, with enough manpower to meet their needs, then who will? If Washington does not act, then the best advice anyone can offer is this: Get sick today; don't wait five years.

B. SOCIAL PROTESTS

23 / MY HARD HAT PROBLEM AND YOURS

Thomas Williams

To come to New York from New Hampshire, where the apple trees were blooming in my own yard, was in itself an almost debilitating shock. The human race is adaptable, as we have all been told, but the impression that still hasn't left me is that New York City is not fit for human habitation. As Mickey Hayes, a crane operator, later told me, "You don't live here—you exist. You got to work here because it's where the money is, but it's not living." The Mohawks and other Indians who work on the high steel, for instance, go home every weekend—some to Caughnawaga on the St. Lawrence, in Canada—a matter of a fearsome seven-hour drive each way.

The building project on the site of the old Astor Hotel is called One Astor Plaza, and will have "New York's Newest, Most Luxurious Motion Picture Theatre and New York Executive Offices of The Walter Reade Organization Inc." Its fifty-four stories will also house many other companies, one on top of the other, and real people will come there, enter luxurious little boxes and be zapped by engines and cables up and down. One Astor Plaza is "The Crossroads of the World"; between Forty-fourth and Forty-fifth on Broadway, an area of mad destruction and madder construction. I found myself staring up at the building's insane verticalities, realizing that all that brutal energy was being expended on

From *Esquire*, October 1970. Copyright 1970 by Thomas Williams; reprinted by permission of Harold Matson Company, Inc.

impermanence. It was all I beams, trusses and open floors, going up forever beyond sanity, into the realm of frozen, screaming vertigo, but at street level an architect's picture of the finished building revealed that it would be decorated by fin-like projections as shoddily fashionable as those on a 1958 Chrysler. It was all process, noise, dust. I thought, too, of a hive of wasps in late summer, when the queen goes mad or dies, and the workers, build insanely, without plan, while the center rots and the hive itself grows outward in grandiose but useless bulges and tumors.

On the street the noises succeeded themselves in variation and intensity—compressor engines, jackhammers, trucks, whistles, horns, the brazen gong of hammered steel that does something to the base of the spine. On the next block, battering rams turned masonry into curves before the bricks fell five stories, spreading huge spinnakers of yellow dust. It is an assault that goes too deep. Everything was shooting up, plummeting down. There was no level, no calm horizon. It was a world in which the perpendicular had ran amok. Fragile men hoisted, on thin cables, steel of such horrendous tonnage that in the mind tender things seemed to bend and softly snap. On the island of the metallic and gaseous avenue a young black man stood shaking with rage, his arms flailing out in oratorical paroxysms, his mouth moving as he screamed his arguments at everything in general—but no sound came out of his mouth. Who needed more sound? After a glance or two he was ignored by everybody who passed.

But the assault on the senses came from everywhere; a girl who sold ice cream from a cart regarded her customers with languorous, stoned beatitude, her hands moving always in slow motion. A blind man with a sign, "Do You Thank God That You Can See?", moved slowly along, shaking his tin cup and smiling gratefully—grateful in every direction, to everybody out there in the light. The movie, *Patton*, was playing at the Criterion; at the Park-Miller Theatre around the corner the bill was, "Male Film Festival—Pledge of Flesh—Male Nude Shorts." On the corner a girl with the head, literally, of an ape handed out leaflets advertising a movie called *Beneath the Planet of the Apes*. A woman at least sixty-five years old minced by in mini-skirt, eye paint of the deepest cerulean, a bouffant blonde wig, pancake makeup over the surface of the moon. She smiled too, constantly; she seemed so wonderfully pleased by life, by her believed appearance of desirability and youth. Many people passed along mumbling or cursing to themselves. I swear I saw a man who had no mouth, or at least I couldn't tell which tortured convolution of his face was his real mouth. And there were hookers, mod pimps, nodders, hippies, soldiers, sly window-shoppers at the porno shops, small, brown-suited, squashed-looking businessmen you thought must sell something vaguely undignified, like urinal deodorant cakes. A well-dressed man in a straw hat stared avidly up at the bulging masonry of the building being destroyed. And for the nose and lungs there was the one greeting, all others being mere variations, and it was the exhaust gas of a million internal-combustion engines.

As I stood in this pandemonium, waiting for the construction workers' lunch break, across Broadway the huge American flag at about the seventh-story level of One Astor Plaza proclaimed . . . something. I was beginning to find out, I think, just what it meant to the men who had chipped in to buy it, who had strung it up there on the steel.

When photographer Bruce Davidson and I had first approached the building, before we knew what our reception would be, I admit to having been in a precarious emotional state. For weeks I had been involved with the students of the University of New Hampshire in the agonies following Cambodia and Kent State—a time of violently alternating emotions that included admiration, fear, love, and for my state and country the nearest I have ever been in my life to total despair. There had been one bad moment when, looking at a blooming apple tree, I was so struck by its mortality, its sure sentence of death by civilization, that I could hardly stand my life.

And now, for reasons I must have had once but could not put together, I was here at "The Crossroads of the World," being assaulted by all the shoddy, polluting impermanence and rot that I feared most, about to have to speak to its doers and makers—a social force that had been represented to me by every source of news as brutal, murderous, know-nothing, war-loving. I was afraid. Not physically afraid; the myth of physical bravery's worth is one of the deepest delusions of mankind. My fear was of confrontation, of psychic violence. My hold upon the idea of man's possible grace is desperate, a juggling act that I continue for the sake of my life.

But we went in, and in the days that followed I talked to many construction workers, at One Astor Plaza, at the gigantic World Trade Center, at projects near Wall Street—to maybe thirty or forty of these men, nearly all with flag decals on their hard hats and flag pins on their shirts. And I suppose I should have known that I would find, not a monolithic force, but complicated men. There was Tommy Galligan, Mickey Hayes (whom they sometimes call "Doc," because he delivered three of his kids himself), John Howard, Lenny Flocco, Bill McLaughlin, Paul Smith, Jimo McKee, Vince Kenny, Mike Rizzo. I should have known because I was once a laborer myself, and quite suddenly remembered the complicated relationships among men who work together. Who was the joker, the buffoon, the apparent leader and the real leader, the quiet, the witty and the loud? It might have been twenty years ago, when I, too, safe in the authority of my work clothes, dirt and sweat, spoke to all the pretty girls who passed, and laughed at all the jokes concerning the job and its characters—wit that through constant variation and refinement becomes economical and sharp.

I talked a lot with Mike Rizzo, who at first came on pretty strong. He is forty-six, has a daughter in high school and a son in the eighth grade. He lives in the Bronx, is a veteran of the 11th Airborne, with one combat jump and two battle stars. He has a dark, weather-cured face the texture of a walnut, and his job is to place in position the steel reinforcing rods before the cement floors are poured.

"If I saw my son carrying a Vietcong flag," he said fiercely, "I'd shoot him myself!"

I said I could hardly believe that.

"All right. Maybe you're right. But my son wouldn't do a thing like that!" His voice grew tighter, exasperated and horrified. "Listen, you know what they did to the flag down there? Some of the guys had a flag up there and these longhair freaks tore it down. I wasn't there, but I heard they *pissed on the flag!* You now know what I mean? I mean those guys were *provoked!* Could you stand there and watch that happen? I'd kill the son of a bitch I saw doing that, I don't care who!"

I said I didn't go along with that kind of put-on, either, mainly because it was stupid. The workers themselves are experts at the put-on; their banter, whether at work or at play, always strikes very delicately near, but not too near, the place where it could hurt. It is a kind of controlled strutting, not vicious, or at least hardly ever vicious, of one's manhood and individuality. They are proud of their work, and of its dangers, but it is essentially repetitious work, and in their conversation they have time to perfect their humor. When they see a young punk blowing his nose in the flag, for instance, they see not only an astounding irreverence, but a crude put-on that breaks other taboos, and the violator is immediately alien, unhuman, expendable.

Over and over, conversation came back to the flag, and I suppose it became obvious to Mike, to Tommy and the others that I didn't vibrate exactly the way they did at the idea of its desecration. Even so, I felt a little guilty at my reticence, because I came to like them all.

A day or so later, after Mike had got across his anger—and to threaten to kill your own son is a gesture, even if only a gesture, that had better be taken seriously—I came to get a sense of his anguish as a man in his society. He used to work with a black, and he came back to this again and again. In many workers I found this preoccupation. He told me how, in an urban-renewal project he worked on, black people had destroyed things, and how the black he had worked with said, himself, bad things about his own race. The exclusiveness of his union in racial matters is there, and it is a touchy subject. They know that in this country the blacks have a gripe, and it is a gripe they can understand.

And even the Church is changing, Mike said, and he's unsure of his place there. His children seem smarter than he was, in some ways, but maybe they got it from television, and they don't *do* anything, they just sit around. Even out on the street they just stand around and don't do anything. He played stickball, kick-the-can, ring-a-levio, swam in the East River. There were parts of the city then that were green and safe. He didn't vote for Richard Nixon; he's a Democrat. But you've got to respect the *office* of the President. And the flag—what else is there but the flag? He's worried about his children getting hooked on drugs. There's no respect for anything anymore. "But you got to respect something! You got to!"

I had the sense that in Mike's desperation he was ready to ask anyone for answers, even me because I represented *Esquire*, and was thus near some kind of power. I felt that I was hearing my own desperation coming back to me in entirely different terms, but mine, exactly mine.

I was told again and again that the construction workers were not pro-war. "Who's pro-war? You'd have to be a nut to be pro-war!" Tommy Galligan said. They resent very much being simplified by the press in this fashion, as they were, for instance, in a New York *Times* editorial. They have their own subtle distinctions, and they don't want to be summed up and slandered by the press any more than the Black Panthers do. I was shown several times the June 1 copy of *Time* magazine, which said that all the workers who marched were on full pay. They told me that a few were, like shop stewards and some others, but that most of those who marched—eighty-five to ninety per cent of the men—were not paid that day.

I was told by them again and again that they're not against demonstrations, that they're not against the students. What they are finding out, I hope, is that quick and superficial press and television reports are nearly always lies, and that there is no lie like a half lie. They are summarized by those picturesquely violent "hard hats" who make the news. Because some students threw things out of the window of Pace College does not excuse those workers who threw things down from the steel at the peace marchers. Everyone is tarred by the same brush. After the anger over the students' having burned buildings (the construction workers, after all, *build* buildings), and after the horror of seeing the flag desecrated, there is no pride in the violence—that there had to be violence. But it is necessary to talk for a while, for more than one day, to reach below the first blast of indignation to where the truth is. Face to face, after a while, one can hear and understand.

Of course they suffer their own broad misconceptions. For instance, John Howard, an engineer who has a son at St. John's University, referred to the radical left—such as the S.D.S. and Yippies —as "liberals." When I said that these people called themselves radicals and hated liberals, he was amazed. He thought the term "radical" was a bad name "we" had pinned on them, like calling the N.L.F. "Vietcong"—something they didn't call themselves. And then, too, there is an old right-wing definition of liberal that comes from one of its secondary meanings in the dictionary, and is more like "libertine." I think of Bobby Seale in Chicago, trying to get Judge Hoffman to understand that the clenched-fist "Power to the People" sign was not a "Black Power" sign, and being gagged for his insistence upon the right of a man to make his own subtleties and distinctions. When we are not allowed this right, we can be manipulated and used against each other.

One worker at One Astor Plaza, an oiler, told me that Bethlehem Steel, which was in charge of the construction, had warned the men about Esquire and about talking to me. And even before that, Tommy Galligan was very suspicious that this would be "a hatchet job"—and I'm afraid I can't blame him. I was asked several times why Esquire wanted to do a piece on the construction workers in the first place, and I said one reason was that Peter Brennan, head of the Building and Construction Trades Council of Greater New York, had told the President in Washington that there would be more patriotic marches by construction workers. This was at the ceremony when Nixon was presented with a hard hat. So, I said, construction workers would remain in the news.

"*Who* said that?"

"Peter Brennan," I said.

"Huh!" This was from a shop steward, and it was clear that no matter how much he agreed with the march of May 20, he didn't much like being made the object of anybody's predictions, not even Mr. Peter Brennan's.

These are, after all, strong men, and nobody owns them. After I'd known Tommy Galligan for a few days he came up to me and pretended to punch me in the gut—a primal gesture of trust that I found moving. He is the one mainly responsible for the huge flag on the steel of One Astor Plaza. He collected the donations from the men (some of the Canadian Indians chipped in, too) and bought the flag. The electricians on the job gave their time to light it at night.

Tommy is thirty-seven, an operating engineer who runs a derrick, one of four that winch huge tonnages of steel to the top of the building. His union—"a good one," he says—is Local 14, International Union of Operating Engineers. He makes between seven and eight dollars an hour, and has a small but attractive apartment in the Bronx overlooking some actual trees and actual grass. He did the wood paneling around the dining alcove, and his handsome wife Pat likes to go to the Washington Square art show and buy real oil paintings. They are both intensely proud of their two children, Tommy, six, and Kerry Ann, four. A color television set dominates the living room, which is full of obviously loved art objects. A wooden plaque on the wall of the dining alcove, decorated with shamrocks, says, "An Irish toast: May you be in heaven a half hour before the devil knows you're dead." Another plaque says, "An Old Gaelic Blessing: May the roads rise with you, and the wind be always at your back; and may the Lord hold you in the hollow of His hand."

Tommy has a high-school diploma, and reads *U.S. News & World Report*, the New York *Post* (mainly, he says, for the sports), the *Daily News*, the New York *Times*, and other publications. He is a former amateur boxer and a boxing buff who thinks Muhammad Ali shouldn't have been stripped of his title until he was actually convicted of something. He is also intensely interested in football. He belongs to the Elks, Lodge 871, in the Bronx.

Pat says she is more angry than her husband at how the construction workers have been treated by the press. And again I don't know why they trusted us to come to their home; I believe that in some ways it was an act of largess, even of bravery.

Mike Rizzo, whom I got to know as well as Tommy, finally called me up and in some shame told me he didn't dare let us take pictures of his home. "If they find out where you live, get your address, some crank'll come and get you. You know what I mean? It's not like New Hampshire, Tom. You know what I mean? I mean I can't put my family in danger like that." A young cop, just that day, had been stabbed to death by a madman who came up to the patrol car, reached in, and stabbed. Mike mentioned that, too, and how it was a jungle you tried to survive in. And of course it was true; the danger was real.

Tommy showed me the police lock on his apartment door, and how it worked. It was the first one I had seen, and it was a shock, because unlike a mere bolt lock (the door had one of those, too), the police lock was an iron bar which fit in a socket in the floor and ran like a buttress to a place near the knob—at a desperate angle that suggested immediate and violent attack from outside. Over the fire-escape window was a steel lattice, locked by a big padlock. Tommy's car, while parked on the street outside, has been stolen more than once. Pat is afraid to take the subway into Manhattan, and she spoke wistfully of houses in calm suburbs. And Tommy said what Mickey Hayes, the crane operator, had said earlier, "This is where the money is. I've got to live here."

But make no mistake, he is deeply angry about disrespect for the flag. On the outside of his door is one of those Elks stickers—"Our flag—love it or leave." He is infuriated by Mayor Lindsay, especially because, at a question-and-answer period which followed a speech Lindsay made at the University of Pennsylvania, the mayor condoned the actions of those who had gone to Canada to escape the war.

"You live in this country, take what it gives you, you take your chances on fighting for it. You take your chances like everybody else!"

Tommy told me then he believes in the domino theory, and that we must get out of Indochina with honor. He believes in a possible Communist invasion of this country, and in a Communist conspiracy within it. But it is possible for me to tell him I don't believe in any of those things, not one, and he will still listen to me; I will not turn into a monster before his eyes.

Above all he wants the flag of the United States of America to be respected, to be loved and honored. It is the flag that matters most, the palpable symbol of what he wants his country to be. I believe that he is confused and made even angrier because his country is obviously not everything that it ought to be. He doesn't know how we can get out of Indochina on the terms he wants. He doesn't know how to make the city a safe and clean place to live in. But he is too intelligent to believe in the blood solutions of the fanatics. He is not a fanatic; beneath his indignation is a generous and fair-minded man.

Of course there are construction workers who are vicious, who relish violence, who would use patriotism as an excuse for the joy of stunning somebody with a pipe wrench. Neither Tommy Galligan nor anyone else, no matter how much he identifies with his own group, can deny it. Violence is too much respected in our country; sometimes I think it is only news, and perhaps our motto should be, as someone suggested, "If you don't understand it, kill it."

But let me try, and I do this in desperation, to speak to both sides here—to Mike and Tommy as well as to those who will accuse me of sentimentality toward a group they have already judged. To the latter I must say that my horror of flag-wavers of any persuasion is as deep as any man's, and before I spoke to them my preconceptions were reinforced by what I can only call sanctimony. And of course it would have been easy to do a "hatchet job." I could have observed many of their poses and possessions with the usual literate and aesthetic smirk, ending with a quite fashionable prediction of apocalypse. People always want to be told what they already think they know, even if the news is as bad as it can be.

Yes, blue-collar workers in this country could be used by the political right to end democracy. Yes, most people in this country have democracy and capitalism so mixed up in their minds they think Bethlehem Steel is part of the Bill of Rights. Most people think of the American military as G.I. Joe on the slopes of Monte Cassino, and of General George Patton as a kind of gruff, lovable Casey Stengel of combat. To many, Lieutenant Calley is only a brave soldier slandered by the "liberal" press, and Richard Nixon is the champion of the little guy. God help me, I can't deny the apocalypse altogether.

But I think that before we descend into despair we must remember that Americans are rarely proud of their prejudices, and as of right now it is still just possible for us to speak to each other without waving flags or spitting on flags. If we do talk, rather than curse or smirk, we might possibly—just possibly—reverse the statistically documented rush to extinction we are in right now, in which population growth itself will forbid the solution of any of our problems, and sheer hunger will rule. If we have, say, only thirty years left, Tommy's beloved son will die at approximately Tommy's own age—thirty-six. Such terrible news, I'm afraid, must quickly be abroad in the land, and must take precedence over whatever honor it is to win a foreign war. I saw no food growing at "The Crossroads of the World," only a blasted landscape and an atmosphere that could barely be breathed.

But a writer who has lost all hope is first silent and then quickly dead, and I found, in the likes of Mike Rizzo and Tommy Galligan—in an underlying humanity more real than any slogan or banner—the energy necessary to write these words.

24 / VIOLENCE IN CHICAGO

Walker Report

During the week of the Democratic National Convention, the Chicago police were the targets of mounting provocation by both word and act. It took the form of obscene epithets, and of rocks, sticks, bathroom tiles and even human feces hurled at police by demonstrators. Some of these acts had been planned; others were spontaneous or were themselves provoked by police action. Furthermore, the police had been put on edge by widely published threats of attempts to disrupt both the city and the Convention.

That was the nature of the provocation. The nature of the response was unrestrained and indiscriminate police violence on many occasions, particularly at night.

That violence was made all the more shocking by the fact that it was often inflicted upon persons who had broken no law, disobeyed no order, made no threat. These included peaceful demonstrators, onlookers, and large numbers of residents who were simply passing through, or happened to live in, the areas where confrontations were occurring.

Newsmen and photographers were singled out for assault, and

From The Walker Report to the National Commission on The Causes and Prevention of Violence, *Rights In Conflict*, Bantam, 1968.

their equipment deliberately damaged. Fundamental police training was ignored; and officers, when on the scene, were often unable to control their men. As one police officer put it: "What
happened didn't have anything to do with police work."

The violence reached its culmination on Wednesday night.

A report prepared by an inspector from the Los Angeles Police
Department, present as an official observer, while generally praising the police restraint he had observed in the parks during the
week, said this about the events that night:

> "There is no question but that many officers acted without
> restraint and exerted force beyond that necessary under the
> circumstances. The leadership at the point of conflict did little
> to prevent such conduct and the direct control of officers by
> first line supervisors was virtually non-existent."

He is referring to the police-crowd confrontation in front of
the Conrad Hilton Hotel. Most Americans know about it, having
seen the 17-minute sequence played and replayed on their television screens.

But most Americans do not know that the confrontation was
followed by even more brutal incidents in the Loop side streets.
Or that it had been preceded by comparable instances of indiscriminate police attacks on the North Side a few nights earlier
when demonstrators were cleared from Lincoln Park and pushed
into the streets and alleys of Old Town.

How did it start? With the emergence long before convention
week of three factors which figured significantly in the outbreak
of violence. These were: threats to the city; the city's response;
and the conditioning of Chicago police to expect that violence
against demonstrators, as against rioters, would be condoned by
city officials.

The threats to the City were varied. Provocative and inflam-
matory statements, made in connection with activities planned for
convention week, were published and widely disseminated. There
were also intelligence reports from informants.

Some of this information was absurd, like the reported plan
to contaminate the city's water supply with LSD. But some were
serious; and both were strengthened by the authorities' lack of any
mechanism for distinguishing one from the other.

The second factor—the city's response—matched, in numbers and logistics at least, the demonstrators' threats.

The city, fearful that the "leaders" would not be able to control their followers, attempted to discourage an inundation of demonstrators by not granting permits for marches and rallies and by making it quite clear that the "law" would be enforced.

Government—federal, state and local—moved to defend itself from the threats, both imaginary and real. The preparations were detailed and far ranging: from stationing firemen at each alarm box within a six block radius of the Amphitheatre to staging U.S. Army armored personnel carriers in Soldier Field under Secret Service control. Six thousand Regular Army troops in full field gear, equipped with rifles, flame throwers, and bazookas were airlifted to Chicago on Monday, August 26. About 6,000 Illinois National Guard troops had already been activated to assist the 12,000 member Chicago Police Force.

Of course, the Secret Service could never afford to ignore threats of assassination of Presidential candidates. Neither could the city, against the background of riots in 1967 and 1968, ignore the ever-present threat of ghetto riots, possibly sparked by large numbers of demonstrators, during convention week.

The third factor emerged in the city's position regarding the riots following the death of Dr. Martin Luther King and the April 27th peace march to the Civic Center in Chicago.

The police were generally credited with restraint in handling the first riots—but Mayor Daley rebuked the Superintendent of Police. While it was later modified, his widely disseminated "shoot to kill arsonists and shoot to maim looters" order undoubtedly had an effect.

The effect on police became apparent several weeks later, when they attacked demonstrators, bystanders and media representatives at a Civic Center peace march. There were published criticisms—but the city's response was to ignore the police violence.

That was the background. On August 18, 1968, the advance contingent of demonstrators arrived in Chicago and established their base, as planned, in Lincoln Park on the city's Near North Side. Throughout the week, they were joined by others—some from the Chicago area, some from states as far away as New York and California. On the weekend before the convention began, there were about 2,000 demonstrators in Lincoln Park; the crowd grew to about 10,000 by Wednesday.

There were, of course, the hippies—the long hair and love beads, the calculated unwashedness, the flagrant banners, the open lovemaking and disdain for the constraints of conventional society. In dramatic effect, both visual and vocal, these dominated a crowd whose members actually differed widely in physical appearance, in motivation, in political affiliation, in philosophy. The crowd included Yippies come to "do their thing," youngsters working for a political candidate, professional people with dissenting political views, anarchists and determined revolutionaries, motorcycle gangs, black activists, young thugs, police and secret service undercover agents. There were demonstrators waving the Viet Cong flag and the red flag of revolution and there were the simply curious who came to watch and, in many cases, became willing or unwilling participants.

To characterize the crowd, then, as entirely hippy-Yippie, entirely "New Left," entirely anarchist, or entirely youthful political dissenters is both wrong and dangerous. The stereotyping that did occur helps to explain the emotional reaction of both police and public during and after the violence that occurred.

Despite the presence of some revolutionaries, the vast majority of the demonstrators were intent on expressing by peaceful means their dissent either from society generally or from the administration's policies in Vietnam.

Most of those intending to join the major protest demonstrations scheduled during convention week did not plan to enter the Amphitheatre and disrupt the proceedings of the Democratic convention, did not plan aggressive acts of physical provocation against the authorities, and did not plan to use rallies of demonstrators to stage an assault against any person, institution, or place of business. But while it is clear that most of the protesters in Chicago had no intention of initiating violence, this is not to say that they did not expect it to develop.

It was the clearing of the demonstrators from Lincoln Park that led directly to the violence: symbolically, it expressed the city's opposition to the protesters; literally, it forced the protesters into confrontation with police in Old Town and the adjacent residential neighborhoods.

The Old Town area near Lincoln Park was a scene of police

ferocity exceeding that shown on television on Wednesday night. From Sunday night through Tuesday night, incidents of intense and indiscriminate violence occurred in the streets after police had swept the park clear of demonstrators.

Demonstrators attacked too. And they posed difficult problems for police as they persisted in marching through the streets, blocking traffic and intersections. But it was the police who forced them out of the park and into the neighborhood. And on the part of the police there was enough wild club swinging, enough cries of hatred, enough gratuitous beating to make the conclusion inescapable that individual policemen, and lots of them, committed violent acts far in excess of the requisite force for crowd dispersal or arrest. To read dispassionately the hundreds of statements describing at firsthand the events of Sunday and Monday nights is to become convinced of the presence of what can only be called a police riot.

Here is an eyewitness talking about Monday night:

> *"The demonstrators were forced out onto Clark Street and once again a traffic jam developed. Cars were stopped, the horns began to honk, people couldn't move, people got gassed inside their cars, people got stoned inside their cars, police were the objects of stones, and taunts, mostly taunts. As you must understand, most of the taunting of the police was verbal. There were stones thrown of course, but for the most part it was verbal. But there were stones being thrown and of course the police were responding with tear gas and clubs and everytime they could get near enough to a demonstrator they hit him.*
>
> *"But again you had this police problem within—this really turned into a police problem. They pushed everybody out of the park, but this night there were a lot more people in the park than there had been during the previous night and Clark Street was just full of people and in addition now was full of gas because the police were using gas on a much larger scale this night. So the police were faced with the task, which took them about a hour or so, of hitting people over the head and gassing them enough to get them out of Clark Street, which they did."*

But police action was not confined to the necessary force, even in clearing the park:

A young man and his girl friend were both grabbed by officers. He screamed, "We're going, we're going," but they threw him into the pond. The officers grabbed the girl, knocked her to the ground, dragged her along the embankment and hit her with their batons on her head, arms, back and legs. The boy tried to scramble up the embankment to her, but police shoved him back in the water at least twice. He finally got to her and tried to pull her in the water, away from the police. He was clubbed on the head five or six times. An officer shouted, "Let's get the fucking bastards!" but the boy pulled her in the water and the police left.

Like the incident described above, much of the violence witnessed in Old Town that night seems malicious or mindless:

There were pedestrians. People who were not part of the demonstration were coming out of a tavern to see what the demonstration was . . . and the officers indiscriminately started beating everybody on the street who was not a policeman.

Another scene:

There was a group of about six police officers that moved in and started beating two youths. When one of the officers pulled back his nightstick to swing, one of the youths grabbed it from behind and started beating on the officer. At this point about ten officers left everybody else and ran after this youth, who turned down Wells and ran to the left.

But the officers went to the right, picked up another youth, assuming he was the one they were chasing, and took him into an empty lot and beat him. And when they got him to the ground, they just kicked him ten times—the wrong youth, the the innocent youth who had been standing there.

A federal legal official relates an experience of Tuesday evening.

I then walked one block north where I met a group of 12-15 policemen. I showed them my identification and they permitted me to walk with them. The police walked one block west. Numerous people were watching us from their windows and balconies. The police yelled profanities at them, taunting them to come down where the police would beat them up. The police stopped a number of people on the street demanding identification. They verbally abused each pedestrian and pushed one or two without hurting them. We walked back to Clark Street and began to walk north where the police stopped a number of people who appeared to be protesters, and ordered them out of the area in a very abusive way. One protester who was walking in the opposite direction was kneed in the groin by a policeman who was walking towards him. The boy fell to the ground and swore at the policeman who picked him up and threw him to the ground. We continued to walk toward the command post. A derelict who appeared to be very intoxicated, walked up to the policeman and mumbled something that was incoherent. The policeman pulled from his belt a tin container and sprayed its contents into the the eyes of the derelict, who stumbled around and fell on his face.

It was on these nights that the police violence against media representatives reached its peak. Much of it was plainly deliberate. A newsman was pulled aside on Monday by a detective acquaintance of his who said: "The word is being passed to get newsmen." Individual newsmen were warned, "You take my picture tonight and I'm going to get you." Cries of "get the camera" preceded individual attacks on photographers.

A newspaper photographer describes Old Town on Monday at about 9:00 P.M.:

When the people arrived at the intersection of Wells and Division, they were not standing in the streets. Suddenly a column of policemen ran out from the alley. They were reinforcements. They were under control but there seemed to be no direction. One man was yelling, 'Get them up on the sidewalks, turn them around.' Very suddenly the police charged the people on the sidewalks and began beating their heads. A line of cameramen was 'trapped' along with the crowd along the sidewalks, and the police went down the line chopping away at the cameras.

A network cameraman reports that on the same night:

I just saw this guy coming at me with his nightstick and I had the camera up. The tip of his stick hit me right in the mouth, then I put my tongue up there and I noticed that my tooth was gone. I turned around then to try to leave and then this cop came up behind me with his stick and he jabbed me in the the back.

All of a sudden these cops jumped out of the police cars and started just beating the hell out of people. And before anything else happened to me, I saw a man holding a Bell & Howell camera with big wide letters on it, saying 'CBS.' He apparently had been hit by a cop. And cops were standing around and there was blood streaming down his face. Another policeman was running after me and saying, 'Get the fuck out of here.' And I heard another guy scream, 'Get their fucking cameras.' And the next thing I know I was being hit on the head, and I think on the back, and I was just forced down on the ground at the corner of Division and Wells.

If the intent was to discourage coverage, it was successful in at least one case. A photographer from a news magazine says that finally, "I just stopped shooting, because every time you push the flash, they look at you and they are screaming about, 'Get the fucking photographers and get the film.' "

There is some explanation for the media-directed violence. Camera crews on at least two occasions did stage violence and fake injuries. Demonstrators did sometimes step up their activities for the benefit of TV cameras. Newsmen and photographers' blinding lights did get in the way of police clearing streets, sweeping the park and dispersing demonstrators. Newsmen did, on occasion, disobey legitimate police orders to "move" or "clear the streets." News reporting of events did seem to the police to be anti-Chicago and anti-police.

But was the response appropriate to the provocation?

Out of 300 newsmen assigned to cover the parks and streets of Chicago during convention week, more than 60 (about 20 per cent) were involved in incidents resulting in injury to themselves, damage to their equipment, or their arrest. Sixty-three newsmen were physically attacked by police; in 13 of these instances, photographic or recording equipment was intentionally damaged.

The violence did not end with either demonstrators or newsmen on the North Side on Sunday, Monday and Tuesday. It continued in Grant Park on Wednesday. It occurred on Michigan Avenue in front of the Conrad Hilton Hotel, as already described. A high-ranking Chicago police commander admits that on that occasion the police "got out of control." This same commander appears in one of the most vivid scenes of the entire week, trying desperately to keep individual policemen from beating demonstrators as he screams, "For Christ's sake, stop it!"

Thereafter, the violence continued on Michigan Avenue and on the side streets running into Chicago's Loop. A federal official describes how it began:

> "*I heard a 10-1 call [policeman in trouble] on either my radio or one of the other hand sets carried by men with me and then heard 'Car 100—sweep.' With a roar of motors, squads, vans and three-wheelers came from east, west and north into the block north of Jackson. The crowd scattered. A big group ran west on Jackson, with a group of blue shirted policemen in pursuit, beating at them with clubs. Some of the crowd would jump into doorways and the police would rout them out. The action was very tough. In my judgment, unnecessarily so. The police were hitting with a vengeance and quite obviously with relish. . . .*"

What followed was a club-swinging melee. Police ranged the streets striking anyone they could catch. To be sure, demonstrators threw things at policemen and at police cars; but the weight of violence was overwhelmingly on the side of the police. A few examples will give the flavor of that night in Chicago:

"At the corner of Congress Plaza and Michigan," states a doctor, "was gathered a group of people, numbering between thirty and forty. They were trapped against a railing [along a ramp leading down from Michigan Avenue to an underground parking garage] by several policemen on motorcycles. The police charged the people on motorcycles and struck about a dozen of them, knocking several of them down. About twenty standing there jumped over the railing. On the other side of the railing was a three-to-four-foot drop. None of the people who were struck by the motorcycles appeared to be seriously injured. However, several of them were limping as if they had been run over on their feet."

A UPI reporter witnessed these attacks, too. He relates in his statement that one officer, "with a smile on his face and a fanatical look in his eyes, was standing on a three-wheel cycle, shouting, 'Wahoo, wahoo,' and trying to run down people on the sidewalk." The reporter says he was chased thirty feet by the cycle.

A priest who was in the crowd says he saw a "boy, about fourteen or fifteen, white, standing on top of an automobile yelling something which was unidentifiable. Suddenly a policeman pulled him down from the car and beat him to the ground by striking him three or four times with a nightstick. Other police joined in . . . and they eventually shoved him to a police van.

"A well-dressed woman saw this incident and spoke angrily to a nearby police captain. As she spoke, another policeman came up from behind her and sprayed something in her face with an aerosol can. He then clubbed her to the ground. He and two other policemen then dragged her along the ground to the same paddy wagon and threw her in."

"I ran west on Jackson," a witness states. "West of Wabash, a line of police stretching across both sidewalks and the street charged after a small group I was in. Many people were clubbed and maced as they ran. Some weren't demonstrators at all, but were just pedestrians who didn't know how to react to the charging officers yelling 'Police!' "

"A wave of police charged down Jackson," another witness relates. "Fleeing demonstrators were beaten indiscriminately and a temporary, makeshift first aid station was set up on the corner of State and Jackson. Two men lay in pools of blood, their heads severely cut by clubs. A minister moved amongst the crowd, quieting them, brushing aside curious onlookers, and finally asked a policeman to call an ambulance, which he agreed to do. . . ."

An Assistant U.S. Attorney later reported that "the demonstrators were running as fast as they could but were unable to get out of the way because of the crowds in front of them. I observed the police striking numerous individuals, perhaps 20 to 30. I saw three fall down and then overrun by the police. I observed two demonstrators who had multiple cuts on their heads. We assisted one who was in shock into a passer-by's car."

Police violence was a fact of convention week. Were the policemen who committed it a minority? It appears certain that they were—but one which has imposed some of the consequences of its actions on the majority, and certainly on their commanders. There has been no public condemnation of these violators of sound police procedures and common decency by either their commanding officers or city officials. Nor (at the time this Report is being completed—almost three months after the convention) has any disciplinary action been taken against most of them. That some policemen lost control of themselves under exceedingly provocative circumstances can perhaps be understood; but not condoned. If no action is taken against them, the effect can only be to discourage the majority of policemen who acted responsibly, and further weaken the bond between police and community.

Although the crowds were finally dispelled on the nights of violence in Chicago, the problems they represent have not been. Surely this is not the last time that a violent dissenting group will clash head-on with those whose duty it is to enforce the law. And the next time the whole world will still be watching.

C. RESPONSES TO CHANGE

25 / I SPY, YOU SPY

Eliot Marshall

Senator Sam Ervin of North Carolina, a faithful guardian of privacy, thinks the government is storing too many facts about too many people in high-speed, quick-reference data banks. The Civil Service Commission, Secret Service, HUD, HEW, Customs Bureau, and Justice Department are some of the agencies that keep files on citizens who are neither federal employees, criminal suspects, nor convicts. "Judge" Ervin believes that Americans suffer a subtle form of intimidation by having their lives recorded in federal files, and he wants to establish a computer regulating agency. He plans to open hearings on data-keeping on October 6 before the Constitutional Rights Subcommittee.

Ervin found good ammunition for his cause this spring when the Army was forced to admit it has been spying on civilian politics and keeping computerized records of potential troublemakers. Former Army intelligence officer Christopher Pyle wrote an article describing Army plans for a large computer at Ft. Holabird, Md. which would serve as a reference bank on citizens who seemed subversive. For several years, Army undercover men have watched political demonstrations—usually antiwar and civil rights rallies. Agents joined the SDS and Black Panthers. Officers investigated Ralph Abernathy's Resurrection City and attended the University of Maryland as full time student/spies. The information they collected was distributed over nationwide Army teletypes, published in a blacklist of troublemakers, and eventually tucked away in files.

From *The New Republic*, October 3, 1970. Reprinted by permission of *The New Republic*, © 1970, Harrison-Blaine of New Jersey, Inc.

When the program was exposed, Ervin and other congressmen threatened to hold public hearings. After several months of congressional harassment, the Army decided in June that it would cut back its domestic intelligence. The order went out as a policy letter signed by a colonel in the Pentagon: the Army will "under no circumstances" collect information on "civilian individuals or organizations whose activities cannot, in a reasonably direct manner, be related to a distinct threat of civil disobedience" beyond the control of local authorities. The Army beat an official retreat, but left behind some grumbling legislators.

Ervin thinks the wording of the Army directive is imprecise and full of loopholes, and he wonders who will fill the intelligence gap created by the Army's departure. The June directive says the Army now "relies upon the Department of Justice at the national level to furnish civil disturbance threat information." To the senator, this looks like "an obvious surrender by the Justice Department." But to those on the inside, it seems to indicate nothing new. A spokesman for Justice says, "We're not doing anything we didn't do before. We have always supplied information to those who would need it." The Army's civilian files are now being held by Justice as evidence in a lawsuit involving Melvin Laird and a man who says his name is on one of the lists. Asked if Justice has incorporated the Army intelligence into its own data bank, the spokesman said, "There's nothing in those files we don't already have." Apparently the Army spying was a case of government overlap: at best, a waste of time; at worst, an invasion of civil territory.

The Justice Department's civil disturbance unit feeds information into an "interdivisional computer" where it keeps intelligence on organizations and people who might cause trouble, where they operate, and why. Other agencies are permitted to look at the files if they show a good reason. Asked if there are any guidelines determining what names go into the computer, the Justice spokesman said there is certainly an "internal" policy: "I think our interest is in the more militant people, the leadership, like SDS, Weathermen types, and Black Panther types." He couldn't be explicit, but he seemed to think that Justice uses a narrower definition of "subversive" than does the Army.

Ervin argues that surveillance and file-keeping in the Army

fashion has a "chilling effect" on the exercise of free speech. When people know that federal police are watching certain activities, they are reluctant to become involved. Where they would normally speak out, they remain silent. And this, says Ervin, is a violation of the First Amendment. In theory, a free citizen should know that as long as he obeys the law, his actions will not earn him a secret government dossier.

The conflict between surveillance and private rights is not just a federal concern; the American Civil Liberties Union has joined battle with local police across the country over the same issue. The New Jersey Supreme Court this June dismissed an ACLU invasion-of-privacy suit against the state attorney general. After the 1968 riot in Newark, the A-G began requiring state police to fill out personality and incident reports whenever they were assigned to a demonstration. Agents attended rallies, investigated those present who interested them, and kept the notes in permanent files. In dismissing the case, the chief justice said the ACLU was worrying about "hypothetical horribles," and that "it would be folly to deprive the government of its power to deal with that tyranny [lawlessness] merely because of a figment of a fear that government itself might run amok." The case is expected to reach the Supreme Court.

ACLU branches in New Orleans and Richmond are also handling lawsuits against local policemen accused of photographing onlookers at antiwar and civil rights meetings. In New Orleans, officers of the intelligence unit allegedly used picture-taking to harass demonstrators. One plaintiff testified that at an antiwar demonstration, "a car full of policemen would ride by slowly and take pictures from the car and they were giggling and laughing . . . and then they would . . . go around the corner and come back and take our pictures again." She said the police cameramen frightened away people who otherwise would have joined the protest.

These methods are untypical; most agents prefer to remain inconspicuous. In Oklahoma this August, the Civil Liberties Union stumbled onto an $18,347 federal grant to a secret state agency. By direct order of Governor Dewey Bartlett, the state military department has been running a surveillance post for two years without the knowledge of the legislature. In applying for funds under the Omnibus Crime Control act, the agency listed its needs for: part-time professional investigators, $470 worth of subscriptions to publications, a secret radio band for communicating with agents in the field, and riot conferences with police chiefs in college towns. It mentioned the presence of black organizations and "antiwar/anti-draft" activities on campuses as evidence of the growing danger to civil order.

Oklahoma civil libertarians believe the governor's agency has disregarded the constitutional rights of 6,000 citizens listed in its files. To them, the selection of suspects seems arbitrary, and the practice of spying on citizens, odious. The ACLU filed an injunction suit against the state in federal court on September 16.

Policemen view surveillance as a practical question. Paul Fuqua, spokesman for the Washington, D.C. police, believes spy-work can't be restricted. "How can you limit it?" he wants to know. "If your best buddy was pushing heroin, don't you think we'd investigate you from top to bottom?" Although he couldn't give details about his intelligence unit, he said that most decisions on surveillance are made by the officer on the case. In a kidnapping, Fuqua said he wouldn't hesitate "to bug the hell out of a suspect's telephone." Fuqua isn't concerned about most "two-bit local intelligence operations," but he admits he is scared by some of the latest spying devices and sophisticated computers. For example, he feels uneasy about a new laser-beam listening system that works from as far as a mile away. When focused on a window, it relays vibrations from conversations in the room, using the windowpane as a microphone. It's a great leap forward in snooping.

Like Fuqua, most men connected with investigative operations are puzzled by Senator Ervin's insistence that "we stand to lose the spiritual and intellectual liberty of the individual" if the trend towards computerized surveillance continues. Anthony Mondello, General Counsel of the Civil Service Commission and a specialist in personal rights, speaks of privacy protection chiefly in technical terms. He foresees advances in coding, thumb-print, and voice identifying devices to prevent unauthorized employees from checking into secret computer files. He has faith in the present system. He believes that public demonstrators are "asking to be photographed," and that there is no significant difference between government files on controversial citizens and ordinary newspaper files. Even Ramsey Clark, often quoted for his liberal legal opinions, sees the computer as nothing more potent than "a highly efficient filing cabinet." People who complain about police computers may simply be asking for "an inefficient police force," says Clark. He thinks it would be better to face the question squarely: "what information will a free society permit to accumulate without the individual's consent?"

Surveillance and blacklisting are ancient tools of government which have suddenly become more effective through high-speed communication and data-retrieval machinery. Computers, teletypes, and radios are making spying efficient and potentially more damaging. One federal official describes in frightening dimensions the computer tapes now being developed. Soon it will be possible to store ten-page dossiers on every American in a tape library the size of a living room. Within ten minutes of receiving a query, the computer could print out a short life history.

The worries of the ACLU may prove to be more than just "hypothetical horribles." And Senator Ervin's hearings may produce more than just a "figment of a fear."

26 / A FASHIONABLE KIND OF SLANDER

Robert Coles

It may seem strange now, six or eight years later, but in respected and moderate circles of the South, and the rest of the nation, the Southern Freedom Riders and the Mississippi Project volunteers of 1964 were thought to be (were declared) wild, impetuous, thoughtless, self-destructive, and masochistic; and the plan to challenge

From *The Atlantic Monthly*, November 1970. Copyright © 1970, by The Atlantic Monthly Company, Boston, Mass. Reprinted by permission.

the state of Mississippi was considered a crazy and romantic scheme, doomed from the start and potentially dangerous, or even ruinous, because of the response that powerful men like James Eastland and John Stennis and their allies would no doubt make.

I would like to single out three of the expressions I just used: *masochistic, crazy,* and *self-destructive.* For years in the South I heard those words directed at civil rights workers, and when I went to Appalachia to work with the Appalachian Volunteers, a similar group of dedicated, youthful political activists, I again heard the same thing. The line goes as follows: What's the matter with them? What kind of people do things like that? Why do they do such things? Do they really think anything will come of antics like theirs, rash and impulsive assaults? They are mistaken if they believe a small minority like them can prevail against the powers-that-be. Maybe they want to lose, though. Maybe they are stubbornly, uncompromisingly bent on the kind of confrontation that can lead only to violence, disorder—and a kind of retaliation that will not only put an end to their protest but set things even further back, create an even worse climate of fear and repression. In short, maybe those youths are irrational, deluded by a host of absurd and dangerous fantasies, violence-prone, and in some serious way, anti-social.

"SICK"

In 1963 I discovered how that kind of approach to activist, dissenting youths works. I heard a decidedly sensitive and well-educated Southern judge send a youthful black civil rights worker to a state hospital, where he was to be "observed," where his "mental status" was to be evaluated, where possible "delinquent" and "sociopathic" trends would be ascertained and studied—and where, perhaps, the young man would begin to get some "treatment." If he received no treatment the youth did have a chance to think, and what I heard from him was for me a professional confrontation of sorts, something I have never been able to forget, especially because I had worked with delinquent youth in the course of my training in child psychiatry: "It's quite a setup they've got. We protest our inability to vote, to go into a movie or restaurant everyone else uses, and they call us crazy, and send us away to be looked over by psychiatrists and social workers and all the rest of them. The questions I've had put at me since I've been here! Were you a *loner* when you were a boy? Did people consider you *rebellious*? Were you *popular* or *unpopular* as a child? When you were younger did you have trouble *taking orders* from your parents or your teachers? Did your mother *discipline* you firmly, or did she more or less let you do as you please? And on and on they go, one question after another, and none of them very subtle.

"The guy doing the questioning told me he is a doctor, a psychiatrist, and I asked him why he wasn't interested in *what* I've done, and the *objective reasons* I've acted as I have. But he said he knew 'all that.' He told me his job is to examine my mind and find out what my 'motivations' are. He kept on asking me whether I feel angry at this person and that one, and if I have a temper, and how do I 'handle tension,' and he wanted to know whether people in 'authority' make me anxious, and whether I have trouble in 'controlling' myself, and whether I 'rush out and act' when I come upon an unpleasant situation, or instead do I stop and think and try to figure out the best possible 'attitude' to have. I wrote them down, as many of his words and questions as I could, because the way he put those questions was to me more abusive than anything I've ever heard from the poor, ignorant red-necks. At least they have the decency to insult you right to your face; so you know exactly where they stand and no one's fooling anyone, least of all himself. That doctor (I can tell from talking with him over a week) considers himself way above the red-neck; in his mind he is a careful, thoughtful, temperate man. He used that word 'temperate' two or three times with me. He kept on contrasting 'temperate behavior' with 'impulsive behavior,' and after we got talking more casually he told me that some people have a 'need'—that's right, a *need*—to disrupt the lives of others, and hurt them, and get hurt themselves. Did I think I was that kind of person?

"Soon you just slip into the whole scene. I mean, you stop noticing all the assumptions a guy like that constantly makes, and you simply try to answer him as best you can. And anyway, if you protest and tell him off, tell him what you think is implicit in his questions and his whole way of thinking, he's not going to take your argument seriously; he's going to go after *you*—and call you 'hostile' and 'defensive' and full of 'problems' and all the rest. He as much as told me so, that doctor did. He said a lot was going on inside my mind, and until I found out what 'really' was prompting some of my 'behavior,' I'd probably continue what I've been doing. He told me he was going to recommend to the court that I not be sent to jail. He said I needed treatment—but he was worried that I would be 'resistant' to it, and that would be 'too bad' for me, and later I would be sorry."

The youth then pointed out to me what I hope is obvious: the smug, self-righteous arrogance he had met up with, the pejorative use of psychiatric terminology, the limitless display of self-satisfaction and condescension, the essentially illogical and totalitarian nature of a mode of thought that claims to have the authority to decide who has a right even to discuss certain matters, and who (whatever he *thinks* he is saying or doing or trying to say or trying to do) is *really* "sick" or "resistant" or seriously in need of "help," and therefore thoroughly, hopelessly suspect. I was prepared to accept much of that from him—I had heard patients endlessly labeled in ways that robbed them of their dignity, and I had seen in myself as a psychiatric resident the awful tendency to dismiss a patient's disagreement or criticism as evidence of just about anything but his or her good judgment. But I was not so prepared to see how convenient it could be for that judge, and many like him, to have people around who would summon all the authority of medicine and science to the task of defending the status quo—which meant putting firmly in their place (a hospital or a clinic) those who choose to wage a struggle against that status quo.

"PARANOID"

Only over time did I begin to realize, often because I was brought up short by some very bright and clearheaded youths, that all sorts of phrases and concepts bandied about rather freely by me and my kind reveal as much about us as about those we describe. What indeed is "mental health"? Who indeed is "normal"? Were slave-holders "normal"? Did Nat Turner have a "problem with authority"? If a man tells me he is going to kill himself, I call him "suicidal" and want to hospitalize him. If a man in Vietnam runs into a burst of machine-gun fire, urging his comrades to do likewise, I call him a hero. If a man wants to kill someone, he is homicidal and needs confinement. If a man drops a bomb on people he doesn't even see or know, he is doing his duty. And if a man is *afraid* he might want to kill someone, he, of course, needs help or guidance or treatment to prevent a fear from becoming a deed; whereas if a pilot should become horrified at the thought of what *he* might do, the bombs he might cause to fall on fellow human beings, he would need the same "treatment"—presumably so that he will get over his hesitations and "do his duty." Certainly if he starts making a lot of noise about his fears and his misgivings he will be sent for "evaluation." And, of course, if the pilot never once has such hesitations and qualms, he is "normal" or "patriotic" or a "good soldier" or whatever.

Such ironies and vexing discrepancies ought to make us all at the very least aware that psychiatric judgments about what is or is not "appropriate" are not rendered in some scientific vacuum, but are made at a particular moment of history and in a given society by men who are distinctly part of that society—namely, its upper middle class.

The Southern youth who was just quoted knew in his bones what it takes some of us longer to realize, if indeed we ever do, no matter how thoroughly we analyze ourselves—that the assumptions we make about a person's social and political behavior have to do with the kinds of lives we ourselves live, and that the doctor in that mental hospital was nothing less than a willing and indeed eager representative of a particular kind of entrenched power, which wanted those protesting its authority discredited and knocked out of commission, one way or another. In the distant past, but also in recent times, dissenters have been banished to prison or sent to their death (or sent to America!) for their noisy, unorthodox, unsettling, and provocative words and acts. Many of us no doubt find such out-and-out repression distasteful, but we are not beyond our own ability to call a person we oppose only thinly disguised names, to insult him and at the same time ignore

the thrust of his declared purposes, his stated intentions, his deeds
—which surely ought to be open for discussion on their own
merits, rather than the merits of one or another person's psychiatric status. We dismiss, belittle, and run down those we disagree
with *substantively* by doing them in *personally*.

For example, in response to a questionnaire put out by a magazine, a substantial number of American psychiatrists were willing
just a few years ago to signify that yes, Barry Goldwater is not
"psychologically fit" to be President of the United States. Later,
we heard that George Wallace might also be "neurotic" and "unstable." I happen to feel, as a citizen, that I would prefer to have
as my friend Barry Goldwater rather than Lyndon Johnson, that
in fact Mr. Goldwater is more open as a person, less self-centered,
and less given to pettiness or meanness—but I voted for Mr. Johnson because in 1964 his position on all sorts of issues seemed far
wiser to me than Mr. Goldwater's. In 1964, to a supporter of
Lyndon Johnson, his moodiness, his arrogance, his secretiveness
were the foibles of a great, warmhearted humanitarian, just as to
Richard Nixon's supporters today, his aloofness, his outbursts of
anger when things have not gone as he likes are the way he
chooses to deal with a difficult job, or the way he responds to outrageous provocations. Put differently, psychological evaluations
inevitably are influenced by our disposition to like or dislike a
person or his views; and that holds for psychiatrists, too—who
can misuse their own professional language and applaud or condemn deeds or individuals with words like "egosyntonic" (which
means "good") and "pre-oedipal" (which means "bad").

Then there are today's students and demonstrators. What we
don't hear about them! They are "products of permissive childrearing practices." They are sons of self-made men who abhor
the materialism of their fathers, and more than that, are struggling
with some version of an "oedipal conflict." They are "immature."
They have "poor ego controls." They are not in touch with
"reality." They are "passive-aggressive." They are "exhibitionistic" or plagued by "omnipotent fantasies." They are "acting
out" one or another "problem." Their words and thoughts and
actions show them "paranoid," even in some cases "psychotic."
Nor are those whose serious and carefully thought out ideas hap-

pen to capture the interest of the young immune from that kind of comment. The distinguished British psychoanalyst R. D. Laing, whose many books and papers require patient study, whose ideas are bold and challenging and singularly free of the banal and the pompous, is called a host of psychiatric names and ignored in all too many centers of psychiatric and psychoanalytic training. The well-known American psychiatrist Thomas Szasz, whose books constantly demand from his colleagues a willingness to look at the way unconventional people are commonly enough labeled "mentally ill" and locked up permanently, is himself called "paranoid" or possessed of a "one-track mind" or an "obsession"—as if men like Pasteur or Freud were not grandly preoccupied and maybe even "obsessed."

Needless to say, there are no limits to the abuses that can be perpetrated in the name of any ideological system. In the Soviet Union social critics and writers and scientists are regularly carted off to psychiatric hospitals, where they are called various high-sounding names and kept locked up. Here things are by no means as blatant and absurd, but with shrill rhetoric becoming almost our daily fare, it is hard to imagine any line of argument as off-limits today. And if young people or political activists are to be condemned for their "personality problems" rather than listened to (and thoroughly applauded or severely criticized) for the substance of what they propose or advocate, then surely we ought to turn the tables and ask some questions about other people—in order to end once and for all a silly and insulting way of dealing with issues.

"PROBLEMS"

What are we to say, for instance, about the "early childhood" or "mental state" of political leaders or business leaders or labor leaders who lie or cheat or order thousands to go off to fight and kill? What kind of "psychological conflict" enables a man to be an agent of the Central Intelligence Agency, or a pilot who drops napalm bombs, or a congressman who wants to use atomic and hydrogen bombs so that a nation will be "turned into a parking lot"? What kind of "oedipal conflict" enables so many people to demonstrate their obvious lack of real concern for millions of poor Americans—out of work, ailing, hungry? Do we ask about the psychological "factors" that enable a man to be hard-driving, competitive, on the rise, always on the rise, often over the backs of everyone else around? Do we question the "unconscious reasons" so many of us "adjust" to the injustice around us, become indifferent, become caught up in what is called a "rat race" or a "grind" even by those utterly uninterested in social change or protest? Moreover, if students are out to kill their "parent surrogates," what indeed about our desire as grown-ups to squelch the young, subtly and not so subtly degrade them, be rid of them—because they inspire envy in us; because they confront us with all the chances we forsook, all the opportunities we have lost, all the tricks and evasions and compromises and duplicities we have long since *rationalized* or *repressed* or *projected*?

So it goes, and so do we all suffer, I believe. Step by step we become the victims of various kinds of slander and invective, some obvious, some indirect and clothed in pietistic, sanctimonious language or in the jargon of the social sciences or psychiatry. Words like "fascist" and "elitist" are hurled indiscriminately and viciously at anyone and everyone, and of course "Communists" crop up everywhere in the minds of some. And if those more political modes of assault don't work, the rest of us, more "moderate" and maybe just as desperate and confused, can always dispense with a bothersome individual or political question by raising our eyebrows and calling into question a person's "psychodynamics" or damning an entire group with some psychological or sociological generalization. Why bother, after all, to remind ourselves that every single human being has "problems," struggles with love and hate and envy and fear and all the rest? Why bother to ask *whose* "law" and *whose* "order" are being assaulted, and for what *purpose*? Why bother asking ourselves what *in fact* so many youths, from so many different backgrounds and regions, are actually saying and asking of us? And finally, why trouble ourselves by asking how it has come about that we have lost faith in our ethical convictions, and so have to attack or defend people and entire political movements by resorting to words and concepts originally meant only to help doctors clarify for themselves the sorrow and pain felt by particular patients?

27 / THE NEW VIOLENCE

Joseph Morgenstern

For the better part of two decades, evidence has been accumulating that violence in the mass media can breed aggressive behavior in the mass audience, especially among children. Supporting documents from last month's report to the Surgeon General on "Television and Growing Up: The Impact of Televised Violence" give us the strongest suggestions to date that violent TV programs can have harmful effects on large groups of normal kids. It's unlikely, though, that millions of outraged parents will lower the boom on the broadcasters. Much of the adult audience is on a violence trip of its own at the movies.

Americans love to watch images of violence in the fun house of the mass media. Violence is the best epoxy for holding an audience together between commercials, the very deathblood of such shows as "Mannix," "Gunsmoke," "Cannon," "Hawaii Five-O," "Adam-12," "Cade's County" and "Mod Squad," not to mention all those dumb, undifferentiated Saturday morning cartoons. A recent study by the British Broadcasting Corp. found that American television programs shown in England have twice as many violent incidents as British productions do.

Occasionally an urban riot, campus confrontation or choice assassination will cause the public or Congress to wonder briefly if all this mayhem in the media is such a good thing for the country, after all. The last time the question arose was in 1969, when Sen. John Pastore (Democrat of Rhode Island) sponsored a $1 million study of media violence and its possible relationship to "antisocial behavior among young people." Historically, the networks' position has been that no such relationship has ever been proved. Just to make sure it wouldn't be proved this time, the broadcasters tried to rig the Surgeon General's study in their favor. To a considerable extent they succeeded.

All candidates for membership on the advisory committee that commissioned the research and later summarized it were subject to vetoes by the three commercial networks. CBS declined to exercise any such veto; NBC and ABC had fewer scruples and blackballed seven candidates. The fourth network of 219 noncommercial (and largely nonviolent) stations (PBS) was not consulted. Two of the twelve committee memberships went to incumbent directors of research at NBC and CBS. Three more went to scholars who had been or still were employed by the networks.

THE LAST WORD

Once the surveys and laboratory experiments were completed, all research data and conclusions were compiled into five large volumes, then summarized by the advisory committee in a 279-page report to the Surgeon General. Whether by intent or ineptitude, the committee misrepresented some of the data, ignored some of it and buried all of it alive in prose that was obviously meant to be unreadable and unread. The five supporting volumes are still being withheld from the public. Thus far, the news media have accepted the committee's summary as the last word on the research. Beneath the misleading headline "TV Violence Held Unharmful to Youth," The New York Times story stressed contradictions in the Surgeon General's report and, with incomplete quotations, gave the impression that televised violence leads to increased aggressive behavior only in small groups of youngsters.

In fact, the summary says much more than this, and the supporting data says more than the summary. The summary dismisses as unsubstantiated the catharsis theory—that viewing filmed violence allows pent-up emotions to be released harmlessly. While the summary does say that the most direct effects of media violence may occur among children predisposed to violence, it stresses that this violence-prone subgroup may constitute a "small portion or a substantial portion of the total population of young viewers." And an overview of one of the five volumes of supporting research says, in an italicized conclusion, that *"the present entertainment offerings of the television medium may be contributing, in some measure, to the aggressive behavior of many normal children. Such an effect has now been shown in a wide variety of situations."*

That conclusion was written by Dr. Robert M. Liebert, a psychologist at the State University of New York at Stony Brook, Long Island. Liebert participated in two of the 23 research studies, has read all 23 and feels strongly that the summary draws inaccurate conclusions from them. "I believe," he says, "that the most reasonable conclusion is that there is a link between televised violence and aggressive behavior for the majority of normal children. The data show no evidence that only a minority is influenced. That is a factual error."

Not all the researchers feel their work was misrepresented, of course, and not all the committee members feel their summary was self-canceling. "Prior to this report," says one of them, Dr. Ithiel de Sola Pool of MIT, "you could not have said that there is a causal relationship between TV violence and aggressive behavior in children. Now we can see that there is a significant causal relationship."

Beyond the baleful light of the box, violence rages in the streets and it's the rage in the movies. Within the past few months a striking new consensus has emerged on movie violence —indeed, on ultra-violence, to borrow a term from the stylish sadists of "A Clockwork Orange." Moviemakers have found ultra-violence ultra-profitable, the mass audience has found it enjoyable —and an influential majority of reviewers has found it intellectually attractive and artistically valid.

In the highly praised "A Clockwork Orange," roving bands of dehumanized hoodlums deal out a cool, affectless violence that includes kicking, stomping, gang rape and beating a woman's brains out with a big phallic sculpture. "Straw Dogs" dispenses with the cool and comes to a devastatingly powerful climax of rape, knifing, mutilation, acid-tossing, shooting, beating and burning. Santa Claus tries to crush a fallen kid's rib cage in "The French Connection." A maniac "hippie" in "Dirty Harry" does unspeakable violence to his victims; what the detective hero does to the maniac hippie is no more speakable and equally visible. Roman Polanski's "Macbeth" dispatches its victims with a vividly slit throat, a broadax in the back, a dagger in the forehead, a sword in the groin. When Macbeth himself was beheaded the other day at the Playboy Theater in New York, a matinee audience of high-school students on a field trip screamed in horrified delight as the thane's hands groped for the head that had already split.

"WHAT THE PEOPLE WANT"

If there's any such thing as ultra-sex, it's still largely confined to peep shows, porno houses and X-rated movies that some violence-laden newspapers refuse to advertise out of deference to their readers' sensibilities. But only one movie has ever been rated X for violence—"I Drink Your Blood"—and that rating was changed to an R when cuts were made. All the James Bond pictures carry GP's—suitable for general audiences, with parental guidance advised—even though 007's witty swashbucklings have turned gross and squalid in the new "Diamonds Are Forever." A kiddie version of ultra-violence has even crashed the Radio City Music Hall, which caters mostly to families and young children. The Hall recently played "The Cowboys," a GP-rated Western in which John Wayne is slowly shot to death by rustlers, then avenged when a group of children torture one rustler and kill them all.

Does this mean the movie industry's rating system is in a state of collapse? Motion Picture Association of America president Jack Valenti maintains that the ratings are still doing what they're supposed to do, marking certain pictures off limits to children and warning parents that certain other pictures may be unsuitable for children. "I don't think it's the rating system that's in collapse," Valenti says. "It may be that parents just don't care any more." A Newsweek survey of theater operators in cities across the nation reveals little or no public dissatisfaction with the ratings or the violence of new movies. "Mores and customs change and movies have become franker," says a manager in Detroit. "Violence is acceptable," says a showman in Chicago. "It's what the people want."

That's no news in itself, of course. Mass audiences have always wanted violence and always gotten it, whether in bear baiting, melodrama, comic books or pro football. Nor is it news that violence, even pornographic violence, is more socially acceptable than sex. In 1949, in a pamphlet called "Love and Death," Gershon Legman wrote: "There is *no* mundane substitute for sex except sadism."

Yet something new did come over media violence in the 1960s. It was the result of an interaction that's always in progress between entertainment and reality. On one side was a convergence of events without parallel in American history—racial strife, assassination, confrontation, the war in Vietnam. On the other side, entertainment stayed in step with the world beyond the studios and gave us the showerbath murder in "Psycho," and the James Bond extravaganzas, with a hero sophisticated enough to lead his audience down hitherto forbidden paths of sex, sadism and stylish decadence. "The Untouchables" flourished on TV, the spaghetti Westerns—made in Spain by Italians—treated American audiences to a level of violence that Hollywood had hardly dared dream of. Roger Corman's "The Wild Angels" rode in on the emerging motorcycle myth. Richard Brooks upped the violence ante in "The Professionals," and Robert Aldrich gave audiences a half-hour high of slaughter in "The Dirty Dozen."

These movies were long on action and short on philosophy, but new attitudes toward violence were beginning to trickle down from literary and scholarly speculations of the day, just as Epicurean and Stoic notions of nature that were popular in Shakespeare's time found dramatic expression in his Edmund and Edgar. This was the decade in which Eichmann was executed, "In Cold Blood" appeared and the English translation of "On Aggression" was published. In the entertainment world it was also the period in which "Bonnie and Clyde" forced a rethinking of the mythology of violence with its daring new notions of criminal behavior and the lyric horror of its climax, and "The Wild Bunch," with another quantum jump in physical intensity, tried to explore the nature of life with the esthetics of death.

PROPHECY OR PARODY

Many critics and moviegoers welcome the new ultra-violence as an extension of such experiments. "A Clockwork Orange" is praised as prophecy, or as a dark parody of the present. The horrors of "Macbeth" are seen as historical truths: lords and ladies were close to savagery and killed as savages. Admirers of "Straw Dogs" feel it illuminates the human condition with its vision of violence as a rite of passage in which a man puts himself in touch with his primal emotions—to become, for better or worse, a man.

A few eloquent dissents from this attitude have been advanced in recent weeks. Andrew Sarris, writing in The Village Voice, found a facile anti-intellectualism in "A Clockwork Orange," and woeful inadequacies in Kubrick's widely hailed technique. Pauline Kael, in The New Yorker, drew analogies between the drug culture's appetite for intense, violent mystery and the mock profundities of "El Topo." Writing about "A Clockwork Orange," Miss Kael condemned the movie's "finally corrupt morality" which betrays Anthony Burgess's novel by making the mod-sadist hero much more human and likable than the contemptible straights he preys on. "How can people go on talking about the dazzling brilliance of movies," her review asked, "and not notice that the directors are sucking up to thugs in the audience?"

One way they can do it is by following the lead of the old New Criticism in literature, confining themselves to matters of style and structure—cool technicians reviewing the techniques of other cool technicians. Ultimate meaning can be a horrible can of worms, and there's no ethical obligation to deal with it if you believe that violent entertainment has no ultimate effect, apart from instruction or healthy catharsis. There's the rub, though. If the effect of TV violence on children has finally been demonstrated, it's not unreasonable to assume that ultra-violence in the movies has some effect on adults. It's not necessarily the same effect, a heightening of aggressive behavior. But neither do these movies necessarily enlighten their audience in ways that they're supposed to.

A film like "Straw Dogs" may put us in touch with our primal emotions, but that's no great trick—the Nazis did it constantly. It also sets up human existence, on a shaky allegorical level, as a simplistic choice between fighting violence with violence or capitulating to it completely. Where's some provision for the uses of intelligence, or at least craftiness? The film puts us in touch with a machismo that's supposed to be unfashionable in sophisticated circles these days, yet persists in philosophical disguise. A man can only be a true male, according to the movie, when he's won his merit badges in rape, combat and murder. It's as if de Sade had rewritten the worst of Hemingway for a special Nasty Edition of Playboy. There's only one possible role for a woman in this

macho-violent setting. She's there to be raped, she wants passion-
ately to be raped, she deserves to be raped and raped she most
certainly is in "Straw Dogs," "Macbeth" and, of course, in "A
Clockwork Orange."

This kind of entertainment is seductive in more ways than
one. With its obscurity, macho bravura or both, it puts you
promptly on the defensive. You can't be much of a man if you
don't dig it, or at least concede its underlying wisdom. Man is
base (and woman is baser), say the pundit artists. How true, how
true, respond the admiring critics, only too glad to get a secure
ride on the hate-humanity bandwagon. "I don't mind saying that
I myself was sickened by my own film," says Sam Peckinpah, co-
writer and director of "Straw Dogs." "But somewhere in it there
is a mirror for everyone." Maybe so, but the mirror is framed in
right-wing gilt. It shows the stereotyped liberal intellectual—
Dustin Hoffman in simpers and specs—as a cowardly, contemptible nerd who won't take a stand till the barbarians are inside his
own house: Neville Chamberlain Meets the New Madmen. "I'm
not a Fascist," Peckinpah has been quoted as saying, "but I am
something of a totalitarian."

He's a lot more candid than some of his colleagues. Don
Siegel likes to be thought of as a tough action director, but the
thread of Fascism in his "Dirty Harry" is as strong as the suspension cables on the Golden Gate Bridge. The gallant, ruthless San
Francisco detective tries to take a crazed killer out of circulation
by fair means or foul, but he's hamstrung by all those dumb rules
on arrest that were handed down by a doddering Supreme Court.
Polanski takes a simple-minded, totalitarian approach to "Macbeth." The language and poetry seem beyond him, so he uses
violence to explain everything. Stanley Kubrick has become a
totalitarian of the arts who crushes other people's intricate moral
ideas into a pulp of mod decadence.

There's a joke about a fake guru who tells all his disciples
that "life is a river." Gurus of the new violence do something of
the sort with stylization. Their techniques—slow motion, surreal
performances, elegant décor, brilliant editing, fish-eye lenses, repeat frames—seem to comment on the action without saying anything. They lend distance, but they also dehumanize victims in the

way that high-fashion photography dehumanizes models, and they create a high-fashion horror that can turn an audience on higher than the real thing. The Vietnamese war could look lovely in slow motion—Skyraiders floating in for the kill like seagulls, fragmentation bombs opening like anemones. But the horror would still be horror, with nothing added but technique. Dancing on a face while singing "Singin' in the Rain" is still dancing on a face. It becomes clear that "Bonnie and Clyde" was both watershed and quicksand. It used technique within a humanistic design and shocked us awake to violence. Now anti-humanists are using the same technique to lull us into dulcet dreams of death.

ETHICAL CULTURE

Purveyors of the new violence can tell themselves and their critics that they're involved in a program of character building, public service and ethical culture, but a few visits to neighborhood theaters suggest that a large part of the mass audience simply loves the violence as violence. The givens are not always the takens. Kids in the balcony at a recent Times Square showing of "Dirty Harry" were stomping their feet with glee at each shooting or beating. One boy was coming on strong as a munitions expert, giving his girl a run-down on the range and impact of each weapon as it appeared. When the massacres ended and the house lights came up, he breathed a sigh of deep satisfaction and said quietly: "That was nice."

That's the part of the ultra-violence trip that many filmmakers and critics don't like to deal with. At least two sets of signals are operating here, and the confusion between them raises some anguishing questions that no one knows how to answer. Where does an artist's responsibility end? With the truthful depiction of his personal vision, or with its social effects? What are the effects of ultra-violent movies, on the cavemen as well as the sophisticates of the mass audience? Once again we don't know, but it's not enough to say that Shakespeare and Marlowe were violent and civilization still survived. Technology has brought a new amplification effect into play. Never before has so much violence been shown so graphically to so many.

CAUSE AND EFFECT

There's a sense of imminent disaster when you're in an audience that's grooving on ultra-violence, and you're tempted to say that things can't go on this way too much longer. They can, of course, and probably will. Today's ultra-violent films will be tomorrow's "Wednesday Night at the Movies" on TV—with anything sexy cut out, of course. If holograms bring free-standing images into our living room, we may have to shampoo the carpet after each new award-winning blood bath. Violence may also crest, as it has before, and cyclically subside. Something of the sort has happened in the rock world, which lowered its amps and pulled back from the abyss that opened at Altamont.

Whether it crests or not, however, media violence demands to be taken more seriously than it has been in the past. We know now, thanks to the Surgeon General's research, that it helps incite children to aggressive behavior. While we don't know what it does to adults, there's an ominous clue in the public's tolerance of horror in the newscasts from Vietnam. The only way we can possibly tolerate it is by turning off a part of ourselves instead of the TV set. It's very possible that incitement to violent deeds is the false danger for adults, and desensitization the real one. "Dirty Harry" didn't necessarily incite that self-styled weapons expert to buy himself a .41 and cut someone down with it. There's no proof—yet—that such ritualized primitivism turns adults on; not even the poor, the uneducated, the violence-prone, the people who can never get themselves together. The more immediate possibility is that it turns us off, like any other drug, that it freaks us out on make-believe fury, keeps us from doing anything constructive with our aggressions, that it frustrates, demeans and diminishes us.

PART FOUR
PROBLEMS OF A
CROWDED PLANET

PROBLEMS OF A
CROWDED PLANET

It is obvious from an analysis of the problems we have covered up to this point that most social problems can be seen from a number of viewpoints and that many have an international dimension. In this section we will deal with problems that seem to have been given particular attention because of their international or world relevance.

There has been much talk about the shrinking globe. We can experience this when we sit in our living rooms and watch, live via satellite, a war in progress halfway around the world. It is difficult for us to believe that men fought in the Civil War for days and even weeks after peace was declared simply because it took that long to get the message across the country. Most of us can sit in our home and within seconds call and talk to another person by telephone almost anywhere in the world. And an increasing proportion of the people of America with moderate or better incomes have traveled to various parts of the world. With these things in mind the problems of international relations take on a new light. It is not just a matter of war or peace. We are beginning to realize that other countries' problems of economics, health, population, and the like affect us all. Of course this is not to suggest that war itself does not take on a different perspective because of our smaller world. It is interesting to speculate what the Viet Nam War would have been like if the only communication devices we had were similar to those used in the Civil War.

The problem of population growth is not a new one. For several generations now we have been warned about the dire possibilities that will confront us if the world continues to grow at its present rate of increase. This has been the one issue, outside of international conflict, that the United Nations has devoted a major portion of its energy toward handling. There seems to have developed a general consensus that population growth is a major social problem. There is little consensus as to what to do about it. Some would say that if we just let nature take its course something will happen to relieve the problems. Others say we must educate the population to the virtues of small families. Racial minorities in the United States have expressed concern over the direction of population control efforts, suggesting that, because they are aimed at low income families where the birth rate is the highest, the programs are systematically reducing the size, and therefore the power, of the minorities, since they tend to be overrepresented in the lower income groups. So one can see there are many facets to the problems of population growth.

But growth is not the only problem connected with population. There are also problems that merge when the characteristics of the population change. With regard to an earlier article on the aged, it could be argued that we were there discussing a population problem, since it has only been in the past decade that we have had enough old people to constitute a significant problem. The article presented in this section on what life will be like by 1980 deals with the same problem.

We have left the topic of urbanization until last. However, the problems of the city have been reflected in articles and topics throughout this book. The problems discussed in almost every section of the book are in one way or another related to the fact that we are becoming more and more an urbanized society. By this we mean that more and more persons are living in or near large cities and are, thus, dependent upon the smooth functioning of the city for their way of life. Most directly, many of the problems we reviewed under the heading of ecology are clearly problems of urbanization. But just as important are problems of interpersonal relationships, as discussed in Parts I and II. The problems of crime, unemployment and poverty are all accentuated in the city, and racial problems cannot be avoided.

Nowhere else in modern society are the effects of change felt more than they are in the city. As we experience the most rapid change in the history of man, it is the city that feels the most severe stresses and strains, and it is the city that will have to be the most flexible and adaptable if we are to withstand the trauma of change.

A. INTERNATIONAL RELATIONS AND WAR

28 / THE WORLD OF THE 70's

Walter Laqueur

The present moment in world politics is one of transition (defined once by a distinguished economist as the interval between two other periods of transition), and it is characterized on the level of theory and action alike by a great deal of confusion, by exaggerated hopes and exaggerated fears, by wishful thinking and groundless pessimism. Certainly one of the main contributing factors to the confusion is what has come to be known in America as neo-isolationism (it has also been called "the foreign politics of neo-humanism")—that retreat from globalism which seems to be the defining mark of the current American mood. The retreat may not in the end go as far as some hope and others fear, but no one can dispute that the impulse behind it is today a major presence in American domestic politics or that its repercussions on the world scene will be widespread and decisive. Although it was no doubt hastened by Vietnam, there is reason to suppose that the new mood would have developed anyway, perhaps inevitably. Any sustained effort to pursue a global policy must be based either on a missionizing ideology of considerable firmness and longevity, or on a carefully calculated plan of action that combines ambition with farsightedness and discrimination. Neither of these preconditions has been much in evidence in American foreign policy.

It is easy to understand neo-isolationism as a mood: Americans have paid a high price for globalism and have received little enough

From *Commentary*, August 1972. Copyright © 1972 by the American Jewish Committee. Reprinted by permission.

in return. It is beginning to occur to some people that the world at large, which in any case has proved incurably addicted to turmoil and perversity, can get along without American help and guidance. But apart from its inherent attractiveness, neo-isolationism has also received justification as the correct ideological response to a new world political situation. Briefly, that new situation has been described as one of "multipolarity." Both the United States and the Soviet Union, it is argued, find themselves declining in relative influence, and both have grudgingly accepted this state of affairs. New centers of power are rapidly emerging in various parts of the world which provide a genuine regional balance. Conditions are now ideal for a true and lasting détente. As they turn away from their obsolete global ambitions and their lunatic arms race, the U.S. and Russia will find it possible at last to attend to their multitudinous problems at home—the former moving toward the realization of the American dream, the latter pursuing its vision of the Communist future. The cold war having been liquidated, the era of truly peaceful competition (and cooperation) in a pluralist world will be ushered in.

Thus, in his report to Congress last February, President Nixon himself announced the end of the postwar bipolar world and pointed to the "increasing self-reliance of the states created by the dissolution of empires and the growth of both their ability and determination to see to their own security and well-being." Recently, Sir Herbert Butterfield, proclaiming it a good thing that we have in the world both a Soviet Union and a United States, said that it would be "better still if we [could] have three such giants or four or five, better again, even, to have seven."* The International Institute of Strategic Studies in its last annual report announced the emergence of a new "great-power quadrilateral," a "genuinely global system with two non-white countries (China and Japan) firmly among the leaders." And an American author has coined the term "pentagonal world" (he was not referring to the place where Melvin Laird works.)

To be sure, not every prophet of multipolarity has regarded it as a panacea for all the world's ills; Stanley Hoffman, for instance,

---

* *The Discontinuities between the Generations in History* (The Rede Lecture), Cambridge, 1972.

wrote in 1968 that "it is all too easy to imagine a multihierarchical system of dizzying instability." But quite apart from the issue of its desirability, it is highly questionable whether the vision of a multipolar world corresponds at all to the facts of international life. For no such symmetry in power between the United States and the Soviet Union as the theory of multipolarity posits has actually been achieved: in the economic and military spheres the United States is still ahead and will in all probability remain ahead for the foreseeable future, while in the political and psychological spheres the Soviet Union is ahead and seems ready to increase its lead. Nor, secondly, are any new centers of power such as are envisioned by the theory of multipolarity likely to emerge during the next two decades. In the survey that follows I shall attempt first of all to assess the relative economic and political positions of the U.S. and the Soviet Union, taking special note of the likely impact of the recent SALT agreements, and then go on to consider the role in the new world situation of Japan, Western Europe, and China. Such a *tour d'horizon* should have the effect of placing in a colder but truer light the notion of an emergent multipolarity in the international system.

I

For over four decades now Soviet leaders have been promising to overtake America in the economic sphere. They have pointed with satisfaction to the advances made by their system as compared with the stagnant, crisis-ridden capitalist world. The official program of the Communist party of the Soviet Union, as it was reformulated under Khrushchev, stated unambiguously that in the decade of the 60's "the Soviet Union will surpass the strongest and richest capitalist country, the United States of America, in production per head of population." This slogan has now been replaced by a more modest one. According to the most recent announcements, the USSR expects by 1975 to surpass the present level of American industrial and agricultural production; this, it is said, will be a "major milestone in the Soviet Union's economic competition with the capitalist countries."

It is not an unrealistic prediction. In 1971 more steel was produced in the Soviet Union than in the United States. In the production of coal the Soviet Union overtook the U.S. as long ago as 1958, and in the production of cement in 1967. The USSR also produces more raw iron and iron ore than the United States, and by 1975 it will probably produce more agricultural machinery as well as more of certain industrial and agricultural consumer goods. The Soviet GNP, no greater than one-third of the American in 1950, today stands at about half that of the U.S.* Present Soviet plans envisage an annual industrial growth rate of 8.9 per cent; agricultural production in 1975 is expcted to be at least 20 per cent above the current level.

These figures are impressive, but there are other aspects to the picture as well, less encouraging from the Soviet point of view. First, although the Soviet Union has gained ground vis-à-vis the U.S. in relative terms, the absolute distance is greater than ever before, and it is likely to increase even if the Soviet rate of growth should double that of the United States. (In 1950 the American GNP was 275 billion dollars greater than the Soviet GNP [in 1966 dollars]; at present it is 500 billion dollars greater or more.)

Secondly, up until recently Soviet planners have concentrated on "traditional," i.e., partly outdated, industries, and are consequently far behind the United States (and Japan as well) in science-oriented industries (electronics, computers, chemicals).

Thirdly, Soviet hopes for overtaking the United States rest on the assumption that America will perform poorly in the 70's while the Soviet Union (with the help of its economic allies) will meet, or exceed, the fairly high rates of growth it has fixed upon. But neither half of the assumption can be taken for granted. American real growth now runs at 6 per cent after two years of stagnation. The recent Soviet record, on the other hand, has been checkered: 1969 was fairly disastrous by Soviet standards (a growth rate of 2.3 per cent), 1970 was excellent (8.5 per cent), 1971 was far from outstanding (6 per cent—partly as a result of a bad harvest). Soviet economists expect that the new protectionist mood in the U.S. will result in a falling rate of growth, with stagnation and perhaps actual decline to follow; it is not certain they will be proved correct.

---

* Most of this advance was achieved in the 1950's; in 1960-69 the Soviet economy made virtually no progress toward improving its relative position vis-a-vis the U.S.

But meanwhile there are several factors working to inhibit the growth of the Soviet economy. Soviet resources in manpower are limited; as a result, progress will depend on a very high, virtually an unprecedented, increase in productivity (36–40 per cent for the Ninth Five Year Plan). This in turn will depend to a large extent on the modernization of Soviet industry, and on the ability of the civilian sector to make dramatic progress in research-and-development in the years to come.

In the last-named area the Soviet Union has far to go. According to a report by Pyotr Kapitsa to the Academy of Sciences several years ago, the Soviet Union, with approximately the same number of scientists, has produced only half the scientific work of the U.S. Andrei Sakharov and his colleagues stated in a memorandum to the Soviet leadership that "we are ahead of the U.S. in the production of oil, gas, and electric power, ten times behind in chemistry and immeasurably behind in computer technology. We are simply living in a different era." To help redress the balance the Soviet government is eager to derive what material benefit it can from Western technology—probably one of the main stimuli behind the current Soviet interest in détente.

This, then, is the economic picture at present. If current trends continue there is every reason to suppose that in basic industrial production the Soviet Union will make somewhat faster progress than the United States for the next few years. But beyond this, what? According to the scientists, a technological revolution, brought about by such impending developments as supersonic transport, weather control, the harnessing of thermonuclear energy in giant generating stations, third-generation computers, etc. While America has been falling behind in traditional industries like textiles and steel production, its lead in the field of computers and electronics has been steadily growing. And since the application of the new technology is very costly indeed, no one is predicting that the Soviet Union will be able to keep up.

Of course, any discussion of economic growth must take into account the increasingly vociferous opposition in the West to the very concept of unrestricted ("exponential") growth. Pollution, adverse climatic effects, the increasing scarcity of mineral and other resources—these, along with the specter of a world population explosion, have been cited as reasons for slowing if not halting the rate of growth in the industrial countries. But only in the West, and specifically in the United States. The Communist aim remains as it has always been: maximum growth. As John Noble Wilford reported from Moscow a few months ago:

> *While the U.S. debates the possible ecological hazards of the Alaskan pipeline, the Soviet Union publishes boasts of the "world's longest gas pipeline." While American nuclear power stations are being stalled by protests, the Soviet Union is building reactors with a capacity of a million kilowatts or more, and is planning many more. While a wave of anti-technology sentiment in the U.S. killed the supersonic transport project and reduced spending for basic research and space exploitations, the Soviet Union is apparently expanding its support in such fields on the ground that science and technology are indispensable foundations of growth and progress. . . .**

The Soviet (and Chinese) attitude is not hard to understand. An economic slowdown at this point would simply perpetuate the Communist world's position of economic inferiority. On some distant day, perhaps, having drawn level with or overtaken the non-Communist world, the Soviets may opt for deceleration—but not until then. Current policies calling for unrestricted industrial growth are deeply anchored in Communist theory and practice, and are not likely to be changed quickly or easily.

In short, as far as the 70's are concerned, it can be predicted with reasonable certainty that the economic balance of power as between the Soviet Union and the United States will remain pretty much as it is. But what of the military balance of power? The essential facts are not in dispute;† the interpretation of them, however, diverges widely.

---

* New York *Times,* March 30, 1972.

† Admittedly there is some doubt as to the precise extent of defense spending in the Soviet budget. Official Soviet statements put it at 8 per cent of the total GNP, while some Western observers go as high as 15.2 per cent (M. Boretsky in "Economic Performance and the Military Burden in the Soviet Union," Washington, 1970). Since the Soviet Union does not publish detailed figures, and since no one in the West can know for certain how much a "defense ruble" is worth, the debate is likely to continue for a long time. (See Alec Nove's "Soviet Defense Spending" in *Survey,* October 1971.)

Broadly speaking, there exist in the United States three schools of thought on the question of strategic arms, and the SALT agreements have scarcely affected the basic arguments of each. The first maintains that as a result of a massive Soviet military build-up since the mid-60's an imbalance has come into being which will grow during the years to come and reduce the U.S. to second-class status unless a major effort is made now to reverse the trend. While the U.S. has settled for parity (or "sufficiency") the Soviet Union has built up its forces beyond the level needed for deterrence and seems to be aiming at superiority. In quantity of arms the U.S. is now inferior to the Soviet Union; if, as a result of further defense cuts, America should also lose its technological lead, an American President may one day end up, to use Secretary of Defense Laird's phrase, crawling to the negotiating table of its victorious enemies.* True, the SALT agreements have put a ceiling on the production of certain arms, but the race to improve the *quality* of arms will continue, as will the effort to increase the power and the accuracy of existing weapons. In this area too the U.S. will be at a great disadvantage, since in circumstances of a pseudo-détente American defense planners will be much harder put than their Russian counterparts to get the allocations they need.

The second school of thought regards this appraisal as alarmist. To be sure, the Soviet Union has caught up with the United States and in some respects has overtaken it, with over 1,600 ICBM's to America's 1,054, and with a stepped-up submarine program that will probably result in numerical superiority of Polaris-type vessels within the year. Nevertheless, the implications of this situation have been overdramatized. In the first place, the Soviet Union reached "rough parity" ten years ago. Secondly, the Soviets themselves face considerable domestic constraints (economic rather than political) on defense spending, and as the SALT treaty shows, they have in fact acknowledged the ruinously expensive cost of achieving a first-strike capacity. Seen from this vantage point, the present Soviet build-up has been a futile exercise in "overkill."

---

* See, for instance, the reports of the Blue Ribbon Defense Panel published in July 1970 and in March 1971; also, "The Military Unbalance" published by the National Strategy Information Center (New York, 1971); and W. Kintner and R. Pfaltzgraff, "Soviet Military Trends: Implications for U.S. Security" (Washington, 1971).

The third school of thought maintains that American defense spokesmen, who constitute a kind of lobby for the military, have always exaggerated Soviet military power in order to get more money out of Congress. Thus U.S. military spokesmen predicted for years that the Soviets were about to develop MIRV's (multiple independently-targetable reentry vehicles), whereas in fact they were lagging seriously behind; as a result the gap in missile warheads widened rapidly in favor of the United States—so much so, according to I. F. Stone, that the Russians now fear "we are trying for some kind of counterforce, preemptive, or first-strike capacity." In any case, in the opinion of the third school of thought, the cold war is over, and in today's world military power is no longer a measure of political power. Now that an agreement has been reached on the limitation of strategic arms, the U.S. should follow through with a drastic reduction of its arms budget, unilaterally if necessary.

Although each of these conflicting views has its own element of distortion and bias, each also contains an element of truth (albeit of unequal weight). The first school of thought correctly stresses the dangers that will confront the United States a few years hence unless it continues to be on guard. American technological superiority in the military field is not all that substantial, and if defense spending on research-and-development falls much below the Soviet level, the consequences could be serious indeed. Yet it is also true, as proponents of the second and third schools have argued, that for the foreseeable future America's position cannot be much affected by quantitative Soviet superiority in any one specific area. Military spokesmen do tend to exaggerate potential peril in order to obtain budgetary allocations, although in a sense it is their obligation to do so, just as it is the duty of a physician to take account of the worst possibility in making a diagnosis of illness. That such an approach has its own dangers goes without saying, and they are not only the dangers of overspending. By stressing Soviet strength and American weakness, military spokesmen in the United States run the risk of creating an adverse political effect abroad, inviting America's European and Far Eastern allies to conclude that the U.S. commitment to their defense is unreliable.

We touch here on a central issue. When military might has been neutralized, as it effectively has, other factors come to assume decisive importance: the appearance and credibility of power, and the readiness to exercise power in the pursuit of national interests. Political power, like justice, must be made manifest to be appreciated. In this respect the image of America as far as the outside world is concerned is more and more that of a nation unwilling to exercise power, a nation beset by a mood of pervasive defeatism, and ridden with internal dissent. On the other hand, the Soviet Union presents itself as purposeful and dynamic, out to win the global struggle, rather than to preserve the status quo. No guilty feelings are expressed in the Soviet Union on the subject of power; on the contrary, there is a great and growing self-confidence, which feeds on the American retreat from globalism.

This description of the situation may seem grossly to overstate American weakness and Soviet strength. But the image counts as much as the reality—in Europe, in the Third World, and, of course, in the Soviet Union—and although as of today the belief that the American ship is sinking has not yet become widespread in Europe and Japan, and the Russians still have a healthy respect for American power, America's image is changing, and for the worse. This is not to say that the Soviet Union will risk a head-on confrontation with the U.S. in order to hasten the process. There is in fact no need for it to do so, even for strategic gain. Other things being equal, future conflicts around the world will be fought by conventional forces and their outcome will be decided by the local balance of power. In most of the potential danger zones the Soviet Union already possesses the advantage, both of geographical proximity and of military and political initiative. In Europe, the Middle East, and Southeast Asia, Moscow can turn on the heat at will. Whether or not it does so, the mere fact that it can makes all the difference in the world.

Thus, irrespective of the statistics on defense spending, missiles, and nuclear submarines, a basic political imbalance has developed between the United States and the Soviet Union.

II

But if there is no symmetry between the United States and the Soviet Union such as the theory of multipolarity asserts, neither is there any real ground for supposing that new superpowers have emerged.

Of the members of the alleged new league of superpowers none has been the subject of more extravagant claims than Japan. "Japan's emergence to its new postwar status," writes Andrew J. Pierre, "is the result of its gradual though impressive evolution to the rank of the third most powerful economic country in the world in the 1970's."* According to Herman Kahn, Japan is bound to become an economic and technological superstate within the next two decades; and Hisao Kanamori, of the Japanese Economic Planning Agency, has estimated that per-capita income in Japan in the early 1980's will be level with that of the United States and almost three times higher than Britain's. To put it even more dramatically, by 1990 Japan's economy will supposedly have overtaken America's, a country with twice Japan's population; the Soviet Union will have been outdistanced long before.

At the time these predictions were being made—only a year ago—it was assumed that Japan would have the technological momentum, the work force (as well as the work ethos), and the export markets necessary to make such growth possible, if not inevitable. Labor shortage, inflation, environmental problems, possible changes in world-trade patterns—all were thought to be of limited significance. Yet within the space of a year this euphoria has given way to more sober assessments. It has been realized, for instance, that an economy so heavily oriented toward exports is unbalanced and vulnerable; Japanese exports now face tariff difficulties in the United States and Europe, and there are limits to what the Far Eastern market can absorb. (Thailand's trade deficit with Japan already exceeds that country's total foreign-exchange reserves.) Some of the present difficulties are probably transient in character, but others are structural and may well inhibit economic growth in the years to come. For Japan, 1971 was a year of multiple shock. Even while some foreign commentators were predicting that the 21st would be the Japanese century, the mood inside Japan was becoming more and more subdued. Suddenly people were asking whether Japan should not seek a détente with Russia or China,

---

* "Europe and America in a Pentagonal World," *Survey*, Winter 1972.

or perhaps both; whether it should not opt for unarmed neutrality; whether it might not be possible to insure Japan's viability as a nation without maintaining a close link with the United States. There is a great deal of soul-searching in Japan, but none of the confidence befitting a superpower.

The Chinese maintain publicly that the present crisis is bound to propel Japan toward militarization. They point to the fact that despite the provision of the 1947 constitution banning the maintenance of military forces, Japanese self-defense units have been established and equipped not only with rifles but with tanks, missiles, submarines, destroyers, and a thousand planes. Between 1972 and 1976, about 16 billion dollars will be spent on expanding and improving the Japanese army. As a result Japan will move from twelfth to seventh place among the world's nations in defense spending. According to some experts Japan will be able to produce Minuteman-type missiles within three years.

Such asessments, however, ignore both the general context of Far Eastern politics and the strong internal forces opposing Japanese remilitarization. Japan spent in 1970 less than 0.8 per cent of its GNP on defense, the lowest figure by far of any country of comparable size and population. (Under the "Fourth Defense" build-up program the figure will rise to 1 per cent.) Paragraph 9 of Japan's constitution prohibits offensive weapons, a conscription system, and sending troops overseas. The constitution can be reinterpreted (or sidestepped) to a certain extent, but popular antimilitarist feeling is strong and cannot easily be overcome.

In foreign policy, Japan for twenty-five years took the American nuclear umbrella for granted. Now there is serious doubt whether America will be able or willing to honor its commitments even if the Seventh Fleet remains and air-force units are stationed as before in the Philippines, Guam, and Okinawa. Statements from Washington proclaiming the end of bipolarism have been echoed by declarations in Tokyo heralding the age of multipolarization and the need for a foreign policy "divorced from ideology." Influential circles on both the Left and the Right favor a revision of the security pact with the United States or its abolition. But the fact is that despite its economic strength, Japan is far from being a major power center and the number of options open to it is very limited indeed. A neutralist policy would probably best correspond to the mood prevailing in Tokyo. The Japanese could sign a nonaggression pact with the Soviet Union at any time, but the gesture would be meaningless. As for China, in view of its distrust of Japan, an exceedingly great effort will be needed before relations between the two countries can be normalized, and the Soviet Union can be expected to view any such effort with disfavor.

Japan has attempted to boost its trade with China. In 1971 such trade reached an all-time high but it still amounted to less than a billion dollars, and there are no real prospects for dramatic improvement. China's total foreign trade is hardly any bigger today than it was in the 1920's, and it will probably not increase by much; the myth of the unlimited possibilities of the Chinese market dies hard. The Soviet Union is only too eager to increase its trade with Japan but it insists on low-interest loans and offers payment in oil over a period of twenty years starting in 1978. Such conditions, needless to say, are not very attractive from the Japanese point of view. This leaves the United States and Europe as Japan's leading customers.

The American economic complaint against Japan is, very briefly, that Japan has refused to liberalize its trade, that it buys mainly raw materials from America and exports highly sophisticated machinery. In Western Europe, where its trade is more limited, Japan faces a similar problem. It has been selling ships, cars, and electronic equipment, while it has bought from Europe whisky, expensive woollens, and confectionery goods. This has resulted predictably in European measures limiting Japanese imports. The Japanese now realize the necessity of having a larger measure of reciprocity and of "voluntary self control," but given the limited size of the domestic market and the structure of Japanese industry this will be easier said than done.

The Japanese dilemma appears likely to resist rapid solution. In all probability economic growth will not continue on the phenomenal level of the past, and in the meantime social conflicts are intensifying and a growing polarization is visible on the domestic front. All in all, Japan offers a striking example of the truth that GNP is not a synonym for power. Japanese political leaders, who believe that their nation has the greatest power potential in the Far East, complain regularly of American coldness and indifference to Japan. But the Soviet attitude has been exactly the same as the

American. The Russians are concerned about China, whose GNP is less than half of Japan's; they do not lose a minute's sleep over Tokyo. Such are the realities of power in 1972.

III

Let us turn next to contemporary Europe, an area of the world characterized at present by two encouraging features: (relative) peace and prosperity. There has been no war in Europe in over twenty-five years and there is no likelihood of there being one. Considering the state of the continent at the end of World War II, the economic and cultural revival Europe has undergone is little short of miraculous. I see in fact no reason to revise a judgment I made two years ago: "Far from 'dying in convulsions,' as Sartre predicted, Europe has shown a new vigor which has astonished friend and foe alike." *

Nevertheless Europe today can hardly be regarded as one of the five pillars of a new "pentagonal world system"; indeed, the very notion of Europe as a center of political power has about it a touch of the ludicrous. The internal situation in many European countries is, to put it mildly, far from stable. In Britain, the political climate has deteriorated during the last year both as a result of the situation in Ulster and because of internal social tensions. No longer is there a consensus on basic issues; an irresponsibility, indeed a silliness, has crept into British politics, reflected for instance in Labour's official attitude to European unity. The Irish, curiously enough, have been more farsighted in this respect. In France, the danger has by no means passed of a reversion to the bad old days of the Fourth Republic; Pompidou's government has demonstrated little real leadership, and has suffered from several embarrassing *affaires*. The less said about the Italian and the Turkish domestic scenes, the better. Even in Germany, until recently a model of stability, the political climate has turned ugly, the polarization become sharper. Chancellor Willy Brandt's party has come under the influence of a new generation of activists, imbued with a sense of purpose and displaying much tactical ability, but in

---

* *Europe since Hitler*, 1970.

ideological inspiration closer to the Communist party than to Social Democracy; whether the new forces take over the party, or alternatively cause its defeat in the next election, the result may well be disastrous for Germany. Franco's reign nears its inglorious end and the Greek colonels will not last forever; it is difficult to imagine that either in Spain or in Greece the transition to democracy will be accomplished peacefully—if it is accomplished at all. Ironically, these two dictatorships have made great economic progress, although this is of course no guarantee of stability. Sweden, and to a lesser extent Norway and Denmark, are affected by deep internal discontent and even in the Benelux countries domestic crisis has become a frequent occurrence. Finally, signs of disintegration have emerged in Yugoslavia, and the question of who and what will follow Tito on the political scene agitates both the Yugoslavs and their neighbors.

An optimist would argue that domestic crises of the kind prevalent in Europe today are part of the normal democratic process. The Labour party, such a person would contend, will ultimately say yes to Europe; Italy will somehow muddle through; Brandt, Heath, and Pompidou realize the need for closer European collaboration; and, given both time and the Soviet Union's preoccupation with China, there is no serious danger that Europe will fall apart.

All this may be so, but the truth is that Europe lives on borrowed time. For reasons I have indicated previously in these pages,* closer European economic cooperation is an immediate, not a long-range, imperative. The continent's present economic strength is deceptive, and can easily degenerate. In the area of foreign and defense policy, Europe has shown an inertia and in some cases a shortsightedness and a paralysis of will which are truly alarming. Senator Mansfield's complaint is after all justified: why should 250 million people, possessing great industrial resources and a long military experience, be unable to organize an effective military coalition to defend themselves?

Not that there is anything basically wrong with Chancellor Brandt's *Ostpolitik*; the agreements with Russia and Poland should

---

* "The Fall of Europe?" January 1972.

have been signed long ago, and in some ways the *Ostpolitik* does not even go far enough. But if the policy itself is sound, the illusions engendered by it should give pause; Brandt himself and some of his colleagues have encouraged such illusions by speaking in terms of a historical turning point in European affairs and by predicting a radical improvement in East-West relations. Yet there is no reason to assume that the *Ostpolitik* will bring about a "real détente," or will help resolve the existing conflicts of interests in Europe. As far as France is concerned, Prime Minister Pompidou and his ministers profess to favor closer European cooperation, and they certainly fear the withdrawal of American troops from Europe, but at the same time they want others to pay the price of unity; the protection of French agriculture is still a more important consideration to them. As it was under de Gaulle, France continues to be the main stumbling block on the road to European unity. The defense policy of the Scandinavian countries has more in common with *Alice in Wonderland* than with reality. Sweden still earnestly insists on neutrality, though it has virtually given up the attempt to make its neutrality credible. Iceland's only contribution to NATO has been the U.S. base at Keflavik which it now is asking to have removed. Denmark spends little more than 2 per cent of its GNP on defense and the ruling Social Democrats want a drastic reduction in that amount. These neutralist leanings would make sense if there were no political pressure and no military threat. But the Scandinavian countries are in fact under constant pressure from the Soviet Union, which has established in the Murmansk-Kola region what the Norwegian minister of defense has called "the world's mightiest complex of bases." Warsaw Pact superiority in the Baltic Sea is five to one and still growing. The Soviet Union has a most impressive naval task force standing by year-round between the coast of Norway and the north of Scotland—neither for fishing nor, in view of the inclement weather, for reasons of health.

The "Scandinavian syndrome" is reflected in Western Europe's attitude to the Soviet proposal for a European Security Conference, the principle of which has now also been accepted by the United States. If the Soviet intention were détente—a reduction of armaments, an agreement on the inviolability of existing borders, collective security, a repudiation of the threat or use of force, promotion of trade, and so on—no sane person could object. The

Russians already have treaties with France and Germany providing for these aims, and they could have similar agreements in a matter of days with every other European country.

But Soviet intentions are a little more ambitious; the Russians do not merely want, as they maintain, to transform relations among European states in order "to help overcome the division of the continent into military-political groupings." On the contrary they want to strengthen the cohesion of the Warsaw Pact countries while keeping Western Europe disunited. They argue that the Communist countries constitute a "natural" bloc, tied together by ideological, economic, and other ties, while the non-Communist countries of Europe have no such common interests and their unity is therefore "artificial." The overriding long-term aim of a European conference as far as the Russians are concerned is not just collective security but a lasting peace on their terms—a Pax Sovietica. Not for a moment do the Soviets contemplate dissolving the Warsaw Pact.

Indeed, the very notion of a European conference has been befogged to such an extent by empty and misleading slogans that one may doubt whether it will prove a proper forum for discussing concrete problems like a balanced reduction of armed forces. At best, as the *Economist* has observed, the European conference promises to be a bore, a sort of mini-UN assembly in which weary politicians exchange weary platitudes. At worst, it could offer the Soviet Union an opening for an aggresively expansionist policy with regard to Western Europe. The whole affair may in the long run be of no consequence. But it demonstrates very clearly the weakness of Western Europe, its inability to take the initiative, to assert its interests, to shape a common policy. The problem facing Western Europe is one of survival, of maintaining its security and independence in the face of the gradual American retreat from globalism. The notion that Western Europe has a major part to play in the new concert of powers is simply unrealistic.

IV

China, in contrast to Japan and Western Europe, is a factor of major importance in the new "international system," not as a global power but certainly within the Asian framework. It offers, as I have remarked, a striking illustration of the fact that economic performance does not count for much as a criterion of political power. For a fairly long time the world has been treated to accounts of the marvelous achievements of Chinese workers and peasants, the wise and farsighted policy of Chinese leaders, the incredible accomplishments of barefoot Chinese scientists. These claims are by now wearing a little thin. Mao and his colleagues have been in power for almost a quarter-of-a-century, yet economically China is still a very backward country. It prides itself on steel production—21 million tons in 1971 (incidentally this is one of the few figures published)—but the capacity to produce 22 million tons existed ten years ago. China's grain harvest in 1971 was 245 million tons, which is less than in 1958, despite the fact that the population has grown by many millions since then. Oil production (about 25 million tons) is small by any standards and will limit the scope of economic expansion in coming years. With a per-capita annual income of about $145 China is still among the poorest countries in the world.

Yet unlike Japan and Western Europe, China has given absolute priority to defense. It staged its first atomic test in October 1964 and its first full-scale themonuclear test in June 1967, thus doing in less than three years what took the French eight to accomplish. In April 1970 the Chinese launched their first satellite, with twice the payload of Sputnik 1. They began building ICBM's in 1965; although progress has not been as fast as expected, they were able by 1972 to deploy a handful of new missiles with a range of up to 2,500 miles (Moscow is less than that distance from Chinese soil).

It is not known whether a preemptive nuclear strike against China has ever been seriously considered in Moscow. But there is no doubt that the Chinese threat figures very prominently in Soviet thought; forty-four Soviet divisions are believed to be presently deployed along the Chinese borders. The propaganda image of the Chinese enemy (in contrast to the American) is that of a tough and ruthless fighter, inflexible, one who will not hesitate to use any devious strategem, any weapon to achieve his aim. However, Soviet leaders seem to be counting on a lack of stability inside China. That Mao and his colleagues might be replaced by a pro-Soviet clique is probably beyond their wildest dreams. But it is not at all impossible that in a struggle for power among rival contenders, and in view of the tensions already existing between the army and the party (and within the party and army), not to mention other centrifugal trends (China's twenty-eight regions in many respects pursue divergent policies), China might again be paralyzed as it was during the Cultural Revolution. Such a development would not, of course, remove the "Chinese danger" altogether, but it would certainly reduce its urgency and would enable the Soviet Union to pursue a more energetic foreign policy elsewhere. Peking's influence on the world Communist movement is likely to shrink as the strictly national components in Chinese Communism become more prominent; the appeal of Maoism outside China (and outside the Chinese diaspora) was always based to a certain degree on a misunderstanding.

Nevertheless, whatever happens on the domestic scene, China will still be the most populous country on earth and its military strength cannot be ignored. It will figure prominently in the political calculations of Russia, Japan, and India. But it will not be a global power for a long time to come.

The American retreat from globalism unquestionably creates a new situation. The balance of power is indeed changing—but not toward multipolarity. While America is in retreat, the Soviet Union still has a globalist policy. As the U.S. opts for disengagement, the Soviet Union increases its commitments. To this extent, regardless of America's economic performance and strategic might, the Soviet Union is now in a superior position. Nor is the hypothesis warranted that new centers of power are about to emerge. A world power (let alone a "super power") must be capable of asserting its interests and purposes beyond its borders, yet with all their economic resources and military potential, Western Europe and Japan are not only lacking in that capacity, but in the area of defense they are even more dependent on outside help than Australia or Brazil. It is uncertain that they will succeed in weathering the coming storms once the American umbrella is removed from over their heads.

There is, in short, no multipolar system emerging, unless one takes the term as a euphemism for the spread of confusion, or possibly chaos. The American retreat is causing new power vacuums in the world. How they will be filled, and who will fill them, is the great question of the decades to come.

29 / THE UNITED NATIONS AND THE COMMON MAN

Nuri Eren

At the San Francisco Conference of 1945, the founders of the United Nations were primarily concerned with formulating controls that would ensure peaceful relations among sovereign governments. But the traumatic experience of the Second World War, in which the minds of men had engaged in conflict long before arms were committed to battle, also had taught them that international peace and security rest ultimately upon the spiritual and physical well-being of individual citizens within the states. From the beginning, therefore, plans were to create a U.N. system of "special agencies" to promote the health, education, and living standards of the average human being. Today, while peace between nations seems as distant a goal as ever, U.N. service to individual citizens has bloomed beyond all expectations and has slowly and quietly fostered, especially in the "underdeveloped" world, an increasing realization of the relation between personal freedom and welfare and global security. Maybe the process of serving the individual rather than the effort of transforming nations will give mankind the universal peace that has eluded it for so long. In this context, the first twenty-five years of the United Nations deserves to be truly celebrated.

First, the U.N. system is helping millions of individuals to improve the conditions of their material existence. In the U.N. system seventeen different agencies specialize in promoting education, health, economic growth, social development, agriculture, ecology, and communications. Almost 90 per cent of the budget flows into these efforts, servicing two-thirds of the world's peoples who are needy, and answering some need or another for almost all of them.

For example, consider the case of Sadik Harbi. Today he functions as a fully qualified primary school teacher. When Algeria became independent in 1962, he was only fourteen. Eighty per cent of the teaching staff in the country had quit because they were French. Harbi was one of those recruited into a crash four-week teacher-training course by UNESCO experts. Later, while the fourteen-year-old taught elementary school, he received further evening instruction in a U.N. training center and used teacher-training materials provided by U.N. agencies. Now, with 15,000 other monitors, he belongs to the new and up-to-date army of primary school teachers in Algeria.

Sadik Harbi's experience was part of a worldwide U.N. effort to spread primary school education to millions of children in under-developed lands. Tens of thousands of peasants have been transformed into teachers like Harbi. In Carthage, Tunisia, for instance, Ridwan Hilali's students love their school. Hilali, along with 3,000 other Tunisians, has been trained in new techniques of education and teaches his classes how to test the soil, value their food, and handle electricity. Four million additional children will be attending schools in Tunisia as a result of U.N. assistance. Meanwhile, in Latin America, U.N. help in founding and modernizing primary teacher-training schools has helped 90,000 teachers, thereby increasing school attendance from twenty-five million to sixty million pupils in nine years. Altogether, U.N. training programs operate in seventy-seven countries.

The effort has been extended to secondary and higher education. For example, Eduardo Lopez of Lima, Peru, is spending this year in Santiago, Chile, at the Training, Experimental and Educational Research Centre sponsored by UNESCO, learning to be a secondary school director. The program calls for 2,000 trainees. When they all return to work they will help an extra five million Latin American children receive secondary education. In Africa the success of the Higher Teacher Training Institute in the Sudan has prompted the founding of additional institutes in seven other African countries. Two million pupils in Africa will benefit from these new teachers.

Thousands of students also are in universities today as a result of U.N. efforts in higher education. The Middle East Technical University in Ankara, Turkey, was founded initially with U.N. assistance and funds. In India the United Nations supports post-graduate engineering studies in eight new regional colleges to help the country to meet its increasing need for technical personnel. In Latin America the United Nations family collected $200-million for upgrading and modernizing university education in the Southern Hemisphere. This program embraces all universities on the continent.

U.N. efforts in health and nutrition also have touched millions. In the African Republic of Mali they call them "United Nations guns." Appropriately, the guns are vaccine injectors and they shoot to save people from communicable diseases such as smallpox, cholera, and yaws—the deadly enemies of Africa and Asia. In India alone malaria cases have dropped from a hundred million to 150,000 a year. The United Nations has vaccinated 226 million persons in ninety-five countries against tuberculosis. It has protected 39 million children from trachoma and five million against leprosy.

Two U.N. agencies, the World Health Organization and UNICEF, with an annual joint budget of $140-million, are especially concerned with health. In the isolated town of Madurai on the south tip of the Indian subcontinent, for example, people are drinking safe milk for the first time in their lives. UNICEF-sponsored milk-processing plants operate in 200 communities around the world. In Thailand's Prae province and in many Andean countries UNICEF plants manufacture iodized salt, the one protection against goiter.

U.N. agencies have created new lands for landless peasants. Ahmad Badawi, a camel herder of eastern Jordan, has turned into a prosperous dirt farmer, thanks to underground water recovered by a United Nations specialist. Farmers in the Vardar River Basin in Yugoslavia, in Sebou River Region in Morocco, in Wadi Jizan in Saudi Arabia harvest rich crops from vast tracts of land reclaimed by U.N. flood-control programs. A United Nations-sponsored five-year project has opened 988,400 acres of virgin forest in Ecuador. U.N. efforts in Nigeria, India, and Brazil have increased the production and export of tropical woods to more than $1-billion a year.

All of these international programs were carefully planned. Of the sixteen organizations in the U.N. family, the U.N. Development Program and the World Bank Group are the key strategists. The Development Program has spent $1.6-billion in research to help a host of nations to use their natural resources more productively.

The World Bank Group has provided the capital for building the technical infrastructure needed to develop these capacities. It has provided millions with electric light and energy, new ports, railways, water supply and sewer systems, telecommunications, new industries, even research centers for technological development. In 1969, the Bank Group provided nearly $1.9-billion toward the development of public services, transportation, industry, and agriculture in twenty-five countries. In the last two decades its contribution to some one hundred nations has totaled almost $20-billion.

The United Nations also has sought to provide the human resources necessary for industrial production. In India, for example, 150,000 workers in forty industries received their training from 4,500 U.N.-sponsored instructors. U.N. institutes operate in more than sixty countries and train thousands of managers and technicians every year. The Institute of Technological Research in Colombia, for example, taught coffee planters a new technique in depulping that helped to bolster Colombian coffees' position in the market. In Ghana more than 100 of the top officials in government services took training from the U.N. Institute of Public Administration.

Another major accomplishment of the United Nations in its first twenty-five years has been its contribution to law in all lands. One revolutionary aspect of the charter signed in San Francisco was its explicit recognition of the close relationship between a nation's decency toward other nations and its decency toward its own citizens at home. The charter also reflected the conviction that the fostering of human rights constitutes one of the essential conditions of international peace and that these rights must be protected internationally. From the first, this concept took a firm hold of the corporate conscience of the U.N. family. Even in the hectic postwar era it influenced many peace treaties. On the recommendation of the United Nations, Bulgaria, Finland, Hungary, Italy, Rumania, and Japan pledged themselves to the observance of human rights in their new postwar constitutions.

But it was the Universal Declaration of Human Rights, adopted by the U.N. on December 16, 1948, that set mankind moving toward an international standard of individual rights. The pursuit has been relentless and unbelievably successful.

First, the declaration's recognition of "self-determination" as a fundamental human right shook the foundations of the international community. The insistence that the subjugation of alien peoples constitutes an impediment to peace led to the independence of some sixty countries within fifteen years. Today, a mere handful of people remain under alien rule, and the U.N. family continues to fight indefatigably for their liberation.

A closer look at the developments within the U.N. system reveals the two-pronged process by which the declaration enabled common man to achieve his elevation to international status. First, the declaration and similar assertions of principle set up standards of behavior for governments in their relationships with their own citizens. Though not binding on the states, these principles influenced legislation and initiated the internationalization of the rights of individual citizens. As a Southwest African testified before a U.N. committee: "Whether the declaration has been binding or not, we have learned through it those rights which are ours to demand."

Ratified by sixty nations and therefore transformed into national law, the declaration affected the fundamental law of citizens' rights in these countries. The result was to spread the liberal ideas of the dignity and worth of the individual. Nine countries cite the declaration as the source of the freedoms to which they commit themselves in their constitutions; forty-one others have incorporated the declaration's freedoms into their own constitutional system. Still other nations, such as Libya, had their fundamental laws drawn up by U.N. experts.

The second prong of the escalation of the individual to an international status is constructional. The principles enunciated by the declaration were gradually transformed into more explicit, binding terms for the enjoyment of these rights by the individual citizen. In the past twenty years the U.N. system produced thirty-seven agreements affecting every aspect of the political, social, and economic life of common man. For instance, the Convention of the Status of Women has influenced life in almost every land. One hundred and thirty countries have granted voting rights to women since 1946. Ninety countries have extended other political rights. In France married women were given the right to own property. In Austria women were allowed to conserve their permanent civil service status after being married.

In fact, principles inspired by the United Nations have left few areas in national legislation unaffected. In 1951 and again in 1954 Ontario's legislature adopted two acts to eliminate discrimination "because of race, color, creed, nationality, ancestry, or place of origin in order to meet the standards proclaimed by the Universal Declaration of Human Rights." In Bolivia a legislative act reaffirmed the equality of opportunity for all and declared that "national education shall be inspired by the Universal Declaration of Human Rights." In Panama a law condemned discrimination as a flagrant violation of the Universal Declaration. In the United States the Civil Rights Act of 1964 and the Economic Act of 1964 include the substantive rights of the U.N. declaration, as do the principles of the Age in Discrimination Employment Act of 1967.

The declaration also has influenced judicial action. The International Court of Justice has referred to it on various occasions. Its principles have pervaded national courts, including those in the United States. The declaration was cited in the New York Supreme Court in 1950 and in the U.S. Supreme Court in 1949. With the enactment of two additional covenants in 1966, the United Nations has completed the transnational legal framework that has increasingly affected individual citizens for the last century. The slow accretion of U.N. services in this area has given the individual an international identity beyond his status as citizen of a state.

The main question now is how effectively the common man's new legal standing can be realized and enforced internationally. The record so far is impressive and encouraging. Operations have begun at universal, regional, and national levels. Intergovernmental groups have been formed to deal with various aspects of citizen rights. A UNESCO Commission for Conciliation and Good Offices settles disputes over discrimination in education. An expert committee of eighteen nations spawned by the Convention on the Elimination of All Forms of Racial Discrimination focuses on complaints in this area. The Fact-finding and Conciliation Commission on Freedom of Information already has dealt with 450 cases involving disputes over freedom of expression. The International Labor Organization (ILO) receives complaints from workers' and employers' organizations about infringements of rights.

Each year a report on rights is compiled. The reports are compiled on a three-year cycle. One year, it is on civil and political rights; the next year on economic, social, and cultural matters; the third year on freedom of information. These reports help to promote and protect those rights through international scrutiny.

The United Nations has evolved a system of hearings and on-the-spot observations by U.N.-appointed missions. In 1963, a U.N. human rights mission visited Vietnam. In 1967, the ILO sent a study group to Spain to examine the trade union situation. In 1969, Secretary General U Thant dispatched a representative on humanitarian activities to Nigeria. More recently, the U.N. constituted a special committee for investigating the human rights of the peoples affected by the Arab-Israeli War.

More significantly, the U.N. has moved to the point of regarding infringement of basic human rights as criminal acts. The General Assembly has branded "apartheid, as well as all forms of racial discriminations," as "crimes against humanity." Previously, of course, Rhodesian and South African infringements had been universally regarded as threats to peace. The General Assembly had adopted thirty and the Security Council six resolutions regarding South Africa; upon Rhodesia the council has imposed economic sanctions and other restrictions.

The regional commissions on human rights have developed effective international machinery for supervision and adjudication in matters concerning the rights of common man. The Inter-American Commission on Human Rights and the European Commission on Human Rights allow individuals to appeal against their own governments. The European commission can receive petitions from any person, nongovernmental organization, or group of individuals claiming to be the victim of a violation by its state. In fact, by the winter of 1968 the commission had received 3,700 such complaints. The European Court of Human Rights constituted by the convention has adjudicated many such cases. In 1967, for example, affirming its jurisdiction in the complaint of 327 French-speaking Belgians about laws requiring education of their children in Flemish, the court ruled that the Belgian practice violated the European Convention on Human Rights, which forbids discrimination in education.

From the beginning, the United Nations remained so committed to the material welfare of the common man that for almost two decades it resisted accepting official responsibility for the individual's political and socio-economic rights. The organization also seemed so concerned with the rights of colonial peoples that it deliberately neglected the non-colonial. But involvement with apartheid and racial discrimination developed political attitudes and practices that paved the way to a more universal involvement. In October 1966, a resolution was passed in the General Assembly inviting the Economic and Social Council and the Human Rights Commission to give urgent consideration "to the ways and means of improving the capacity of the U.N. to put a stop to violation of human rights wherever they might occur." In 1968, the evolution progressed one step further when the Human Rights Commission adopted a resolution for handling complaints by individuals against their own governments "in cases revealing a consistent pattern of gross violation."

The final step in implementation and enforcement will be the appointment of a High Commissioner for Human Rights. Also proposed are an Organization for the Promotion of Human Rights and finally an International Court for Human Rights. The realization of all of these projects will not and should not free the individual from the control of his state. On the contrary, these groups will reinforce his legal status within his own nation in the same manner that the development of the nation-state reinforced the ties of the individual with respect to his family through institutionalizing marriage and inheritance laws.

In the quarter century of its existence the United Nations can claim certain achievements in ordering the life of mankind. For instance, it has learned to **deal** with the problems of contemporary society and environment in a universal and transnational manner. It has developed institutions with transnational outlooks and means. It has forged a corporate conscience responsive to all mankind that imposes on all states a sense of international accountability for whatever they do abroad, as well as at home.

But its service to common man tops all these achievements. In a world where giant organizations threaten to dissolve the individual into a nonperson, it has lifted the worth and dignity of the common man into international status. Maybe this achievement more than compensates for its failure to order a world without war.

Perhaps this is the beginning of a new era in which men bonded across their national boundaries by the same freedoms will eventually feel and live as citizens of one world. For initiating this era, the San Francisco meeting twenty-five years ago can be rated as one of the most important events in the history of man.

30 / IS NUREMBERG COMING BACK TO HAUNT US?

James Reston, Jr.

> *"If certain acts in violation of treaties are crimes, they are crimes whether the United States does them or whether Germany does them, and we are not prepared to lay down a rule of criminal conduct against others which we would be unwilling to invoke against ourselves."*
>
> —Associate Justice Robert Jackson,
> chief prosecutor at the Nuremberg Trials.

This statement has come back to haunt us. At Mylai on March 16, 1968, Charlie Company, First Battalion, Twentieth Infantry, Eleventh Brigade, conducted an operation that has raised fundamental questions about the important principles of international conduct that we as a people articulated at the close of World War II. Can we face the problems of command responsibility, policy responsibility, and cultural responsibility? If we can, where then does the blame stop? Who or what should be on trial?

Massacres are not unprecedented in war: There is some doubt that modern war can be waged without them. But the Mylai in-

From *Saturday Review*, July 18, 1970. Copyright © 1970 Saturday Review Inc. Reprinted by permission. See also James Reston, *The Amnesty of John David Herndon*, McGraw-Hill, 1973.

vestigation has brought the matter into the realm of law, and law progresses by precedent.

Perhaps the most pertinent precedent occurred on February 16, 1945. Early on that morning, a company of Japanese troops arrived in the Philippine village of Taal in Batangas Province, and mounted machine guns. The officers questioned the villagers about the guerrillas operating in the area. When they got no answers, they fired into the hutches, and set them on fire. Later, villagers were herded into a ravine and more than 200 were killed with grenades and machine guns. The same pattern was followed in the adjacent villages of San José, Rosario, Cuenca, and Bauan.

The context of these massacres is important. Four months earlier, the combined units of the Third Amphibious Force and the U.S. Seventh Fleet landed at Leyte Harbor on the Philippine island south of Luzon. After a beachhead was established, Gen. Douglas MacArthur waded ashore with his famous comment, "By the grace of Almighty God our forces stand once again on Philippine soil." Later in the day, in a radio broadcast, he appealed to the Philippine people:

"As the lines of battle roll forward to bring you within the zones of operations, rise and strike. For your homes and hearths, strike. For future generations of your sons and daughters, strike. In the home of your sacred dead, strike. Let no arm be faint. Let every arm be steel. The guidance of Divine God points the way. Follow in his name to the Holy Grail of righteous victory."

And strike they did. The American invasion sparked the co-ordination of guerrilla activities throughout the Philippine Islands. By the time the Americans landed on Luzon (January 20, 1945) the guerrillas were strongest in Batangas Province, the southwestern tip of that island. In the mountains outside Taal, two divisions of American-supplied guerrillas were taking shape. This force launched attacks on Japanese posts and supply areas, sabotaged bridges and rail lines, and thus presented the supreme commander of the already disintegrating Japanese forces in the Philippines, General Tomoyuki Yamashita, with a formidable problem.

Shortly after the Luzon landings began General Yamashita had issued orders to "suppress" or "mop up" the guerrilla activity in the islands. (It was this order that formed the basis for his prosecution as a war criminal a year later.) In Batangas, however, this was not easily done. The mountainous jungle was the natural habitat for a growing guerrilla movement, and the landings of American forces outside Manila in January put them between Batangas and General Yamashita, who had fled to the northern town of Baguio. This virtually cut Yamashita's communications with the Batangas command.

Nonetheless, having been told that the suppression of the guerrillas in his area was behind schedule, the commander of a Batangas battalion, Colonel Fujishige, in an attempt to shut off civilian cooperation with the guerrillas, began a campaign of suppression that led to massacre, rape, and torture. An American prosecutor was to repeat the refrain at a trial a year later: "They were massacred—shall we say suppressed!"

The relevance of the Batangas Province massacres by the Japanese in January, February, and March 1945 to the Mylai massacres by Americans twenty-three years later lies not so much in the similarity of the atrocities, but rather in the war crimes trials that followed the Japanese actions and the principles that evolved from those trials. For not only the perpetrators were tried for these massacres, but also General Yamashita himself. As the first major Japanese figure to be tried after the American victory on September 2, 1945, General Yamashita was not charged for ordering the Batangas massacres or even knowing about them, but simply for failing to control the troops under his command.

"The Accused," said the indictment, "a general of the Imperial Japanese Army, between 9 October '44 and 2 September '45, at Manila and other places in the Philippine Islands, while commander of armed forces of Japan at war with the United States and its allies, unlawfully disregarded and failed to discharge his duty as commander to control the operations of the members of his command, permitting them to commit brutal atrocities and other high crimes against the people of the U.S. and of its allies and dependencies, particularly the Philippines, and he (the Accused) thereby violated the laws of war."

General Yamashita's trial began in late October 1945, barely a month and a half after V-J Day. The prosecution launched its case by parading scores of witnesses who testified to their mistreatment by Japanese troops, particularly in Manila and in Batangas. *The New York Times* reported that "The court continued to hear stories of so many atrocities that people just sat dazed in their seats." But this technique (also used at the Bertrand Russell war crimes trial held in Stockholm in 1967 to protest American bombing in Vietnam) was to be expected after the opening statement of the U.S. prosecutor, Major Kerr:

"I am frank to say, Sir, that this case will not be an easy one to hear, nor a pleasant one to try. We Americans are a Christian nation; we are even a sentimental nation. It certainly shocks each one of us to confront the truly horrible acts of beings in the form and shape of man that we must present to the commission in this proceeding . . . . [We do not] select instances on the basis that they are the most horrible, the most nauseating, that might be presented to the commission. If we bring before the commission a witness in a stretcher, permanently mutilated, physically ruined for life, it is not because we are endeavoring to impress the commission through the use of shocking evidence; it is simply because the witness has a story of factual information which the commission should hear, and because that witness . . . is a competent and desirable exhibit of the ruthlessness of those who conquered the Philippines."

After several weeks of gruesome tales from Philippine civilians, the trial moved to cross-examine the principals themselves. Colonel Fujishige, the commander in Batangas, was questioned about the killing of women and children and readily admitted giving orders to kill all persons who opposed the Japanese. "There were many instances," he said, "where women bearing arms inflicted considerable damage to my forces. When I was in an automobile, a child threw a hand grenade at me. . . . I told my troops that if they were attacked by armed women and children that of necessity . . . they must be combatted."

Technically, Colonel Fujishige was on safe legal ground. The Hague Convention No. IV of 1907, which served as a main legal precedent for the Yamashita, Tokyo, and Nuremberg trials—as it will in the Mylai trials—supports him: "The inhabitants of a territory (says Article 2) which has not been occupied, who, on the approach of the enemy, spontaneously take up arms to resist the invading troops . . . shall be regarded as belligerents if they carry arms openly and if they respect the laws and customs of war."

The concept of command responsibility, which grew out of the Yamashita case, carries culpability beyond complicity in atrocities.

The prosecutor contended only that the accused must have known about atrocities because they were so widespread, just as the American high command in Vietnam must have suspected atrocities there. However, to the prosecution in 1945, it was immaterial if Yamashita knew how his orders were being carried out.

"These orders from Yamashita to 'mop up,' 'suppress' the guerrillas," said Major Kerr, "obviously resulted, in the Batangas area, in the mass killings which followed some time later. Of course, these orders did not say 'massacre all civilians.' He unleashed the fury of his men upon the helpless population, and, apparently, according to the record, made no subsequent effort to see what was happening or to take steps to see to it that the obvious results would not occur—not a direct order, but contributing, necessarily, naturally, and directly to the ultimate result.

"We maintain, Sir, that if the Accused saw fit to issue a general order to suppress guerrillas under circumstances as they existed, according to his own testimony, he owed a definite absolute duty furthermore to see to it that they did not open wide the gates of hatred of his men, leading them to wreak vengeance upon the civilian population. Obviously he did not to that. That is part of his responsibility."

The defense argued that General Yamashita's communications had been cut. The Americans were between him and his Batangas command. His forces were disintegrating. And the guerrillas had exhausted the patience of the Japanese.

Major Kerr: "The defense cries that Yamashita was too far away from the scene of the battle, too far removed from the actual perpetrators, justly to be charged and punished for crimes of those under him. Yet his very government, his entire nation may legally be held responsible—even farther removed from the perpetrators and from the scene of the crime. We say it is in accordance with all the established principles of responsiblity in the field of international relations that the commanding officer as an individual be held responsible."

The prosecution not only bore down on Yamashita's responsibility for his troops, it also argued that their actions were an inevitable result of the kind of war the General had waged. Major Kerr: "The Defense saw fit to refer to the victims of the Japanese as the victims of war. Victims of war! Is this warfare? We have another explanation for it. We say they were victims of Yamashita! They are victims of the type of warfare that was conducted by Yamashita, by the troops under him."

On December 7, 1945, four years after Pearl Harbor, General Yamashita was sentenced to hang. Two-and-a-half months later, after the failure of an appeal to the Philippine and U.S. Supreme Courts, in the town of Los Baños, fifty miles from Batangas Province, that sentence was carried out. In subsequent trials sixteen soldiers were tried for their parts in the Taal massacre. Six, including Colonel Fujishige, were hanged; one was shot; two were given life sentences; one was sentenced to thirty years, another to twenty-five years, and a third to twenty years. Four were acquitted. The two platoon leaders, Second Lieutenants Fukuoka and Hosaka, received the lightest sentences, twenty-five and twenty years, respectively. The company commander, Warrant Officer Kobayashi, received a life sentence. The stiffer penalties were reserved for the higher staff officers.

"General Yamashita's record was a blot on the military profession," General MacArthur said shortly before the execution. "Revolting as this may be in itself, it pales before the sinister and far-reaching implication thereby attached to the profession of arms. *The soldier, be he friend or foe, is charged with the protection of the weak and unarmed.* . . . *When he violates this sacred trust, he not only profanes his entire cult, but threatens the very fabric of international society.*"

In one of the last interviews with Yamashita before his death, the subject of MacArthur was raised, and Yamashita was to say, "After all, it could have been him."

Since the investigation implicating fourteen high-ranking officers in the Mylai incident, some commentators have argued that the U.S. Army is applying the principles of Nuremberg to itself. However, the Mylai charges do *not* squarely meet the question of war crimes in Vietnam; it would be closer to the truth to say that the Mylai investigation evades the real responsibility. The charges so far are against the instruments of the Pentagon policy in Vietnam, rather than against the policymakers. Nuremberg concentrated on the latter.

War crimes were defined at Nuremberg and Tokyo as follows:

1) *Class A: Crimes Against the Peace:*   Namely, planning, preparation, initiation, or waging of a war of aggression, or a war in violation of international treaties, agreements, or assurances, or participation in a Common Plan or Conspiracy for the accomplishment of any of the foregoing. [The planning of aggressive war was considered the "supreme crime" in the postwar trials.]

2) *Class B: Crimes Against Humanity:*   Namely, murder, extermination, enslavement, deportation, and other inhumane acts committed against any civilian population, before or during the war, of persecutions on political, racial, or religious grounds in execution of or in connection with any crime within the jurisdiction of the Tribunal, whether or not in violation of domestic law of the country where perpetrated.

3) *Class C: War Crimes:*   Namely, violations of the laws or customs of war. Such violations shall include, but not be limited to, murder, ill-treatment, or deportation of slave labor or for any other purpose, of civilian population of or in occupied territory, murder or ill-treatment of prisoners of war or persons on the seas, killing of hostages, plunder of public or private property, wanton destruction of cities, towns, or villages, or devastation not justified by military necessity.

If he is found guilty, Lt. William L. Calley would, by the standards of the Nuremberg, Tokyo, and Yamashita trials, be a low-grade, Class C war criminal. But if Lieutenant Calley is on trial for brutality, so is the search and destroy policy on trial for brutalizing him. In *Casualties of War*, Daniel Lang describes the effect of that policy on American troops:

> *Day after day, out on patrol, we'd come to a narrow dirt path leading through some shabby village, and the elders would welcome us and the children come running with smiles on their faces waiting for candy we'd give them. But at the other end of the path, just as we were leaving the village behind, the enemy would open up on us, and there was bitterness among us that the villagers hadn't given us warning. All that many of us could think at such times was that we were fools to be ready*

to die for a people who defecated in public, whose food was dirtier than anything in our garbage cans back home. Thinking like that—well, as I say, it could change some fellows. It could keep them from believing that life was so valuable—anyone's life, I mean, even their own. I'm not saying that every fellow who roughed up a civilian liked himself for it . . . he'd start defending what he'd done many hours ago by saying that, after all, it was no worse than what Charlie was doing.

The brutality of war, however, and the criteria of culpability under the Nuremberg and Yamashita precedents are not limited to the policy of search and destroy. The Mylai area had, according to Maj. Gen. William Peers, who was in charge of the Pentagon's investigation, traditionally been "under Communist domination." It was therefore subject to intense bombardment from the air.

By the end of 1967, said Jonathan Schell, the author of two books on Vietnam, "the destruction of society in Quangngai Province was not something we were in danger of doing. It was something that was nearing its completion. About 70 per cent, by my estimation, of the villages in that province had been destroyed." Most of this destruction, Schell explained, had been done by American aerial bombardment, prompted by reports of village cooperation with the Vietcong.

Most Americans are aware of the impersonal slaughter that takes place from the Vietnamese stratosphere, but many are unaware of its systematic intensity, or of other elements of random brutality:

The TPQ program (night bombings). Every province in I Corps including Quangngai is authorized five to twelve radar-guided bombings per night. These tactical bomber strikes are based on the scantiest intelligence of enemy activity at a specific map coordinate. A former intelligence agent who worked in this program said enemy hospitals were second only to fixed supply installations when selecting target priorities for TPQ strikes. Destroying enemy hospitals was stressed as a high priority in our Cambodian operations by Vice President Agnew in a recent television interview. And yet the American public was so outraged when several mortar rounds hit our hospital at Camranh Bay early in 1969.

Operation Thor. In a twenty-four-hour period in the spring of

1968, sixty B-52 strikes, the largest number of these "arc light" strikes in the entire war, cut a three-kilometer-wide swath across South Vietnam below the DMZ. No attempt was made to determine what villages lay along this patch. Such are the dimensions of "military necessity" in Vietnam.

Relocation. In the spring of 1967, American reconnaissance planes flew over a ninety-square-kilometer area of the central highlands which was inhabited by the nomadic Montagnards and known as a regrouping area for VC infiltration into the coastal area around Nhatrang and Tuyhoa. The purpose of this mission was to identify every inhabited place. Shortly after the flights, troops of the American Fourth Division moved into the area, rounded up some 4,000 Montagnards, and took them to a newly built village called Edapenang. The Montagnards were relocated so that they could not serve the enemy as bearers and food production personnel, and so the jungle could be opened for unrestricted bombing raids and big operations like Dakto and Hill 875, where American forces sustained 1,645 casualties. Through cultural ignorance we provided water from wells rather than the stream water that Montagnards were used to, built individual family housing rather than the customary long houses, and moved people during their planting season so that they had to be fed for eighteen months. As a result, the population of Edapenang dropped from 4,000 to 1,000. Edapenang was the pet project of the Fourth Division commander in 1967-68, General Peers.

Phoenix program. The emphasis of this operation, which has been incorrectly reported as assassination, is on "bringing in" VC cadremen from villages. One device used toward this end is the "metal trace detection kit," a CIA machine in which ultraviolet light is supposed to detect "tissue aberrations" either on a trigger finger or on the shoulder where a rifle butt would be placed. In 1968 the kit was taken into hamlets in I Corps area, villagers rounded up, a poncho set up like an old-time camera, and each villager forced to submit his body to the test. By an ex-intelligence agent's testimony, all the villagers' hands looked splotchy, and as a consequence the Vietnamese commander ordered them all taken out and tortured with the water treatment until they provided information. The machine required an expert to determine any significant tissue aberrations; there was none on the scene when the agent observed the use of the kit; nonethless, villagers were tortured on the basis of amateur interpretations. When the American agent protested to his commander, the superior shrugged it off. "Oh, what the hell," he said, "it's their show."

It is the high-technology warfare that the United States is waging in Vietnam, not the face-to-face "gratuitous brutality," in Hannah Arendt's term, of Company C that causes the wholesale killing of Vietnamese civilians. It is therefore not surprising that Col. Oran K. Henderson, now charged with making false statements and false swearing, testified to the Pentagon in 1969 that he had seen the bodies of only one woman and two children in Mylai and believed that they had been killed by artillery, or that Col. Thon That Kien, the Quangngai Province chief, also tried to convince himself that stray artillery fire had killed all those civilians. Civilian death by artillery or air strike in a free fire zone is an accident of war; killing civilians with an M-16 is a crime if anyone should dare to press charges.

Where does the culpability for Mylai stop—with Calley, with Westmoreland, with McNamara, with Johnson and Nixon, or with the whole American people? The Hague Conventions of 1899 and 1907 were based on a brand of warfare that could imagine a Lieutenant Calley but not a B-52. And the postwar trials of the Axis figures were careful to avoid charges against the enemy that were applicable also to ourselves. If the Allies had been vanquished in that war, any war trials would surely have centered on the area of aerial bombardment and high-technology weaponry, particularly the saturation bombing of Japanese and German cities and the use of the atomic bomb. Dr. Richard Falk, the international law professor at Princeton, has pointed out the irony that the day the United States signed the charter for the International Military Tribunal at Nuremberg, August 8, 1945, was the day it dropped the atomic bomb on Nagasaki. With this gap left unplugged in the annals of war crimes proceedings, the policy of high-technology warfare has developed in Vietnam without touching the conscience of America.

The Defense Department admits no responsibility. The Peers report devotes an entire chapter to the Pentagon directives and troop information pamphlets regarding the Hague and Geneva conventions and a soldier's duty to respect the Vietnamese and their customs, concerning the need to "handle an enemy captive firmly, promptly, but humanely" and to protect him against "violence, insults, curiosity, and reprisals of any kind." But any Vietnam veteran will tell you that the cards on the treatment of POWs and civilians are handed to the incoming soldier with the same bureaucratic unconcern as are his new fatigues, scrip, and salt tablets.

What is significant, therefore, is not the paper policy but the practice. Which will be more important for the combat soldier: the Nine Rules for humane treatment of the Vietnamese on a card in his wallet, or a pep talk about taking revenge on the gooks the night before an operation into Pinkville?

The fundamental question of the Calley trial relates to the Yamashita trial: Does the kind of war that we are fighting in Vietnam make Mylais inevitable? No Vietnam veteran is shocked by Mylai. He knows that there was more killing at Mylai than elsewhere but that it was not unique in our search and destroy operations. The circle of responsibility goes beyond Calley and his company. (Not that the criminal responsibility need be larger. A crime must have its direct perpetrators.) The political, moral, and command liability will remain unanswered in the trials of those now charged.

The relevant area of consideration is the new concept of justice that the United States introduced at Nuremberg: crimes against humanity. The sheer weight of death and devastation in Vietnam now transcends all political discussion. One million Vietnamese civilians, according to Senator Edward Kennedy, have become casualties of war since 1965. For those crimes no man—not Calley, not Westmoreland, not Johnson or Nixon—stands alone in the dock, but the whole American nation. The technology that is the American wonder at home is the American horror in Vietnam. The American people has approved of its use in both places.

In 1947 the philosopher Karl Jaspers approached the question of German guilt in a way that is pertinent to the question of American responsibility today. He talked of four areas of guilt: criminal, political, moral, and metaphysical. Under his definition, an orgy of accusation about individuals who were responisble for our war policy will not satisfy justice, though those individuals share a higher political liability than General Yamashita.

Jaspers wrote, "We are responsible for our [the Nazi] regime, for the acts of the regime, for the start of the war in this world-historical situation, and for the leaders we allowed to rise among us."

This is the political responsibility that all Americans share. The metaphysical responsibility comes when injustices are committed in our presence with our knowledge. The acceptance of this responsibility, Jaspers says, can lead to a transformation of human consciousness where pride is broken and arrogance is impossible.

"Because of the great diversity in what we believed all these years," Jaspers said to the defeated German people, "what we took to be true, what to us was the meaning of life, the way of transformation must also be different now for every individual. We are all being transformed. But we do not all follow the same path to the new ground of common truth, which we seek and which reunites us. In such a disaster everyone may let himself be made over for rebirth, without fear of dishonor. What we must painfully renounce is not alike for all—so little alike that one man's renunciation may impress another as a gain. We are divided along different lines of disappointment."

The Vietnam War is transforming Americans also, but it is not clear what we will become as a result. Will we allow this country to revel in more vainglorious causes or seek to reclaim our original ideals? Mylai could lead to a new maturity in our recognition that Americans are humans like everyone else, capable of nobility, but also capable of bestiality, and that when our technology places upon us the highest responsibility in the world we must work toward a climate where the nobler instincts can flourish once again.

B. POPULATION

31 / WHAT U.S. LIFE WILL BE LIKE BY 1980: THE MEANING OF POPULATION SHIFTS

U.S. News & World Report Staff

Ahead for the 1970s are dramatic shifts in the U.S. population, shifts that will bring vast changes in the pattern of American life.

Now getting under way—and certain to grow in years just ahead—is a boom in the number of young adults.

That's the age group which is going to dominate the coming decade, shaping markets for business, influencing politicians, affecting styles of living.

In numbers alone, young adults—people in their 20s and 30s— will outpace all other age groups.

Between now and 1980, the horde of young adults will grow by 18 million, up 34 per cent. People in all other age groups will increase by 9 million or a mere 6 per cent.

In other words, 2 of every 3 Americans added to the population in the coming decade will be young adults.

It all stems from the baby boom in the years just after World War II. These Americans now are coming of age, moving through the colleges, marrying, starting and raising families.

The impact. Young adults spend and borrow freely—for cars, clothing, recreation, housing and the myriad products that go into new homes and apartments. Styles and fashions, increasingly, will bear the stamp of younger people.

Jobs in rising numbers will have to be found as high-school and college graduates enter the nation's work force. These new jobs will require heavy investment by business.

Reprinted from *U.S. News & World Report*, January 11, 1971.

27 MILLION MORE AMERICANS BY 1980 . . .

As of July 1— U. S. Population
1980 232.4 million
1979 229.2 million
1978 226.2 million
1977 223.2 million
1976 220.3 million
1975 217.6 million
1974 214.9 million
1973 212.4 million
1972 209.9 million
1971 207.6 million
1970 205.4 million

Population growth is speeding up again after more than a decade of slowing. Reason: Americans born in the baby boom just after World War II are coming of marrying age and starting families of their own.

. . . AND MOST OF THEM WILL BE YOUNG ADULTS

CHILDREN AND TEEN-AGERS	1970	78.1 million
	1975	79.3 million
	1980	82.2 million

GAIN, 1970-80: 4.1 million, or 5%

YOUNG ADULTS, 20-39	1970	53.6 million
	1975	62.1 million
	1980	71.7 million

GAIN, 1970-80: 18.1 million, or 34%

MIDDLE-AGED GROUP, 40-59	1970	45.4 million
	1975	45.3 million
	1980	45.2 million

DECLINE, 1970-80: 200,000, less than 1%

PEOPLE 60 AND OVER	1970	28.3 million
	1975	30.8 million
	1980	33.3 million

GAIN, 1970-80: 5 million, or 18%

Two thirds of the growth in American population during the 1970s will come in the young-adult group—the people who will be marrying, raising families, looking for new homes, borrowing and spending money on a wide variety of products and services.

Basic data: U. S. Census Bureau

The bright promise of an affluent young population will not be realized, of course, if youthful workers find no work waiting for them.

Politicians, too, are taking notice. Election campaigns, more and more, will have to be oriented to younger voters. By 1980, half the U.S. population of voting age will be under 40 years old.

Urge for action.   It's the view of many social scientists that today's restless students, once they start careers and raise families, will settle down and work within the American system.

Still, businessmen and governments at all levels can expect more pressure for change from young adults—people with flexible ideas and habits and, as a group, better-educated than their elders.

Younger people will be pressing for more action to meet social needs, demanding a bigger say in running things.

Marriages will continue to boom, with a resulting surge in the number of new households. By 1973, the number of weddings will surpass the record of nearly 2.3 million set in 1946.

The baby population.   Births, after declining for more than a decade, are now starting to move up again. The trend to smaller families is likely to continue, but the rising number of families being formed will push total births to new highs.

Another baby boom, as a result, will take hold later in the 70s, creating a bigger market for the things babies and growing children need.

As for other age groups—

The teen-age boom will come to an end in the 1970s. There will be about the same number in 1980 as now, limiting growth opportunities for businesses catering to this age group's requirements for records, clothing, other items.

Among younger children of school age—5 years old and up—the next decade will witness an actual decline in numbers.

You can already see the effects of the leveling off in the school-age population. The teacher shortage of just a few years ago now is turning into a surplus of teachers.

One result: Americans can look forward to slackening pressure to raise local school taxes.

College enrollments, on the other hand, are soaring—partly because of an increase in the college-age population, partly because a larger share of this group is attending college. Today's enrollment of 7.9 million will reach 12 million by 1980.

People in their 40s and 50s—the ones that provide much of the leadership for this country's business—are to drop in numbers by

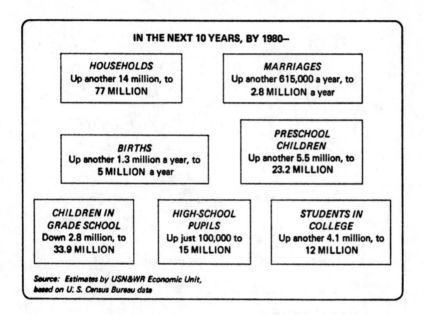

IN THE NEXT 10 YEARS, BY 1980—

HOUSEHOLDS
Up another 14 million, to
77 MILLION

MARRIAGES
Up another 615,000 a year, to
2.8 MILLION a year

BIRTHS
Up another 1.3 million a year, to
5 MILLION a year

PRESCHOOL CHILDREN
Up another 5.5 million, to
23.2 MILLION

CHILDREN IN GRADE SCHOOL
Down 2.8 million, to
33.9 MILLION

HIGH-SCHOOL PUPILS
Up just 100,000 to
15 MILLION

STUDENTS IN COLLEGE
Up another 4.1 million, to
12 MILLION

Source: Estimates by USN&WR Economic Unit, based on U. S. Census Bureau data

1980. That could keep the supply of top managers rather tight—or open up new opportunities in executive suites for younger Americans.

It's in the middle-age bracket that average incomes are the highest and spending per person the heaviest. People in their middle years tend to move into bigger houses, spend more for services, including medical care, travel, college for their children, eating meals in restaurants—in general, upgrading their living standards.

A decline in the number of people in their 40s and 50s could restrain the market for some types of goods and services.

But economists, looking ahead, say that management's need for people in this age range should push their pay—and spending—sharply higher.

More older people.   Move up another bracket—to those over 60—and you find a rapid climb is in store, second in rate of growth only to the young-adult group.

The surge in prospect promises greater demand for apartments, medical care, nursing homes and added strain on hospitals. Also likely from this expanding bloc: More pressure to broaden Social

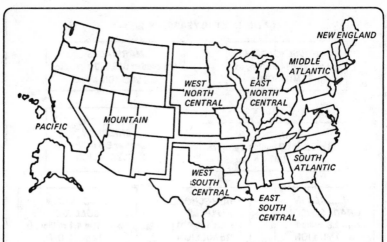

HOW YOUR REGION WILL GROW IN COMING DECADE

REGION	NOW	1980	GAIN
NEW ENGLAND (Maine, New Hampshire, Vermont, Massachusetts, Rhode Island, Connecticut)	11,848,000	13,000,000	10%
MIDDLE ATLANTIC (New York, New Jersey, Pennsylvania)	37,153,000	40,600,000	9%
EAST NORTH CENTRAL (Ohio, Indiana, Illinois, Michigan, Wisconsin)	40,253,000	44,000,000	9%
WEST NORTH CENTRAL (Minnesota, Iowa, Missouri, North Dakota, South Dakota, Nebraska, Kansas)	16,324,000	17,400,000	7%
SOUTH ATLANTIC (Delaware, Maryland, D.C., Virginia, West Virginia, North Carolina, South Carolina, Georgia, Florida)	30,671,000	36,100,000	18%
EAST SOUTH CENTRAL (Kentucky, Tennessee, Alabama, Mississippi)	12,804,000	13,800,000	8%
WEST SOUTH CENTRAL (Arkansas, Louisiana, Oklahoma, Texas)	19,322,000	22,000,000	14%
MOUNTAIN (Montana, Idaho, Wyoming, Colorado, New Mexico, Arizona, Utah, Nevada)	8,282,000	10,000,000	21%
PACIFIC (Washington, Oregon, California, Alaska, Hawaii)	26,525,000	33,100,000	25%

NOTE: Figures are resident population, excluding Americans abroad.

Source: 1970, U. S. Census Bureau; 1980, estimates by USN&WR Economic Unit

Security benefits—and to raise taxes on younger people to cover the cost of those added pensions.

But Government benefits and the growth of private pension plans are removing the need to stash away every extra penny. Older people thus are becoming more independent financially.

Merchants, as a result, are showing increasing interest in the sales market now expanding among older people—a market not just for the necessities of life but for luxuries, such as travel, books and recreation, fashionable clothing, cosmetics.

Outward push. Where will Americans live? The trend to the suburbs is continuing apace. Many smaller towns that once were considered part of a big city's suburbs are becoming fair-sized cities on their own.

Further pull of people to suburbia will mean more housing, shopping centers, plants and commercial buildings in outlying areas. It will also bring growing congestion and the problems of providing more public transportation and utility services.

Big cities, if trends of the 1960s continue, will grow slowly or lose population. But medium-sized and smaller cities are likely to add population at a good clip.

As the map on this page shows, the outlook is for the States of the South and West to show the fastest growth in the coming decade. Americans have the urge, census experts report, to move toward warmer climates and toward the shore.

Population in the Northeast and the central part of the country is to show the smallest gains.

Yet these areas will still contain the majority of Americans, still provide the biggest markets.

Toward 1980—. Over all, America's net population growth—the result of births, deaths and migration—is again speeding up after more than a decade of slowing. The net growth of 2 million in 1968 was the smallest since 1945.

Larger increases now lie ahead. By 1979, the annual growth will be back over 3 million, heading for new records.

By 1980, the total U.S. population will be about 232 million— and nearly 1 in every 3 Americans will be in his of her 20s or 30s.

More and more, the U.S. will become a nation of young adults.

32 / THE POPULATION BOMB: CAN THE U.N. DE-FUSE IT?

James Avery Joyce

A curious fallacy about population seems to have arisen: The poorer the nation, the higher its birth rate, and the more developed the nation, the lower its birth rate; therefore, the obvious way to limit world population is to make all nations richer.

The more developed countries have frequently been cited as evidence to support this simple logic. Both the United States and the Soviet Union are down to about 1 per cent population growth per year (which means that they will double in approximately 70 years). The rate of population increase in Norway, Sweden and Denmark has dropped steadily over the years and now stands at about 1.5 per cent. Australia and New Zealand, with similar social patterns, have nearly the same rate. Japan has cut its birth-rate in half, from 2 to 1 per cent, since the war. Declining death rates, of course, push the population growth rate up somewhat, but the downward trend generally prevails as prosperity grows.

But what about the developing world? Will economic growth alone solve the population problem? Will increasing affluence produce a new balance of nature, checking man's proliferation so that it will be in accord with his environment?

Paul R. Ehrlich, author of *The Population Bomb*, disposed of this argument neatly in a recent *Saturday Review* article in which he remarked that "it might seem logical to attempt to solve the population problem in the underdeveloped countries by developing those countries so that they, too, will undergo a demographic transition and reduce their birth rates. But analysis shows this to be a dubious proposition." He reasons that it is extremely questionable whether "internal resources could be mobilized quickly enough to permit the industrialization of the entire earth at any meaningful rate." But, more important, he says that even if worldwide industrialization could be accomplished in some 50 years, the total

From *War/Peace Report*, April 1971. Reprinted by permission.

population of the underdeveloped areas would then be four times its present level. And, he adds, there are no present signs that the "overdeveloped" countries are willing to develop the underdeveloped ones.

The more one looks at world population figures, the clearer it becomes that the accelerating growth must be halted at once. It cannot be left to the forces of nature. According to the U.N.'s latest *Population Studies* (No. 41), the world's population totaled almost three billion in 1960 and 3.6 billion in 1970. It may reach 4.5 billion in 1980, 5.4 billion in 1990, and 6.5 billion by the end of the century. In these totals, the population of more developed regions accounts for the following figures: 976,000 million in 1960; 1.1 billion in 1970; 1.2 billion in 1980; 1.3 billion in 1990; and 1.5 billion in 2000. These figures increase at average annual rates of 1 per cent, with the rate declining somewhat near the end of the century. The population of less developed regions accounts for the following figures in the U.N. study; two billion in 1960; 2.5 billion in 1970; 3.3 billion in 1980; 4.1 billion in 1990; and five billion in 2000. These figures increase at annual rates of 2.4 per cent, diminishing to 2 per cent by the end of the century.

HIGHEST RATE YET

Although these projections may be debatable, it is significant that they suggest *a higher rate of world population growth during the 1970s than in any preceding decade.* Thus, the Second United Nations Development decade, from 1970 to 1980, may witness the fastest growth of human numbers in all the history of mankind. The numerical increase may be even higher in subsequent decades because, even though the rate of growth may decline, the population base will be larger.

Consequently, the urgency of the problem has dominated all the recent debates on population within the United Nations. The only question that matters is: What can be done *now*? What sort of population planning can be designed and integrated within the Second Development Decade to prevent its objectives from being defeated or frustrated by the fact that added numbers of people will outpace new economic programs?

The most common answer, of course, has been summed up in the phrase "family planning." But family planning is a very complex matter. On a global scale it is a mammoth task, in organization, personnel and finances.

Just as the problem is looking more and more unmanageable, though, a breakthrough seems to have occurred. It is the creation of the U.N. Fund for Population Activities, or Population Fund as it is frequently called. It is too early to assess yet whether this new element can be said to be revolutionizing the strategy of world population control or whether it is merely a temporary palliative. But its concept and goals are impressive.

The Population Fund, originally known as the Trust Fund for Population Activities, was established in 1967 by Secretary General U Thant to enable U.N. bodies to respond more effectively to the needs of member states for population programs. The primary role of the Fund is to make countries aware of their needs for population control and then to finance and coordinate assistance efforts. The Fund is overseen by Paul G. Hoffman, administrator of the U.N. Development Program.

Financed from voluntary contributions, the Fund's resources grew from less than $5 million in 1968 to $15 million last year. The 1971 budget will probably exceed $25 million, and by 1975 it should reach $100 million. During the Second Development Decade, the Fund hopes to spend about $700 million on population programs entirely in the developing world.

By the end of 1970, the Population Fund was involved in the support of about 200 projects, including a $1.7 million program in family planning in Pakistan and a $400,000 effort to provide contraceptive supplies and expert advisers on family planning services to the United Arab Republic.

The Population Fund's eight-point policy program for 1971-74 includes assistance in the collection of basic population data; demonstration projects in family planning connected with existing material and child health services; large-scale family planning programs such as those presently being financed in Pakistan and Mauritius; pilot projects on new contraceptive techniques; social science research; inclusion of family planning in current social and economic projects; a review of laws relating to population ques-

tions; and an information campaign to awaken the public conscience and broaden its understanding of population problems.

The Fund does not execute its projects directly. It turns them
over for execution to the U.N. and its various agencies, such as
UNICEF, UNESCO and the World Health Organization. Naturally,
the Fund plans programs that are tailored to the specific needs of a
country which seeks its help. At the present time, for example, the
Fund is supporting the first census ever to be taken in Africa south
of the Sahara, where up to now less than 10 per cent of the births
and deaths have been recorded. The Fund is providing advisers,
training, equipment, and sometimes the salaries of the numerators.

The Fund's most ambitious project to date is the $1.7 million
family planning program in Pakistan, in connection with Pakistan's
fourth five-year plan. Pakistan itself is investing $146.7 million in
family planning during this period, but the Fund will be supplying
boats, jeeps, scooters, and bicycles to make field workers mobile.
It will provide advisers and resources for training and research, and
will pay $200,000 for supplies of birth control pills this year alone.
It is also sending 40 uterine aspirators for abortions. Similar
nationwide projects are being planned for Ceylon, India, Indonesia,
Iran, the Philippines and Thailand.

Last year the Fund moved into a new field when the Shah of
Iran launched a comprehensive birth control program as part of his
country's overall economic planning. A team of demographic and
information-media experts from several U.N. agencies, headed by
Britain's former U.N. representative Lord Caradon, spent two
months in Iran preparing a blueprint for Iran's future population
policy.

Since Iran's present population of 28 million may become 60
million by the end of the century if the present growth rate continues, the proposals of the Caradon mission are being awaited both
in Iran and the other Asian countries (where half of the world's
population lives) with unusual interest. For more and more of the
Asian governments are abandoning a wait-and-see attitude in favor
of commitment to population control through national policies of
family planning sponsored and supported by the Fund. If this
trend grows in Asia and elsewhere, the U.N. may be able to make a
breakthrough toward de-fusing the population bomb.

33 / CITIES
CAN WORK

Edward N. Costikyan

> *Why are the mayors all quitting?*
> *Why are the cities all broke?*
> *Why are the people all angry?*
> *Why are we dying of smoke?*
> *Why are the streets unprotected?*
> *Why are the schools in distress?*
> *Why is the trash uncollected?*
> *How did we make such a mess?*
> —Anon.

This bit of verse sums up with commendable clarity and directness the problems of the cities as we enter a new decade. The answers are less clear, and the solutions still more obscure. But a misunderstanding of the causes of the trouble has led most urbanologists to a wholly ineffective and unlikely cure. For the nearly universal prescription would have the federal government provide massive financial assistance and take over as many city governmental functions as can possibly be palmed off upwards.

I doubt that the federal government will provide money in sufficient amounts to reconstruct our cities within the near future. Although some of a city's money problems, such as the costs of welfare, properly are financed in whole, instead of only in part, by the federal government, massive increases in federal aid would *not* solve a city's problems, but rather would be quickly ingested by the money-consuming monster that city government can become. Therefore, the causes of the crises within our cities demand a different type of federal help for two reasons: The predominant cause of city crises is the collapse and destruction of the political machine. The second cause is the shortage of a supply of cheap labor essential to the growth and life of any city.

The political machine was the institutional backbone of city government during the period in which our cities were built. It played a multitude of governmental roles. And it gave the average citizen the direct access to government services, which he cannot find today.

The base of the machine was the captain of the election district or precinct. He was in charge of a one- to two-block area for the party. And he was in charge year round. If a resident had a problem—a leaking ceiling, no water or heat, a son in trouble with the law, a shortage of cash or food—he turned to his neighbor the captain. The captain, if he himself could not deal with the problem, took the constituent to "the leader" at the local clubhouse. There the problem was explained, and the leader undertook to solve it. If it was a leaky roof, the leader called someone he knew in the appropriate city department—often someone the leader had placed there —explained the problem, and got action.

This power of lateral invasion into the bureaucracy made efficient administration of a large city possible. It kept the bureaucracy hopping. But it also encouraged corruption. The average citizen, however, was willing to tolerate a degree of corruption as the price of his having ready access to government services. But the more affluent members of society (the backbone of every reform movement), seeing in this lateral access to government services (and not needing those services) potential and actual corruption, set out to destroy that access and the system that produced it.

By and large, these efforts have succeeded in their intent. But we will never know whether their success represents, on balance, progress or retrogression, for all the histories of the political machines and their workings have been written from a reform orientation. It should be observed, however, in the absence of fairer contemporaneous data, that the political machines built the cities, paved their streets, dug their sewers, and piped their water supply systems. Furthermore, under the administration of the machines, mass transit systems, school systems, and massive developments of new housing were constructed.

It would be laughable to suggest that any of our present city administrations could accomplish one-tenth of what the political machines accomplished during the period from the Civil War to World War I.

The machine was also the source of manpower to staff the city government. Of course, the city jobs available to the machine were part of its lifeblood. But the reservoir of people with some training in city government was also a resource for the city—a resource whose absence today has contributed to the "mess" referred to in the verse. People untrained in government try to learn what it is all about while on the job, wandering in and out of office at a pace that staggers the minds of the citizenry. By and large, these untrained people find themselves unable to effectively control or direct the bureaucracy, and frequently they quit in frustration.

The reform answer to the machine as the personnel pool for government was the creation of a competing source of manpower: civil service. As long as civil service and the machine remained in competition for the staffing of the government, the administrative result was good. But with the collapse of the machine, civil service has monopolized the field, and the administrative results have been disastrous, for the bureaucracies have a double layer of protection that deprives any elected official of the power to get the bureaucrats to do their jobs. One layer is the impossibility of firing a civil servant. The other is the civil service unions, which have such power over the city—in the absence of alternative sources of manpower—that in the final analysis the bureaucracies are in a position to dictate to elected officials and their appointees. The bureaucrats can specify what they will and will not do (such as inspect boilers during a cold wave), what they will wear, and where they will work. The elected official (or his appointee) is at their mercy.

And these bureaucracies of unionized civil servants are strangling the cities. In New York City, for example, the police force has been doubled in the past fifteen years, although the population figures have remained almost constant. Fewer, not more policemen are on the line. There are supposedly six policemen for every one-to two-block election district in Manhattan. Tell that to a New Yorker and he'll laugh at you. He hasn't seen one of those policemen on the beat for years—unless it's to protect Khrushchev or Castro or the President of the United States. And then the question is, "Where did they all come from?"

There are fewer than 3,000 policemen assigned to duty on New York City streets (in cars or on foot) at any one time. (Put aside whether those assigned are where they are supposed to be.) One night last year, according to former Mayor Robert Wagner, there was not a single policeman on duty on the streets of Brooklyn. And the cost of all this "protection" has been estimated to be about $39 per citizen in New York City, as compared with about $13 per capita in a city of 100,000 people. When Mayor John Lindsay tried to change an archaic state statute that stipulated police be assigned to only three equal shifts, the police union first fought him in the state legislature, and lost. Ultimately, however, the union won by simply refusing to go along, and the fourth shift, which increases the number of police on duty during high crime periods, is now "voluntary" and is paid overtime.

The same phenomena of high costs, large numbers of employees with few on the line, rigidity, and immunity from discipline by elected officials or their appointees are found in every city department.

The cost of all this leaps and leaps. In New York City, the cost of providing essential services goes up every year by about 15 per cent, while revenues rise by less than 5 per cent. The result is the annual budget gap with which city dwellers are familiar, and which causes the cry for more federal money. New York City's budget, at $3-billion in 1965, is more than double that five years later. This $3-billion increase has not been absorbed by the cost of new services, but by the cost of existing programs. More federal aid will not solve the problem created by the capacity of the present bureaucracies to absorb more and more money for the same, or perhaps less, service.

The destruction of the political machine has left the unionized civil service bureaucracies with the same control over the life of the city that the machine once enjoyed and abused sufficiently to lead to the growth of civil service.

Finally, the destruction of the machine has left some governmental functions without anyone to perform them. The city's election machinery, for example, was once operated by the political parties. The parties, rather than the city, not only trained the election inspectors but paid them (the city paid a pittance, and still does, but the parties no longer can transform this pittance into reasonable compensation). The parties saw that the polls were open when they should be, and that the voting machines worked. True, the parties sometimes abused their power. There were conflicts of interest in primary elections where one faction or another selected the inspectors. (In the first primary in which I was elected a district leader, my opponent selected the thirty-two Democratic inspectors who, with thirty-two Republican ones, operated our sixteen polling places. I won, nonetheless.)

But the parties no longer are capable of performing this governmental function. And although some critics attribute breakdowns in the electoral machinery to the venality of the political machine, in fact, it is the result of incompetence.

The political consequences of the destruction of the machine are far more obvious than the governmental ones. The wave of upset victories in recent city primaries and elections all over the country is the obvious product of the death of the political party machines and party loyalty and party discipline.

The solution to all this is *not* the recreation of the political machines, an impossible task given the level of competence of their present leaders and personnel. Rather it is to stimulate alternative methods of performing the necessary governmental and political functions that the machines once performed.

The second major cause of the crisis of the cities has been the loss of a supply of cheap labor. This loss has not only escalated municipal government costs, but has posed the most serious threat to the capacity of the cities to survive.

Eliel Saarinen in his book *The City: Its Growth, Its Decay, Its Future* pointed out that the basic function of a city is to provide places for people to live and work. Indeed, without places to live, there can be no city.

The loss of a supply of cheap labor has eliminated the capacity of the city (here I mean not the city government, but the totality of its institutions) to provide the places for people to live. In New York City, residential construction has come to a halt—literally, not figuratively, for construction capital and labor can far more profitably be devoted to commercial construction, where rents of $16 per year per square foot can be earned.

Unless some solution is found to this problem, the city is doomed to a slow death as its existing supply of residential housing decays and becomes uninhabitable, and the city's people are pushed out.

The second major problem created by the loss of a supply of cheap labor has already been noted—the 15 per cent increase in the costs of city government each year. Once city employment was attractive to ambitious young men as well as to security-seeking citizens. There was a surplus of cheap labor. Jobs were impermanent in a non-unionized volatile economy, and many offered little in the way of a future. Lower paying government jobs were attractive. They provided security and a step up the ladder. That is no longer true. To get people to work for it, the city must now compete with and attempt to match the private sector. As a result, the costs of city government have skyrocketed, and will continue to skyrocket sufficiently to absorb all that giant transfusion of federal aid to the cities that everyone calls for, and that is supposed to be on the way.

Again, the solution is not to re-create a supply of cheap labor by having a nice little recession (a solution the Nixon administration more and more appears to be pursuing). Rather the creation of alternative work forces, not drawn from the existing high cost labor supply, seems essential.

So much for the causes of the crisis. What are the cures?

On the governmental level, the first task is to create a device to perform the function once provided by the machine of giving the citizen direct lateral access to his government. The most popular proposal to accomplish this has been called decentralization. I prefer to call it reallocation of government functions. The proposal is that each government function will be assigned to the lowest and smallest governmental entity qualified to perform it. Under this approach, basic government services, such as police patrolling, street cleaning, and parking and housing enforcement, will be overseen by a local administrator in charge of a district of about 100,000 people. Other services, such as those dealing with air and water pollution, would be administered on a regional basis. In between, city or county governments would perform those functions they are best capable of.

The details of such a reorganization of city government are far too complex to deal with here. But essential to the proposal is the notion that the local administrator be elected by and be responsible to the voters whose streets he is supposed to keep clean and safe, that the existing civil service bureaucracies be eliminated, that their functions and personnel be reassigned to the appropriate level of government—local, city, county, or regional—and that the elected administrator of each level of government be given substantially greater power over those he supervises than city officials now have over unionized civil servants, who also possess a fair amount of political power.

Finally, the proposal envisages the creation of local district councils consisting of approximately eighty committeemen. These committeemen would each represent an election district (or precinct)—one to two city blocks (about 1,500 people). The committeemen would be part-time city employees elected by their neighbors. They would act much as the old captain did; if there were a problem about a leaky roof or a dirty street, the committeeman would be the person to see. He would have direct access to the local administrator, as his predecessor the captain had to the leader. Similar proposals have been made elsewhere. In Los Angeles, a similar recent proposal gives the committeeman the unwieldy but descriptive title of "neighborhoodman."

Since the committeeman would be an elected official, he would be far more sensitive to constituents' problems than any remote unionized civil servant downtown. And if the committeeman was not more sensitive, he could hardly survive the next election.

It is hoped that this reallocation of government functions will achieve a number of salutary effects:

—humanizing the presently impersonal government furnished by most cities to their citizenry;

—eliminating the bureaucratic rigidity and waste of manpower that have characterized increasingly centralized city government;

—placing responsibility for city government on identifiable individuals subject to popular control and, when appropriate, to removal from office by those they are supposed to be serving;

—reducing the cost of government by eliminating the layers of administrators, which result, for example, in less than 10 per cent of the New York City Police Department's personnel (and analogous percentages in other departments) performing line duty.

Without such a reorganization of city government, I do not believe massive federal aid—if it ever comes—will solve the problems of the cities. And, although the cities need the money, I'd rather not wait for it. Instead, I would suggest that two other steps be taken by the federal government to help cities solve the basic problem of staying alive.

First: On the city governmental level, there is a tremendous need for short-term, vigorous, young manpower to deal with the emergencies that every city constantly faces and the special emergencies it faces from time to time. The city's existing manpower cannot meet or effectively deal with these emergncies.

Consider: If teachers make demands that a city cannot or should not accept, and they go on strike, what happens? The city capitulates, and up go the costs of government. If there is a cold wave and a rash of complaints about lack of heat, and building inspectors cannot keep up with the volume or refuse to try, what happens? People stay cold. If sanitation men go on strike and there is a health crisis, what happens? Unless the mayor can find a way to blame it on the governor, the city capitulates.

And what of the many areas in every city similar to those in New York City, such as Bedford-Stuyvesant in Brooklyn, Harlem in Manhattan, and Hunts Point in the Bronx, where local government has broken down and the city's total existing manpower, even if it were working at full strength, could not deal with a particular area's problems unless it worked sixteen hours a day and disregarded the remainder of the city?

The answer to all these situations is a special emergency force, consisting of young men and women who would devote two to three years of their lives to serving their city just as they are now asked to serve their country. They could quickly be given sufficient knowledge of city government to spot housing violations and to file complaints. They could move into a problem area, take it over house by house, and clean it up. They could provide extra police protection in high crime areas; collect garbage, if that were necessary; patrol the streets, if that were necessary; arrest narcotics pushers (which would be necessary); and bring help and guidance to the oppressed city dwellers who live in degradation. They could collect the rents, and make the repairs the absent landlords refused to make. Some could first complete their educations and then bring medical and legal services to the people and places that need it. No picnic, it would be hard and sometimes dangerous work. What mayor would not rejoice at such an emergency force?

The possibilities are limitless. It is clear that a force such as this is necessary if the cities are ever going to undo the damage that time, bureaucracy, and lack of money and manpower have already done.

Federal sponsorship of such a program, including financial help and especially exemption from the draft, would do more to revitalize our cities than any big gobs of money we are likely to see from Washington.

The most rewarding dividend, however, would be a generation of graduates of the emergency force. Undoubtedly, some would stay in government. And all would have a working knowledge of the problems of government that would act as a bulwark against the electoral appeal of the demagogues we can confidently expect to proliferate as television increasingly becomes politics' principal medium of communication. Furthermore, it might supply some of the meaning to life that so many of our young people seem to be seeking.

Second: The housing problem. If city governments were to operate to perfection but their present failure to build and maintain residential housing were to continue, the cities would soon die, for private enterprise, using the money and manpower available at present, simply cannot meet the cities' housing needs.

When a similar condition existed during the 1930s in the electric industry in the South, the federal government found a solution. Through the Tennessee Valley Authority and the Rural Electrification Administration, the federal government did what private industry could not do. And, while TVA was a yardstick, it was more than that; it was a stimulus to industrial growth and expansion throughout the entire South.

The cities need a federal yardstick program to build housing at rational costs. If industry and labor cannot do the job—and they simply cannot, given today's costs—let the federal government do what it did in the South in the 1930s: unabashedly go into the business of doing what the private sector cannot do.

This move would raise many problems. Vested interests in some labor unions would protest, as would construction firms and bankers. But basically all construction labor, building companies, and real estate bankers are at present devoting their efforts to commercial projects. They cannot build or finance housing at commercial construction costs, and they have not set up for themselves two scales of costs that would permit the production of expensive commercial buildings and less expensive housing. Accordingly, the cost of building housing is the same as the cost of building commercial structures, but the returns on commercial construction are many times higher. Small wonder that housing construction has stopped and private financing for housing has dried up, while new office buildings spring up one after another.

We need a federal yardstick operation with self-renewing federal money, and, if necessary, the creation of a new housing construction work force to build the millions of dwellings the cities will need in the coming years. The creation of such a housing work force might well go a long way toward solving the impasse between the black man and the existing construction unions. There is no stimulus like competition, or even the threat of it, to produce action where action is needed.

This kind of federal assistance would be far more effective than the pie-in-the-sky massive assistance most urbanologists call for. For as cities get larger and larger, their actions more and more seem to resemble those of the dinosaur—or what we imagine the dinosaur to have been in its declining years: large, clumsy, slow-moving, unable to deal with small enemies, too big to be viable, afflicted with hardening of the arteries. The extinction of the dinosaur ultimately resulted from its inability to function and to regenerate itself.

Cities are already in that condition. They are not performing their basic purpose of providing places for people to live, and because of this failure they are dying. Hungry dinosaurs would probably have been kept alive a little longer if there had been a beneficent federal government to provide food. But extinction would have remained the dinosaur's fate.

Our cities will survive and be governable only if those we elect have effective power over those who are supposed to do the work, only if those we elect are responsible and accountable to the people who elect them, and only if the federal government gives the kind of help that will make manpower available to do the work that survival requires.

34 / THE CITY
IN AFRICA

Jonathan Power

Until very recently the sacred measuring rod of success in an under-developed country was considered to be Gross National Product, not least by the eggheads of such a revered source of development wisdom as the World Bank. But at last the jargon of economic development has begun to change. Earlier this year when the world's leading development experts met to discuss the Pearson Committee report, Robert McNamara, the World Bank's president, sounded a new note.

He challenged the august assembly to stop thinking of success as a 5 per cent growth rate. "What do such figures mean," he said, "when we remember that even for the affluent, life is beset by smog, pollution, noise, traffic congestion, urban violence, youthful disaffection and a terrifying increase in the drug problem? . . . What we must grasp is that gross measures of economic strength and gross measures of economic growth . . . cannot measure the soundness of the social structure of a nation." How far this thinking penetrates into the World Bank, however, is a moot point. One of its senior officials said to me after the speech with a cynical smile: "We're making the best of both worlds. We have a radical rhetoric which appeals to the aid lobby and conservative policies that satisfy the bankers."

Nevertheless, the argument of McNamara's speech was brought back to me as I was driving along through the Sierra Leone country-side. I had been given a lift by an airport engineer who had studied at a London polytechnic. I had got him to talk about Guinea. "You know, their educated people are worth nothing," he said. "But look at me. I am an engineer at the airport. I have a car, a mileage allowance. I can afford to buy you a beer, a whiskey, whatever you want." I could not help but think as he talked on that in twenty or thirty years' time, when this ethos has supplanted traditional African rural villages, Sierra Leone and so many other African

From *Commonweal*, April 28, 1972. Reprinted by permission of Commonweal Publishing Co., Inc.

countries would probably be facing savage class tensions, and maybe in a hundred years' time cities as unbearable as New York and Chicago.

But is it absolutely necessary that development has to lead to urbanization and severe social stratification? The answer seemed to be staring at me as I looked through the car window. On either side of the road the traditional dwellings of wattle and thatch that characterize so much of the African countryside had been supplanted. There were now sturdy houses—still constructed from traditional materials, apart from the metal roof—but how different they looked. They were tall and square, with a wooden veranda on which the children were playing with clay marbles. The rough-hung doors and high open windows that allowed a minimum of light had been replaced by elegant wooden entrances full of intricate carving, wide window frames with shutters to be closed at night. Every so often through the palm trees I could see a carpenter at work shaping more doors, tables and chairs. The little shops which once sold only soap, paraffin and rice were now heaped with brightly colored cloth, fish neatly arranged in circular rows, meat and eggs.

And this was not the town. The nearest piece of urban living was 15 miles away, with three miles of river in between. But it was only in the towns of Africa that I had seen these "luxuries" before —luxuries which seemed meaningless beside the open sewers that linked the decrepit, tin-shack, overcrowded houses to the street. What I was now seeing was rural development, not based on the salary of an airport engineer or government clerk, but on catching fish, selling coconut and growing tomatoes. And how much more gentle and stable it all looked.

Yet to my driving companion this was a lower kind of life. To be "educated" or "Western" a young man in Africa has to move to the town. The colonial education system gave him urban skills and urban values. Even today only a handful of African countries teach agriculture in school. Hundreds pour into the towns every day, hunting jobs that do not exist, African cities are growing at an alarming rate, but often for social reasons, not economic ones.

Our Western cities, horrid as they are, at least had an economic cause: they grew because of the stimulus to industrialization from the agricultural revolution. Manufacturing developed in the villages and market towns and only later, as the demands for bigger urban units mounted, did the large towns develop. The proportion of the population living in cities of over 20,000 was invariably smaller than the proportion of the working force engaged in manufacturing. In France in 1856, a not atypical example, 10.7 per cent of the population lived in urban areas, but 29 per cent worked in industry. But in Africa we find more people living in towns than there are working in industry. In Tunisia in 1956, a UN survey showed that 17.5 per cent of the people were in cities, but only 6.8 per cent of the labor force was working in industry.

By 1980 it is estimated that Dakar, Abidgan and Accra alone will each have a million inhabitants—22 per cent, 20 per cent and 8.5 per cent of their country's total population respectively. Yet only 5 per cent of their population will be engaged in industry. (In Latin America and Asia this imbalance between manufacturing and urban population is even more marked, but there rural overpopulation and archaic land ownership structures are primary causes.)

But even if African cities could achieve a Western-type balance between population and industry, what would be the point? Traditionally we have been brought up to think of cities as synonymous with economic activity, industrialization and modern civilization. Large concentrations of people subdivided into a myriad of economic tasks, served by railways, factories and banks, could produce goods at a far greater rate than could the rural economy with its peasants, blacksmiths and carpenters. Yet our own cities have either failed, or are on the point of failing. The social costs have overwhelmed the economic benefits. How meaningless it is, for example, to say as some do, that Chicago's black population has a higher average income level than any other black group in the world. Because in Chicago three or four thousand dollars a year means nothing.

It is not enough to stop the garbage piling up on the streets, or rats taking over the stairways. It does not stop the murder rate being almost one a day. It is nothing when rent and the price of food are exorbitantly high, higher than for whites who live in the better part of town. It is nothing when you have to buy a car to get to work because there's no decent public transport. And yet the god of GNP per head lives on.

So as I drove along through the Sierra Leone bush I could not help but think that the answer must lie on the land and with the small successful family farmers I could see beside the roadside.

(After all, modern farming with its sophisticated division of labor is merely an extension of the town and incapable of absorbing much surplus population if it is to be "economic.") The small family farmer, the crofter, however, has enormous potential. Subsistence farming, a dirty word in the economist's vocabulary can be in fact carried out at quite a high level. Farmers who literally did subsist on maize, beans, and small game, can within a matter of five or ten years widen this to include poultry, fish, fruit trees, green vegetables, and oil palms.

This, together with the simultaneous development in a small village of about a hundred persons of a blacksmith, weaver and carpenter, can mean houses can be improved, a dispensary supported, and the standard of living raised in situ—just what I was seeing out of the car window.

It is also a pattern of life that can easily absorb a growing population for relatively small injections of capital: fertilizer, improved seeds, or a simple pump for irrigation; output can be raised sharply. Fertilizer can produce 200 per cent to 400 per cent returns in the first year. Improved seeds can double or triple yields at the next harvest. (It is, of course, this very concept that Julius Nyerere is pioneering with his villagization program in Tanzania.) Clearly this prescription is no panacea. It cannot answer every need. But it is a question of emphasis.

Does the town grow first and drag the countryside along in its wake with all its frightening social consequences? Or does rural economic activity gradually quicken its pace, steadily but surely pulling together the elements needed for a better life, until the town is ready to emerge as a natural extension of the social and economic life of the countryside?